The Hybrid Tsinoys

American Society of Missiology
Monograph Series

Series Editor, James R. Krabill

The ASM Monograph Series provides a forum for publishing quality dissertations and studies in the field of missiology. Collaborating with Pickwick Publications—a division of Wipf and Stock Publishers of Eugene, Oregon—the American Society of Missiology selects high quality dissertations and other monographic studies that offer research materials in mission studies for scholars, mission and church leaders, and the academic community at large. The ASM seeks scholarly work for publication in the series that throws light on issues confronting Christian world mission in its cultural, social, historical, biblical, and theological dimensions.

Missiology is an academic field that brings together scholars whose professional training ranges from doctoral-level preparation in areas such as Scripture, history and sociology of religions, anthropology, theology, international relations, interreligious interchange, mission history, inculturation, and church law. The American Society of Missiology, which sponsors this series, is an ecumenical body drawing members from Independent and Ecumenical Protestant, Catholic, Orthodox, and other traditions. Members of the ASM are united by their commitment to reflect on and do scholarly work relating to both mission history and the present-day mission of the church. The ASM Monograph Series aims to publish works of exceptional merit on specialized topics, with particular attention given to work by younger scholars, the dissemination and publication of which is difficult under the economic pressures of standard publishing models.

Persons seeking information about the ASM or the guidelines for having their dissertations considered for publication in the ASM Monograph Series should consult the Society's website—www.asmweb.org.

Members of the ASM Monograph Committe who approved this book are:

James R. Krabill, Anabaptist Mennonite Biblical Seminary
Roger Schroeder, Catholic Theological Union
Craig Ott, Trinity Evangelical Divinity School

RECENTLY PUBLISHED IN THE ASM MONOGRAPH SERIES

Byungohk Lee, *Listening to the Neighbor: From A Missional Perspective of the Other*

Keon-Sang An, *An Ethiopian Reading of the Bible: Biblical Interpretation of the Ethiopian Orthodox Tewahido Church*

Birgit Herppich, *Pitfalls of Trained Incapicity: The Unintended Effects of Missionary Training in the Basel Mission on Its Early Work in Ghana (1828–1840)*

"The original study of Dr. Juliet Uytanlet on hybrid 'Tsinoys,' (coined word from a Tagalog word meaning 'Chinese,' and Filipino) is one of the finest studies on the current Chinese Filipinos who reside in the Philippines, and outside of the Philippines. The 'Tsinoys' hold a Filipino passport, but ethnically belong to the Chinese people. Using descriptive ethnographic research as a tool to discover how they view themselves, Dr. Uytanlet was able to demonstrate their hybridity in language and mindset. The pendulum of swinging at times to Chinese mindset on the right, to swinging to the Filipino mindset on the left is quite challenging for many second-, third-, and fourth-generation Chinese Filipinos. This study points out who are the 'Tsinoys' today. It is really an important study on the identity of the 'Tsinoys,' and also the urgent issues facing them. Dr. Uytanlet illustrates her scholarly ability in analyzing and presenting difficult data so that the 'Tsinoys' may understand themselves, and further scholarly research can be done based on her work. Moreover, her work also presents challenges and recommendations for Churches that are willing to understand and touch their lives. The work is the best study on understanding the Chinese who are residing in the Philippines. I highly recommend to publish this important work!"

—Joseph Shao, President, Biblical Seminary of the Philippines;
General Secretary, Asia Theological Association

"The book is a valuable addition to the studies on the Chinese Filipinos. The wealth of information gathered from ethnographic research should broaden our perspectives and understanding of the Tsinoy and how they evolved from the generation of sojourners to the present generation Chinese Filipinos rooted in Philippine soil, grounded in Philippine society, yet proud of their racial and cultural origins. Most importantly, it enlightens readers on the processes and social negotiations that result into a unique culture, blending the Filipino and the Chinese."

—Teresita Ang See, Executive Trustee, Kaisa Heritage Center,
Intramuros, Manila

The Hybrid Tsinoys

Challenges of Hybridity and Homogeneity as Sociocultural Constructs among the Chinese in the Philippines

Juliet Lee Uytanlet

Foreword by Michael A. Rynkiewich

PICKWICK *Publications* • Eugene, Oregon

THE HYBRID TSINOYS
Challenges of Hybridity and Homogeneity as Sociocultural Constructs among the
Chinese in the Philippines

American Society of Missiology Monograph Series 28

Pickwick Publications
An Imprint of Wipf and Stock Publishers
199 W. 8th Ave., Suite 3
Eugene, OR 97401

www.wipfandstock.com

PAPERBACK ISBN: 978-1-4982-2905-0
HARDCOVER ISBN: 978-1-4982-2907-4
EBOOK ISBN: 978-1-4982-2906-7

Cataloguing-in-Publication data:

Uytanlet, Juliet Lee.

The Hybrid Tsinoys : Challenges of Hybridity and Homogeneity as Sociocultural Constructs among the Chinese in the Philippines / Juliet Lee Uytanlet;
foreword by Michael A. Rynkiewich.

xvi + 200 pp. ; 23 cm. Includes bibliographical references.

ISBN 978-1-4982-2905-0 (paperback) | ISBN 978-1-4982-2907-4 (hardback) |
ISBN 978-1-4982-2906-7 (ebook)

American Society of Missiology Monograph Series 28

1. Chinese—Philippines—Ethnic identity. 2. Group idenity. I. Title. II. Series.

DS666.C5 U95 2016

Manufactured in the U.S.A.   06/29/16

Special Permissions

Many thanks to Teresita Ang See and Kaisa Para sa Kaunlaran, Inc. for the permission to include four tables (tables 1 and 18–20) that were originally published in *The Chinese in the Philippines: Problems and Perspectives* volume 3 into this work. I also want to thank the Lilly Library of Indiana University in Bloomington, Indiana, for giving the permission to publish a picture of Sangleys in the Boxer Codex (figure 1) for this book.

To God who is so good to me that my cup overflows.

Also, to my husband, Samson, and our son, Johann.

Finally, to my late father, Lee Loh, who was a sojourner from Fujian, and my mother, Lily Soo, whose parents were sojourners from Guangdong.

"***Di ba*** redundant ***yun?*** Hybrid ***na,*** Tsinoys ***pa. Pareho lang yun di ba?*** (Isn't the title redundant? They are hybrids, and you even added the word 'Tsinoys.' Aren't those two carried the same meaning?)"

—COMMENT ON THE TITLE OF THE BOOK
BY A YOUNG KAISA VOLUNTEER

Contents

Figures and Tables

Technical Notes

The employment of the Minnanhua or Amoy language for this work is based on John MacGowan's *English and Chinese Dictionary of the Amoy Dialect* and Maryknoll Language Service Center (http://www.taiwanese-dictionary.org/). The traditional Chinese characters were used instead of the simplified version. However, Pinyin was used for the Romanization of the Chinese Putonghua. In some texts in Minnanhua or Pinyin, the author maintains the usage of widely held spelling.

Language Font Guide

English: Times New Roman

Filipino: ***Bold Italicized Times New Roman***

Minnanhua: *Italicized Times New Roman*

Putonghua Pinyin: Times New Roman

Putonghua characters: MingLIU 華語

Other languages: *Italicized Times New Roman*

Foreword

By Dr. Michael A. Rynkiewich

PERSONAL IDENTITY, AS A reflection of group or ethnic identity, has always been a matter to be negotiated, not a given. That is because there are always two persons involved in identity formation: the self and the other. One may project one's identity, but others may reject, revise, or even try to replace that identity. In the world of mission, the identity of the Christian congregation is as important as the identity of those with whom the church is in ministry and mission. Here, Dr. Juliet Lee Uytanlet explores the significance of identity in the Philippine Chinese church for its engagement in mission.

Dr. Uytanlet takes a fine-grained ethnographic approach to develop a taxonomy of terms to parse the heavily populated space between Chinese and Filipino. She deploys the terms *hybridity* and *homogeneity* to capture the disparate dreams of the community: to be fully integrated into Filipino society and yet to retain a clear Chinese identity. Perhaps all of us want to be unique and yet want to belong. The contours of a Christian Chinese ministry in a Filipino context are shaped by this journey.

In this age of globalization, migration, and diaspora, some scholars imagined that there would be a levelling of culture; that soon everyone would look, act, and think the same. This has proved not to be the case, and Dr. Uytanlet confirms that ethnicities persist and perhaps even proliferate in the face of globalization. That is, the Chinese in the Philippines resist, reject, and reinvent globalizing influences and thereby shape their own identity. They persist through adaptation as hybrids, they find their own space, mixed yet unmixed.

Through this process, new hybrid cultures and identities constantly are emerging. That means that the church's mission model must also constantly be emerging, never set in stone. Following Dr. Uytanlet's lead, the church may be able to situate learning about self and about the other as a continuous mode of being. The alternative is to risk losing touch with who they are and who they are in ministry with. I hope that this work will be an inspiration for others to explore the intricacies of identity formation in strategic mission situations.

Acknowledgments

> Praise the Lord, my soul; all my inmost being, praise His Holy
> name.—Ps 103:1

THANKS BE TO GOD the Father for his abounding love and faithfulness that carry me through to the fruition of this work. It is the great, great love of Jesus and his mighty grace that saved me and enabled me to finish. Praise be to You, O Holy Spirit, for Your presence and strength. Glory be to God.

At the onset of this dissertation, I took up the challenge of my mentor, Dr. Michael A. Rynkiewich, to write something that will "prove important for the next generation."[1] He firmly believes that the interplay of anthropology and missiology must continue.

> As the world changes, so must we find out where people are and go to them, whether they are settled or in transit. . . . Urbanization and globalization have been two of the most dominant forces shaping the world at the end of the twentieth and the beginning of the twenty-first century, and many people are aware that they will affect the deployment of missionaries from here and out.[2]

However, it was the reading of Jan Nederveen Pieterse's book on *Globalization and Culture* that summer of 2011 in preparation for Dr. Steven Ybarrola's class on the Indigenous Church in an Age of Globalization that sparked my interest on the topic of cultural hybridity. Many

1. Rynkiewich, "New Heaven and a New Earth," 40.

2. Ibid.

thanks to Dr. Ybarrola for his classes and counsel on the areas of ethnicity and ethnography. With his permission, I included his lecture on Data Collection Method in doing ethnographic research methodology in this work.

Dr. Rynkiewich's expertise in cultural anthropology and missiology guided me throughout the process of my writing the proposal and this dissertation. His encouragement and confidence in me made a big difference in this phase of my studies. I deeply appreciate his patience and kindness in helping me achieve my goal to finish. He has been a mentor I will want to emulate as I mentor other students in the future. It is truly a privilege to have the opportunity to study under him. I also want to thank Dr. Eunice L. Irwin and Dr. Howard A. Snyder for their valuable input and comments that helped tighten my arguments and improved this dissertation.

I want to thank the Biblical Seminary of the Philippines (BSOP) for allowing me to take a full year without a teaching load just so I can concentrate in my writing since my family returned to the Philippines in April 2013. Many thanks to the BSOP Board of Directors and Board of Trustees, faculty, administrative staff, library staff, and students for their prayers and encouragement. BSOP has been a pleasant and peaceful place for me to focus and write. Special mention to our president Dr. Joseph Shao, whose words in Minnanhua "*tiòh lūn lòh khì* (must persevere to the end)" always remind me to just persevere and never give up.

I thank all my professors in the E. Stanley Jones School of World Mission and Evangelism (ESJ) of Asbury Theological Seminary. My journey will not be the same without the precious dynamics of sitting in classes, listening to lectures, and interacting with my colleagues. I also appreciate the friendships and support of the ESJ Ladies' Friday Noon Fellowship.

My fieldwork in the summer of 2012 would not be possible without the generous grant given by Mr. William and Mrs. Phyllis Johnson. Many thanks for their prayers, support, and faith in me since I embarked on this doctoral program. I am honored to be a Johnson International Scholar.

I cherish the untiring kindness and counsel of Rev. Danny and Hensie Reyes, Rev. Dr. Vicente and Helen Sia, and Rev. Dr. Wilson and Marissa Gonzales for me and my family all these years. Likewise, I am superbly blessed for the prayers and encouragement of my dear high school friends and their spouses: Michael and Jamelyn Wang, Terence and Carolina Sy, and Joderick and Anne Cafe. I also want to thank Dr.

Andrew and Grace Liuson for their unwavering support since I entered full-time ministry to the present.

Many thanks to Dr. Elaine Vaden of Langham Partnerships who not only ministered to my husband Samson as he is a Langham Scholar but also to me when we were still studying in the United States. Our dear neighbors and friends in Wilmore have made our journey there less "unhomely." Special thanks to Dr. Robert and Ellen Stamps, Caleb Wang and Aurora Kuo, Shinji and Mariko Nakagawa, Thomas and Meng Meu Lau, Andy Ponce, Luke Hsieh, Patricia Walker, Patricia Richmond, Dame Simanjuntak, Sammy and Micah Kim, Susangeline Patrick, Jane Langat, Grace Gichuru, Ruth Tipton, Song Hwa Chae, Juseon Maeng, Hyun Jin Lee, Nam Seng Koh and Jessica Chen, and Jeremy Chew and Jane Ong Bee Bee.

I value the help and assistance extended to me from 2010 to 2015 by Teresita Ang See and Meah Ang See of Kaisa Para Sa Kaunlaran, Inc. They accommodated me in the midst of their busy schedules and for that I am truly grateful. I highly regard the conversations with these esteemed elderlies: Mr. Antonio O, Mr. Ong Siong-Cho, and Mr. Tan Tian-Siong. Similarly, I appreciate the discussion with Ms. Benita Ong of World News Publication 菲律賓世界日報. Many thanks to Rev. Dr. David Cheung for providing helpful electronic correspondences in the summer of 2011 and Rev. Dr. Stewart Young for giving constructive comments on my study in 2013. I am truly grateful for all the scholars and their writings from which this material is built upon.

My sincere thanks for family and friends in the Philippines who aided me in my fieldwork. I am still amazed how I was able to find all the 112 informants in sixty-six days. I am indebted to all my informants, their participation in this study is priceless. Special mention to Pr. Jeanette Yu Chua and Angie Tan Chua for the numerous informants they had referred to me. Finding the New Immigrants was easy with the help of Natalie Ang who also served as my translator since my knowledge in Putonghua is limited.

I found myself accountable to Pr. Jennifer Hao and Teena See while writing in the Philippines. Their prayers and cheers boosted my motivation to write. I thank the following for their care and concern upon our return to the country: Andy and Dr. Jean Go Du, Pr. Anita Tan, Rev. Benjamin and Rebecca Young, Benita Chua, Pr. Danny and Adelaine Balete, Gary and Marites Sio, Pr. Lily Lim, Pr. Marianner Ferrer, Pr. Mary Chua, Wilson and Alice Ngo, and Rev. Un Hock and Jennifer Wee. Special mention to the BSOP administrative staff for their wonderful assistance in our transition and adjustment period. I also want to thank the following for simply being our friends: Von and Angeli Sy, Jeffrey and Claire Ang, Anson and Michelle So, Genesis and Michelle Tan, Mary Santos Heu, Ivy Co Say, Dr. Jocelyn Yao, Joyce Ong, Chryslin Lao, Sven Lim, Hans Arevalo, Cherie Yu, and Dr. Marjorie Golekoh.

Thanks to Christian Bible Church of the Philippines and to Rev. Jeremiah and Kashin Cheung for the hospitality during my field work in the summer of 2012. I also want to thank the pastoral and administrative staff of the following churches and Christian institutions: Chinese Congress on World Evangelization Fellowship Philippines (CCOWEF), Gerizim Evangelical Church, United Evangelical Church of Malabon, United Evangelical Church of the Philippines, and Youth Gospel Center of the Philippines.

I want to take this opportunity to thank the people dearest to me. First of all, thanks to my husband, Samson. He was the first to believe that I could finish a PhD. He encouraged me from the beginning of this journey and helped me in countless ways. I would not have arrived this point without him. He inspires me to be a faithful servant of God. Thank God for a suitable partner. Many thanks to our darling Johann who has been very patient all throughout my busyness in writing. He never fails to pray for me and make me laugh when I am tired, stressed, or discouraged. He is our joy and precious gift from God.

I want to thank my late father, Lee Loh, who taught me by example the joy of telling stories; to my mother, Lily Soo, who taught me how to love and to sacrifice; and to all my eleven siblings and their spouses (Celia and Johnny, Rudy and Pei Chen, Amalia, Rosy and Joseph, Henry, Nancy and Andrew, Shirley and Michael, Emy and Sammuel, Gina and Andy, Katherine and Howard, and Juvy and Ian) and their precious children both in Taiwan and in the Philippines whose confidence in me and love for me pushed me to give all my best.

To all the Chinese Filipinos, may this study be of help to you in any way but most especially in realizing the need to know God and his Son Jesus Christ.

1

Introduction

"ARE WE IN CHINA?" I asked my older sister Nancy. I was curious at age four, so I asked further, "Is the Philippines part of China?" She laughed and said, "What are you talking about?" She then looked at me somewhat puzzled, wondering whether my question was out of stupidity or naivety. I guessed she remembered I was just four so she continued, "We are in the Philippines and the Philippines is not part of China." I wanted to ask more questions. I honestly wondered why the Philippines had more Chinese people than Filipinos, or so I thought then.

I saw Chinese people every day and everywhere in Manila Chinatown in the 1970s, particularly in Binondo.[1] All our neighbors were Chinese. The stores carried Chinese names and Chinese characters. I heard Minnanhua 閩南話 spoken everywhere, at home and even in school.[2] We only used the Filipino language when we spoke with Filipinos. Some Filipinos in our area could even speak and understand Minnanhua so that we did not have to use Filipino at all. On top of these, we had Chinese restaurants, Chinese bakeries, Chinese movie theaters, Chinese bookstores, Chinese fire departments, Chinese supermarkets, Chinese drug stores, Chinese inns, and all kinds of Chinese shops.

Most of the Filipinos I met while growing up were my teachers in school or house helpers at home. We lived near the Divisoria Market

1. Binondo was the first officially established Chinese town or Chinatown in the Philippines in 1594. Today, it is the oldest that is still in existence. See, "Binondo's Byways," 142.

2. Minnanhua is the Chinese language spoken by many Chinese Filipinos since most of them or their ancestors came from Fujian, China. It is also known as Amoy or Hokkien.

where there were many *istambay* (goofer) waiting for work.[3] There were many **kargador** (porters) and **tindera** (saleswomen), **kutchero** (coachmen) and **maglalako** (peddlers). Eventually, I understood that I did live in the Philippines. However, my surroundings caused me to think I was in "little China," a sort of nested community—in China in the Philippines.

As I grew older, I realized there was a bigger world outside Binondo or my "little China." I found myself probing further. I could not understand why we needed to study Pŭtōnghuà (Putonghua henceforth) 普通話 or Mandarin when I lived in the Philippines.[4] Why was I not able to speak Filipino fluently?[5] When I did speak Filipino, why did the people who heard me call me *barok*?[6]

When I became a Christian, I was actively involved in Youth Gospel Center of the Philippines, a student center that reaches out to the Chinese schools in Binondo. I also attended United Evangelical Church of Malabon, a Chinese church. My world continued to revolve around my Chineseness even as a Christian. I entered St. Scholastica's College, which is a Catholic school exclusive for girls. It was only then that I comprehended that the Chinese in the Philippines are a minority. Among the Filipino majority at college, many were better off than the Chinese and many were as well educated. Eventually, I learned to appreciate their culture and friendships. I have gained many Filipino friends both in college and through Philippine Campus Crusade for Christ's ministry. However, I remain in the Chinese community even until today as I serve and teach

3. The word *"tambay"* or *"istambay"* is derived from the English "stand by." It is a derogatory term often used to refer to those who are jobless or out of school.

4. Putonghua (common language) is the standard language used in China. It is popularly known as Mandarin. It is also known as Guóyŭ 國語 (national language) in Taiwan and Huáyŭ 華語 (literally China language) in the Philippines. This work will employ Putonghua instead of Mandarin to be consistent with the use of Minnanhua to refer to the Hokkien or Amoy language.

5. Filipino is the national language of the Philippines. It is mainly based on the Tagalog language. The term Filipino also refers to the people of the Philippines. There are 78 languages and 500 dialects identified as being spoken in the country. Eight major languages used are Tagalog or Filipino, Visayan, Ilocano, Hiligayon or Ilonggo, Bicol, Waray, Pampango, and Pangasinense. Abinales and Amoroso, *State and Society*, 11. The Philippines has diverse groups of people. There are indigenous ethnic groups, tribal groups, and non-indigenous ethnic groups where the Chinese Filipinos are categorized.

6. The labelling of someone who cannot speak straight Filipino was called a **barok** based on the movie *Barok* (1977) starring Chiquito. It was about a caveman whose Filipino was broken and funny.

in the Biblical Seminary of the Philippines, which is a Chinese seminary. I am very clear that my calling at present is to serve and minister to the Chinese in the Philippines.[7]

It is important for me to understand the uniqueness of the Chinese in the Philippines as I continue to serve among them. It is my desire to write a contemporary profile of the Chinese in the Philippines with the aim of sorting out identity issues. In the long run, I hope that this research will help churches and pastors better understand the very people with whom they are in ministry and mission.

RESEARCH PROBLEM

The term "Tsinoy" was coined during the fifth anniversary celebration of Kaisa Para Sa Kaunlaran, Inc. (Kaisa henceforth) in August of 1992 mainly to differentiate the Chinese Filipinos who are already rooted in Philippine society from the new immigrants from mainland China.[8] Since then, it has been widely accepted by many as an ethnic label to refer to the Chinese in the Philippines or *Tsinong-Pinoy*. The word Tsinoy means *Tsino* (Chinese) and *Pinoy* (Pilipino or Filipino).[9] For this study, I employ the term Chinese Filipinos most frequently to refer to all the Chinese in the Philippines.

The interviews seem to suggest that the Chinese Filipinos are conflicted as an ethnic minority in the Philippines: they want to be integrated in mainstream society and yet they want to maintain their cultural identity. Throughout the centuries, they have constructed a unique blend of identity that primarily reflects their Chineseness mixed with Filipino and Western cultures. This mixing or hybridity is inevitable especially in this age of globalization where more cultures meet and influence each other. However, even in the midst of this cultural mixture, the desire to be homogenous as a particular ethnic group with particular cultural beliefs and practices remains of utmost importance for many Chinese Filipinos.

---

7. The Chinese Filipinos are a minority in the Philippines with a population of 1.2 million. They comprise 1 to 1.2 percent of the total population. See, "State and Public Policies," 155.

8. Kaisa Para Sa Kaunlaran, Inc. (Unity in Progress) was created on August 28, 1987, as a cause-oriented non-government organization. It aims to serve as a bridge between the Chinese community and mainstream Philippine society for nation building. See, *Tsinoy*, 243–45, 250.

9. *Pinoy* is the colloquial term for Filipino.

This research investigates the notions of hybridity and homogeneity as sociocultural constructs in the development of current ethnic identity/ies of Chinese Filipinos. This project employs a descriptive ethnographic research method to discover how they see or define themselves in terms of ethnicity and how their perspectives affect other aspects of their lives.

There are many written records in the Putonghua about their identity, contributions, problems, and perspective. However, at the turn of this century, the Kaisa and other Chinese Filipinos have undertaken the task of investigating, recording, writing and publishing books, articles, periodicals, and magazines about the Chinese Filipinos in English. Still, unprecedented changes in global flows of people, goods, and ideas create a new situation for Chinese Filipinos. More research is necessary and more books can be written as Chinese Filipinos seek to rediscover their heritage and uniqueness and face the challenges ahead.

RESEARCH QUESTION

The resilience of the Chinese Filipinos in maintaining their ethnic identity is noteworthy. This positive trait, however, sometimes creates problems considering that they have settled in the Philippines and coexisted with Filipinos throughout the colonial era of Spain, United States, and Japan. Their loyalty to the Philippines has been questioned. Their ambivalent status during the colonial periods had led to massacres, deportation, hostilities, and immigration restrictions that only further strengthen throughout the centuries this group's unity and camaraderie.

It seems that their ethnocentric tendencies have led to a cultural inclination to preserve their heritage. This is still the primary motivation to be different from the Filipinos and homogenous among themselves. Such choice is evident in their continuing use of Minnanhua and even in the persistence of some cultural practices such as endogamy, ancestral worship, and other traditions. Their ethnic identity coincides with other aspects of their lives shaping their experience in family, community, business, education, charity, and religion. The Manila Chinatown is an obvious symbol of their resilience throughout the centuries in the country and continuing adherence to their culture and identity even in the age of globalization.

Then again, the Chinese Filipinos today are no longer "pure" Chinese in their cultural orientation in the sense that they are no longer exactly the same as the Chinese in China, Hong Kong, or Taiwan or even the same as other Chinese in diaspora. In this research, I propose that the Chinese Filipinos have constructed a culture exclusively of their own, a hybrid of selected cultural practices and new identities. They cannot evade the fact that they are influenced by their host country. In particular, the second-, third-, and fourth-generation Chinese Filipinos demonstrate their hybridity in language and mindset. From the interviews, they seem confused whether they want homogeneity in hybridity or homogeneity and hybridity at the same time. Or, are they simply competent in contextualizing themselves to respond in different occasions and situations? This unique blend of culture is as complex as the world we now live in.

To essentialize or generalize for the sake of getting a big picture at times is necessary, but we need to be reminded that there are many subcultures within a culture. In other words, there are "layers of cultures" within culture. Further, aside from the mixing of cultures, the mixing of "blood" or inter-ethnic marriage has contributed to hybridity instead of "purity." This raises two questions which will be the focus of my research.

The first research question is whether the Chinese in the Philippines at present still see themselves as a homogeneous group and/or purist. In line with this, how do they describe themselves in terms of ethnicity and nationality? Do all Chinese, especially those still holding Chinese citizenship, agree with the term "Tsinoy"? Is preserving one's ethnic identity necessarily ethnocentric, or simply appreciating and celebrating one's cultural heritage? How does this ethnic identity affect other aspects of one's life?

The second research question is whether they see themselves as hybrids and no longer purist? Do Chinese Filipinos view hybridity or the mixing of cultures or even of "blood" as a challenge or threat? Can the hybrid Tsinoy culture still be considered a Chinese culture? Who are the Tsinoys today? How do the Chinese Mestizos identify themselves, as Chinese or Filipinos, or both at different times?

DELIMITATIONS

The scope of this research focuses primarily on the issue of hybridity and homogeneity as a way of seeing one's ethnic identity among the Chinese Filipinos. Hybridity is defined in this study as the result of mixing of "blood" or mixing of cultures and/or cultural elements. Homogeneity is being monocultural, a homogenous group, or practicing one culture. I will study the Chinese Filipinos who live in Metro Manila only; not including Chinese Filipinos or other Chinese immigrants in other cities in the Philippines, or in other countries. I study from an insider's perception of ethnic identity, looking for emic categories particularly as related to hybridity and homogeneity. Consequently, I struggle to develop an outsider's perspective. I will focus on how cultural elements such as language, marriage, and family among Chinese Filipinos affect their understanding of who they are ethnically. I am also interested in how Chinese Filipino Christians perceive ethnic identity, and how this understanding relates to both church functioning and the church in mission. I am not studying how Confucianism, Daoism, or Buddhism might relate to ethnic identity.

This study is by no means an exhaustive representation of the sentiments and views of all the Chinese in the Philippines, not even all the Chinese in Metro Manila; but through the life histories that are presented here, some sense of the Chinese immigrants' experience is gained. The details in the narratives certainly provide a deeper understanding of the Chinese in the Philippines than mere stereotyping and labeling by outsiders.

RESEARCH METHODOLOGY

The subsequent portion will lay out the research methodology used for this dissertation. The research method is the structure by which the data was gathered, studied, and analyzed. However, the theories in chapter 3 will serve as the parameters for this research and will also help give meaning to the data gathered.

Research Approach

Cultural anthropology is an important discipline by which we can study the relationship of culture and humankind. Clifford Geertz believes cultural anthropology is best practiced through interpretative methodology as one deciphers the embedded meanings in a particular culture.[10] Michael Rynkiewich cites the recent neuroscience research that leads Stephen Reyna to suggest that "our understanding of the world is based on layered interpretative schema, beginning with neural networks and rising up to the symbolic networks that we call culture."[11] To be human is

---

10. Geertz, *Interpretation of Cultures*, 5.
11. Rynkiewich, *Soul, Self, and Society*, 12.

to continuously interpret and reinterpret the things, events, and symbols seen, heard, or felt around him/her. Such interpretations establish meanings and from such meanings humans craft worldviews and cultures. As one discovers "self" in relation to his/her society, he/she can position oneself in the interplay of human and cultures.

For Geertz, doing anthropology is more than just "establishing rapport, selecting informants, transcribing texts, taking genealogies, mapping fields, keeping a diary, and so on."[12] He adds,

> But it is not these things, techniques and received procedures that define the enterprise. What defines it is the kind of intellectual effort it is: an elaborate venture in, to borrow a notion from Gilbert Ryle, "thick description."[13]

That is, according to Geertz, the end point of doing anthropology is writing ethnography. Ethnography is explicating explications. He admits that in doing ethnography one is really constructing explanations based on the constructed explanations of people,

> That what we call our data are really our own constructions of other people's constructions of what they and their compatriots are up to . . . Right down at the factual base, the hard rock, insofar as there is any, of the whole enterprise, we are already explicating: and worse yet, explicating explications. Winks upon winks upon winks.[14]

Realizing that ethnography is not complete and will never be complete and that its data are the ethnographer's analysis and not necessarily that of the subject, this methodology has its limitations. Nevertheless, it has its advantages as it involves onsite research and firsthand observation of the subject of study. Such raw data are precious and crucial for analyzing and interpreting human and cultures.

In his *Writing Culture*, James Clifford writes that ethnography is

> actively situated between powerful systems of meaning. It poses its questions at the boundaries of civilizations, cultures, classes, races, and genders. Ethnography decodes and recodes, telling the grounds of collective order and diversity, inclusion and

---

12. Geertz, *Interpretation of Cultures*, 6.

13. Ibid.

14. Ibid., 9.

exclusion. It describes processes of innovation and structura-
tion, and is itself part of these processes.[15]

Critics of ethnographies call such works fictions. Clifford agrees but
situates the word "fiction" in the logic of "something made or fashioned"
shifting importance to preserving meaning rather than the "inventing of
things not actually real."[16] He acknowledges that interpretive social scientists view good ethnographies as "true fictions," but sadly, it is "usually
at the cost of weakening the oxymoron, reducing it to the banal claim
that all truths are constructed."[17] Consequently, ethnographic truths are
"inherently partial—committed and incomplete."[18] Ethnographers are
likened to the Cree hunter testifying that he is not sure whether he can
tell the truth but definitely he could tell what he knew.[19]

Further, Clifford reveals the emerging new figure in doing ethnography, not an outsider as has been expected but an insider, an "indigenous ethnographer." "Insiders studying their own cultures offer new
angles of vision and depths of understanding. Their accounts are em-
powered and restricted in unique ways."[20] Clifford posits that the diverse
post- and neo-colonial rules for ethnographic practice do not necessarily
produce "better" ethnographies. Instead, anthropology no longer can
claim automatic authority to its "object" of study who are "the primitive
people who cannot speak for themselves."[21] He concludes that ethnography is a "hybrid textual activity: it traverses genres and disciplines."[22]
It is more than just a literature, it is always writing. I see myself as an
"indigenous ethnographer" doing an ethnographic study on the Chinese
in the Philippines.

Data Collection Method

To go about this ethnographic research, I employ the process prescribed
by Steven Ybarrola. He discusses that ethnography is "immersing oneself

15. Clifford, "Partial Truths," introduction to *Writing Culture*, 2–3.
16. Ibid., 6.
17. Ibid.
18. Ibid., 7.
19. Ibid., 8.
20. Ibid., 9.
21. Ibid., 9–10.
22. Ibid., 26.

in another culture to learn the meaning 'natives' give to the world around them."[23] He lays out the key methods as follows.

RESEARCH METHOD LITERATURE REVIEW

Prior to fieldwork, it is important to learn as much as one can about the history and current situation regarding the culture, society, and geographical setting of the subject of one's study. This stage fits well with reading and research activities taking place during preparations for the qualifying exams and the proposal hearing.

MAPPING OR SOCIAL MAPPING

This refers to seeing how things are spatially related to one another. It is finding where things are, or where to find the subject. It is locating the subject and acquiring general information. For this research, the Manila Chinatown is of primary focus with its very nature an enclave for the ethnic Chinese for centuries in the country. However, informants living in other cities in Metro Manila are critical in understanding how these Chinese outside the enclave see themselves and live their lives. Consequently, I have informants both living in Manila Chinatown and in the Metro Manila area.[24]

PARTICIPANT OBSERVATION

Participant observation is to find out who, when, where, why, and how people meet and interact. I went to places where these Chinese Filipinos are usually found or hang out. It gives more information in understanding who they are or who they see themselves to be. I visited Chinese schools, churches, Christian institutions, Chinese daily newspaper, Manila Chinatown, Binondo, San Nicolas, Tondo, Divisoria, Chinese cultural centers, bookstores, libraries, museum, Manila Chinese Cemetery, malls, and coffee shops.

23. Ybarrola, "Opening Session."

24. Metro Manila is also known as the National Capital Region. It is composed of sixteen cities and one municipality. It had a population of 12 million people in 2010. National Statistics Office, "Population and Housing."

INTERVIEWING INFORMANTS

Ybarrola notes that it is not enough for researchers to just observe behavior, "but must get at the meaning people give to their behavior." This is acquired through interviews. Interviews are formal or informal. Casual conversations are helpful but finding "key informants" who provided in-depth interviews is most important. For this research, informants are classified according to six categories with at least five informants for each category and sub-category whether individual or group interviews. The categories are as follows:

a. Old Immigrants

b. New Immigrants (Adults and Youth)

c. Tsinoys (second, third, and fourth generations)

d. Chinese Citizens and Overseas Chinese Filipino Workers

e. Spouses of Mixed Marriages (Chinese and Filipino spouses)

f. Chinese Mestizos (first, second, and third generations)

I have interviewed Christians and non-Christians, male and female, young and old. I employed the help of family and friends with snowball sampling to find referrals. To avoid biases, I also limited the people I personally knew. By God's grace, I listened to and personally interviewed a total of 112 people in 66 days, 86 of which were my key informants (see appendix A, List of Key Informants). Pseudonyms are provided for all key informants for their protection.

LIFE HISTORY INTERVIEWS

These interviews are more in depth on the life experiences of key informants which generally focus on a particular topic. This research employs life history interviews of 86 key informants to show how they perceive their identities whether as purist or a hybrid.[25] The questions are prepared in such a way as to acquire information primarily about their family ties, language usage, community, and perception of their ethnicity.

DEMOGRAPHIC DATA

These data are important in a more urban environment. Hence, for my research I collected information on the demographic makeup of the

25. See appendix A, List of Key Informants.

Chinese in Metro Manila such as data on ethnicity, race, gender, age breakdown, socio-economic information, occupation, language knowledge and use, and inter-ethnic marriage patterns. I rely and employ census data and published research works on Chinese Filipinos.

DIGITAL RECORDING AND PAPER BASED QUESTIONNAIRES

Ybarrola reminds that one must be prepared for the unexpected and so note-taking at all times is necessary since we cannot rely on our memory.[26] I used a sound recorder, a video camera for the interviews, and a camera for still shots. I also used paper-based questionnaires for basic information. A rudimentary questionnaire was developed for all informants of all categories and an additional questionnaire unique to each category.[27] However, not all informants filled out the paper-based questionnaire due to limitation of time; not everyone agreed to have their photographs taken, and not everyone allowed the interview to be recorded on video.

Analytical Framework

In *The Cultural Experience*, David McCurdy, James Spradley, and Diana Shandy present the core tasks of ethnosemantic ethnography, which are discovering folk terms, eliciting taxonomic structure, and discovering meaning. Ethnosemantic research is the method by which we try to make sense of the "meanings" given by the people we are studying. After I discover the folk terms in the data, I classify them into categories and try to find meanings in them. In finding meanings, McCurdy et al. discuss the importance of details, focusing on the data acquired, and identifying cultural themes. When the ethnographer "hits the wall," he/she must be reminded of the details acquired from the field. That is, the answer is always back in the data. One must look carefully at the details for people, places, times, things, events, actions, and feelings. Look for contrast and stories.[28]

As the expression goes, "the devil is in the details," so one must remember the importance of details. Conversely, one must be aware of the tremendous amount of detail that can be gathered. Hence in making classification, one needs to stay focused and stay within the parameters of the research. The theories on ethnicity and hybridity in chapter 3 will serve both as guide and boundaries to keep the study focused.

26. Ybarrola, "Opening Session."

27. See appendix B for the basic interview questions.

28. McCurdy et al., *Cultural Experience*, 33, 48–51, 67–70.

To discover cultural themes, one must return to the notes and look for similar or reoccurring themes. These are found in "broad value statements" or based on "principle of contrast." Another way is to discover "cultural strategies," ways that people form concepts and face challenges. Challenges are problems faced by the people in their daily lives.[29]

Finally, I took note of past histories of perceptions on Chinese Filipinos. I looked into the significance of physical signs like complexion, facial features, dress, hairstyle (like the queue), language, and religion. These are embedded in works written about the Chinese during the Spanish Period or American Period. I did not look into theater, the arts, or music performed by or about Chinese, though these would be good topics for subsequent research.

SIGNIFICANCE OF THE STUDY

It is my hope that through this research, I will be able to make the following contributions:

a. This research will provide an anthropological study of the ethnic identity of the Chinese Filipinos living in Metro Manila through the use of ethnographic research methods. This study is constructed to discover the way that the Chinese Filipinos see themselves, whether as Chinese, Filipinos, or both.

b. This research will contribute to the literature on cultural hybridity and ethnic identity. This research focuses on whether the Chinese Filipinos remain essentially "purist" or have over the course of time and globalization constructed or reconstructed their culture into a "third culture" or hybrid cultures. There is also the possibility of multiple identities. The Chinese Filipinos make the choice to present a particular self as they negotiate boundaries, thus compartmentalizing their life in response to different social and cultural issues.

c. In this project, I will construct a profile of the present Chinese Filipinos by classifying them based on the data collected. The research aims to learn about their uniqueness and distinctiveness as opposed to simply grouping all Chinese Diaspora in one category.

d. Lastly, with a fresh view of Chinese ethnicity, it may be that the Chinese churches will benefit from its findings in three ways. First, this

29. Ibid., 77–82.

research will help them have a deeper understanding and knowledge of the people they want to evangelize, disciple, and serve. Second, this research will aid these churches in understanding their role in local and global missions. Third, this research will be helpful in addressing issues concerning multilingual services, Filipino memberships, and exclusivity among Chinese churches.

DEFINITION OF KEY TERMS

Chinese Mestizos—Mixed blood or half bred between Chinese and Filipinos.

Constructivism—The theory that ethnic identity is constructed rather than already existing *a priori*. It is the theory that ethnic identity develops situationally, is negotiated, and deals with establishing and maintaining boundaries. As Aletta Norval says, it is "historically evolving, culturally variegated" yet nevertheless "has a powerful structuring influence on individual experience."[30]

EnRAWGen—English Reading and Writing Generation; coined by David Cheung describing the second- and third-generation Chinese Filipinos who tend to read and write in English and mix Minnanhua, Filipino, and English in conversation.[31]

Filipino—Filipino refers both to the people and one of the two official languages spoken in the Philippines. The other being English. See also Tagalog. "Early Filipinos" is the term used for this study to refer to the Filipinos before Spanish Period.

Fujian 福建 or Hokkien—Fujian is a province of China located on the southeast coast. Fujian is the Putonghua expression while Hokkien is the Minnanhua expression. The term "Hokkien" can refer to the people in this region or the language used, thus interchangeable with the term Minnanhua.

Hoan-á—A derogatory term in Minnanhua used to refer to the Filipinos by Chinese Filipinos; means "barbarians."

---

30. Norval, "Politics of Ethnicity and Identity," 277.
31. Cheung, "Chinese Filipino Profile," 2, 6, 9, 11, 13.

Huáqiáo 華僑—The Putonghua expression referring to Overseas Chinese. In Minnanhua, the expression is read as *Huakiao* and it literally means "Chinese who lives abroad." The Huáqiáo, Sojourner, or Overseas Chinese is the immigrant who arrives from China. He/she is the first generation of his/her family. He/she considers the Philippines a temporary home, a transient place. He/she desires to return to his/her homeland and seeks to earn money in the country to send back home. These are precisely the longings of the early immigrants during the Spanish period and American era.

Huárén 華人—Putonghua expression that refers to the Chinese in the Philippines or globalized Chinese or international Chinese who may stay in the Philippines or move elsewhere.[32]

Hybridity (cultural)—The result of mixing of "blood" or mixing of cultures and/or cultural elements.

Homogeneity (cultural)—Mono-cultural, homogenous, or practicing one culture.

Indio—Refers to Filipinos during the Spanish Period by the Spanish.

Jiuqiáo 舊僑 (Old Immigrants)—Putonghua expression for immigrants from China before the 1970s who are mostly from Fujian province. They are also called G.I. or "genuine **intsik**" or Chinatown Chinese. Many of them left China with empty pockets but with strong determination to succeed. They are fluent in Minnanhua and in Putonghua if they are educated. They are not necessarily very fluent in Filipino or English.

Kaisa Para Sa Kaunlaran, Inc. (Unity in Progress)—Kaisa was founded by Teresita Ang See and many other Chinese Filipinos on August 28, 1987, as a cause-oriented non-government organization. It aims to serve as a bridge between the Chinese community and the mainstream Philippine society for nation building.

Putonghua 普通話—Also known as Mandarin. It refers to the standard language of China. It is known as Guoyǔ 國語 (national language) in Taiwan and Huayǔ 華語 (literally China language) in the Philippines.

---

32. Wickberg, "Anti-Sinicism," 176–77.

Minnanhua 閩南話—Putonghua expression that refers to the language of the Hokkien people, who sometimes call the language *Ēmn̂g ōe* or *Banlam ōe*. It is the lingua franca of the majority Chinese Filipinos. Minnanhua is known as Amoy by Westerners. Amoy is the English transliteration for *Ēmn̂g* or Xiàmén 廈門.

Pinoy—The colloquial term for the Filipino.

Primordialism—Ethnic identity stemming from social givens such as those defined by Clifford Geertz. Geertz defines primordial theory or primordial attachments as people joining together by virtue of givens like blood ties or kinship, race, language, customs, or religions.[33]

Tagalog—Refers to the major ethnic group in the Philippines. It also refers to their language. The Filipino language is largely based on the Tagalog language.

Taidiok-á 大陸人—Minnanhua expression; a derogatory term meaning "from mainland."

Third Culture—Volkmar Gessner and Angelika Schade define it as "long drawn out relationships and negotiations, especially characteristic of international organizations, can lead to a development of a common, third culture."[34]

Tsinoy—Coined by Kaisa as an ethnic label to refer to the Chinese in the Philippines or **Tsinong-Pinoy**. They identify themselves as Filipinos (**Pinoy**) with Chinese (**Tsino**) racial origin or culture.

Unhomely—Derived from Homi Bhabha's concept of the unhomed. The unhomely is not homeless but marks deeper historical displacement just like a Chinese who does not feel at home in the Philippines or China.[35]

Xinqiáo 新僑—Putonghua expression referring to the new influxes of migrants from China to the Philippines. *Sinkiao* is the Minnanhua rendition. See refers these Huáqiáo as Xinqiáo (New Immigrants) who came

33. Geertz, *Interpretation of Cultures*, 259.
34. Gessner and Schade, "Conflicts of Culture," 259.
35. Bhabha, *Location of Cultures*, 13.

during the 1970s onward. They are mostly from Fujian reconnecting with relatives.[36]

REVIEW OF RELEVANT LITERATURE

There are references to the Chinese in Philippine history books such as those by Patricio Abinales and Donna Amoroso, Conrado Benitez, Renato Constantino, John Leddy Phelan, William Henry Scott, and many others. Most of their accounts focus on the Chinese during the Pre-Hispanic Period and Spanish Period of Philippine history. These accounts give an important background for the study which are discussed in chapter 2. The following literature review on Chinese Filipinos is divided into three groups: books written by non-Chinese, by Chinese but not from the Philippines, and by Chinese Filipinos themselves.

Books by Non-Chinese on Chinese Filipinos

There are books specifically on the Chinese in the Philippines written by non-Chinese, such as the introductory chapter of Alfonso Felix Jr. in *The Chinese in the Philippines*, the writings of Edgar Wickberg, and Cristina Szanton Blanc's chapter on "Modern Asians" in Ong and Nonini's *Ungrounded Empires*.

Felix argues that the Chinese were not wanted in the country despite their contributions in economy and politics. Hence, the massacres and expulsions on many occasions during the Spanish Period limited their numbers. During the American Period, laws were enacted that oppressed and suppressed the Chinese; for example, laws preventing them from intermarrying with Filipinos, from traveling to the provinces without permit, from obtaining Filipino citizenship, and excluding them from numerous occupations even in retail trade. Felix concludes that the history on the relationship between the Chinese and Filipinos was a history of massacre and discrimination. He cites his own experiences with the Chinese that further confirmed the animosity between the races.[37]

The second point Felix raises is about the exploitation of the Chinese by the different government officials in different eras and the exploitation of the Filipinos by the Chinese which further widened the gap. "For generations, the Chinese and ourselves have held each other in mutual

---

36. See, "Influx of New Chinese Immigrants," 138.

37. Felix, "How We Stand," 1:3–5.

contempt. We expect no ethics from them and they expect us to behave like savages."[38]

Felix then asks an important question: What should be done with the Chinese? Massacre them as Hitler did the Jews, deport them all back to China, or Filipinized them by prohibiting them to speak their dialect and practice their culture? He confesses that his first language is Spanish, since he is of Spanish descent, but his loyalty is to the Philippines. He then proposes that "if we want them to be loyal to us, we must allow them to live as we do, to have the rights we also have."[39]

Wickberg wrote books and articles on Chinese Overseas. With regard to Chinese Filipinos, he focuses on the economic and social changes during the mid- to late-nineteenth-century Philippines that affected the life of the Chinese in the Philippines. He advocates the study of Chinese in other parts of Southeast Asia to further understand the Chinese in the Philippines.[40]

Wickberg classifies the Chinese identities based on historical periods in the chapter "Anti-Sinicism and Chinese Identity Options in the Philippines." After the mass naturalization of 1975, the present Chinese can be classified into five groups: (1) Huárén is the term for the Chinese in the Philippines or globalized Chinese or international Chinese who may stay in the Philippines or move elsewhere. (2) The Chinese in Manila Chinatown who are focused on the Chinese community affairs. (3) The Huáqiáo or Chinese Overseas or Sojourners who are declining in numbers. (4) The Filipinos of Chinese background which is the growing group. (5) The Chinese-Filipinos or Tsinoys who are mostly middle-class and born in the Philippines. They seek integration into the Philippine societies.[41] This classification is very helpful in categorizing and understanding the Chinese throughout history to the present. However, missing in this classification is the cultural aspects that hold their beliefs and practices, as well as their narratives of issues and struggles that will help us discover who they say they are.

Szanton Blanc talks about "new imaginaries" used by Chinese capitalists to redefine themselves. Lee Kuan Yew was the first to develop the Confucian model of capitalism. This model combined capitalism with an

---

38. Ibid.

39. Ibid., 4–10.

40. Wickberg, *Chinese in Philippine Life*, 239–41.

41. Wickberg, "Anti-Sinicism," 176–77.

authoritarian state as opposed to a democratic state like in Westernized countries. This reformulation of the Chinese Diaspora as the triumphal capitalist paved the way for Chinese immigrants to reposition themselves in countries where they have settled.[42] In the case of the Chinese in the Philippines, however, the "imaginary" that they control the economy of the country has led to kidnappings. Granted that there are high profile Chinese Filipinos in the business world (e.g., Henry Sy, George Ty, Lucio Tan, and John Gokongwei), still most of the Chinese Filipinos are medium and small entrepreneurs or regular employees.[43]

Szanton Blanc described the Tsinoys as a complex group of people. They were in a different situation as compared to those of their Straits counterparts. They were still wrestling with discrimination, identity, and community issues. Hence, the "new imaginaries" might not necessarily describe these Tsinoys who were mostly in the middle class and not super rich tycoons.[44]

Books by Chinese but Not from the Philippines

In addition, there are other Chinese who are not from the Philippines but have written about the Chinese in the Philippines or the larger Chinese Diaspora.

Chee Kiong Tong has written a very good survey of the Chinese in Southeast Asian countries. His work provides us with a sense of the larger context of the Chinese Diaspora. He assessed in 2010 that there were 18–20 million ethnic Chinese in Southeast Asia. He points out the relation of the numbers with the whole population of the host countries. For example Indonesia has the largest number of Chinese in the world outside of China and Taiwan. It has more Chinese than Hong Kong. But the Chinese are a minority since they only comprise 3 percent of the total population of 240 million. The United States ranks fourth but the Chinese there are equivalent to only 1 percent of the whole population. Singapore ranks fifth though the Chinese comprise 80 percent of its entire

42. Szanton Blanc, "Thoroughly Modern 'Asian,'" 264–67.

43. Henry Sy and family has a net worth of $12.7 million; Lucio Tan, $6.1 million; John Gokongwei, $4.9 million; and George Ty, $3,700 million. Brown, "Philippines' 50 Richest."

44. Szanton Blanc was present in the first Tsinoy National Convention of the Kaisa in August of 1994. Szanton Blanc, "Thoroughly Modern 'Asian,'" 272–79.

population. Malaysia has 26 percent Chinese, Thailand has 10 percent, and the Philippines has 1–1.2 percent.[45]

Overseas Community Affairs Council of Taiwan recorded that there were 41 million Chinese Overseas in 2012 not counting the people of Hong Kong, Macau and Taiwan: 74 percent reside in Asia; 19 percent in Americas; 4 percent in Europe; 2 percent in Oceania; and 1 percent in Africa.[46]

The top ten countries with the highest number of Chinese in 2012 are as follows: Indonesia (8.1 million), Thailand (7.5 million), Malaysia (6.8 million), USA (4.2 million), Singapore (2.8 million), Canada (1.6 million), Philippines (1.4 million), Myanmar (1 million), Vietnam (1 million), and Peru (990,000).[47]

Focusing on Chinese Filipinos, Tong's assessment is that the Chinese in the Philippines are essentially still very Chinese, especially given their concern with "blood" ties. He proposed that "a more nuanced understanding of the Chinese identity and ethnic relations is necessary."[48] As for Chinese identity, he argues for both primordial and situational theories.[49] I agree with Tong that the Chinese Filipinos are still essentially Chinese but as I mentioned earlier, I see their Chineseness has evolved into a hybrid of cultures. Therefore, the hybridization was not only happening among the Chinese Mestizos that Tong highlighted in his research. Rather, cultural hybridization is also happening even among "pure" Chinese born and raised in the Philippines.

Aihwa Ong and Donald Nonini view "Chinese culture," Chinese family values or guanxi 關係, and "Confucian capitalism" as "discursive tropes" rather than essential Chinese characteristics. The authors observe the Chinese Diaspora as a people with "flexible accumulation" or flexibility in responding to situations, a "third culture"[50] that requires de-

45. Tong, *Identity and Ethnic Relations*, 1, 83; See, "State and Public Policies," 155.

46. Overseas Community Affairs Council, "Overseas Chinese."

47. Overseas Community Affairs Council, "Overseas Chinese: By Country." The Kaisa and See are more conservative in assessing the total population of the Chinese Filipinos in the country. They maintain that the total population is around 1 to 1.2 million.

48. Tong, *Identity and Ethnic Relations*, 201, 209–14.

49. The situational approach, emerging from the theoretical work of Frederik Barth (1969), "emphasizes the fluidity and contingency of ethnic identity, which is constructed in specific historical and social contexts." Brettell, *Anthropology and Migration*, 106.

50. Third culture is defined as follows: "Long drawn out relationships and

territorialized ethnographies.[51] Using David Harvey's definition, flexible accumulation "rests on flexibility with respect to labor processes, labor markets, products, and patterns of consumption."[52] Such flexibility enhances and increases the mobility of people, ideas, and commodities that speed globalization and aid in the transition to global capitalism. These dynamics produce "third cultures" as transnationals face intercultural problems and confront the reality of living and negotiating in two different cultures. Gessner and Schade quote John Useem: "This third culture is not merely a mutual accommodation or amalgamation of two separate, parallel cultures, but the birth of something new as far as behaviours, lifestyles, worldviews, etc. are concerned."[53]

These anthropologists are calling for a new approach in engaging transnational studies as another way of viewing Chinese immigrants. They are seeking ethnographies that are grounded in historical reflections and contextualization of Chinese Diaspora yet departing from the Orientalist's approach wherein ethnicities are fixed, timeless, and defined by the binary opposition of East-West.[54] In her book *Flexible Citizenship*, Ong argues that in the era of globalization, "individuals as well as governments develop a flexible notion of citizenship and sovereignty as strategies to accumulate capital and power."[55]

Flexible citizenship refers then to the "the cultural logics of capitalist accumulation, travel, and displacement that induce subjects to respond fluidly and opportunistically to changing political-economic conditions."[56] The Chinese in Hong Kong and Southeast Asia have evolved in different circumstances to escape upheavals. They have improvised themselves and become flexible and mobile.[57] But, I wonder, can this restructuring of the Chinese Diaspora identity be really understood apart from the primordial ties?

---

negotiations, especially characteristic of international organizations, can lead to a development of a common, third culture." Gessner and Schade, "Conflicts of Culture," 259. The word "third culture" was first used by John Useem, John Donoghue, and Ruth Hill Useem (1963) in the book *Men in the Middle of the Third Culture*.

51. Ong and Nonini, "Chinese Transnationalism," 5–9.

52. Harvey, *Conditions of Postmodernity*, 147.

53. Gessner and Schade, "Conflicts of Culture," 260.

54. Ong and Nonini, "Chinese Transnationalism," 9–14.

55. Ong, *Flexible Citizenship*, 6.

56. Ibid.

57. Ibid., 6, 94.

Lynne Pan has written a good account of Chinese Diaspora tracing way back to the fifteenth century. In chapter 8, she uses the term "Hybrids" to describe the Chinese Mestizos and their contributions in the Philippines. She also uses this term to classify the Chinese "half breeds" in Thailand, Indonesia, and New Zealand. She reasoned that having Chinese blood may not necessarily mean being Chinese in identification. Such was the case of Jose Rizal, the Philippine National Hero. Rizal was a fifth-generation Chinese Mestizo. He unsuccessfully sought to have the categorization Chinese Mestizo changed to *indio puro* as he was about to sign the document informing him of his death sentence. To be categorized as a Chinese Mestizo was to suggest that he was not even a real Filipino or *indio*. Nevertheless, the Chinese have long celebrated Rizal's ancestry as proof of his Chineseness and therefore claimed that he was the greatest Chinese contribution to the Philippines.[58]

On the other hand, Corazon Cojuangco Aquino used her Chinese ancestry to gain the support of the Chinese community when she became the President of the Republic of the Philippines in 1986. The World Kho (Co) Clan Association of Southeast Asia and North America visited her in Manila to congratulate her and give her a sizeable gift for her government. The Khos (Cos) claimed her as a kinswoman even with the fact that she was very much Filipinized as she belongs to the fourth-generation Chinese Mestizos.[59] Clearly, bloodline or blood ties may not always be a ground for ethnic identification, but perhaps this cannot totally be disregarded.

Amy Chua's parents are ethnic Chinese from the Philippines who migrated to the United States. Her controversial book *World on Fire* put a spotlight on the Chinese Filipinos. Unfortunately, she paints an inaccurate picture of this ethnic group by generalizing them all as rich and enjoying their own wealth. This makes the kidnapping situation of the Chinese community the latter's own fault. The thesis of her book is grounded in the assumption that these "market-dominant-minorities" are hated and eventually oppressed and even killed by the impoverished majority as she enumerates the different ethnic wars from different parts of the world.[60] Her work is a case of stereotyping the Chinese in the Philippines as a wealthy minority at the expense of the majority poor Filipinos.

58. Pan, *Sons of the Yellow Emperor*, 165.

59. Ibid., 153–54.

60. Chua, *World on Fire*, 1–12.

Books by Chinese Filipinos

Conversely, there are many works about the Chinese in the Philippines written by Chinese Filipinos themselves. These are materials with an emic point of view. The following are some of the written materials.

Teresita Ang See is one of the founders of the Kaisa. In her third volume of *The Chinese in the Philippines*, See talks about issues like identity, association, business, education, religion, culture, and language. See presents the surveys of Gerald McBeath in 1969 and compared them to her own surveys made in 1989 and 1995.

Table 1. Religious Affiliation of Chinese Filipinos by Teresita Ang See

	Catholics	Protestants	Chinese Religions*
Gerald McBeath 1969	71%	15%	2.3%
Teresita Ang See 1989	66.6%	11.5%	9%
Teresita Ang See 1995	70%	12.9%	2%

Originally published in Teresita A. See, *Chinese in the Philippines*, 3:181.

*Mixture of Christianity, Buddhism and Chinese Folk Religions

She concludes that the Chinese Filipinos are predominantly of Christian religions and not Buddhist, Daoist, or practicing Chinese Folk Religions. Eighty-five percent of the Chinese Filipinos are locally born and raised in the Philippines. Many of them have attended Chinese Christian schools and Catholic colleges and universities, hence are exposed to Christianity. However, she also recognizes that the Chinese Filipinos have a tendency to be syncretistic by accepting all religions and practicing all beliefs to avoid bad luck. Moreover, she observes that during death and funerals, the Chinese Filipinos employ rituals in ancestral worship to ensure that the demised has a good afterlife.[61]

In the chapter "Influx of New Chinese Immigrants to the Philippines: Problems and Challenges," See identifies the problems brought about by the new influx of Chinese migrants. She also gives a clearer picture of the distinction between the old and new migrants after 1995. This

---

61. See, *Chinese in the Philippines*, 3:181–86.

material contributes to our understanding of the Chinese Diaspora in the Philippines and the problems of kidnappings and citizenship.[62]

In the chapter "The Case of the Chinese in the Philippines," See presents the Chinese during the Spanish and American colonial periods. She also lays out arguments against the myth of Chinese economic control proposed by Amy Chua. Lastly, See narrates the story of the formation and vision of the Kaisa. According to See's report, 52 percent of Tsinoys live in Metro Manila. More than 90 percent consider the Philippines their home country. There is a huge difference among Chinese in Metro Manila and in the provinces as well as new immigrants and second and third generations. See classifies the Chinese in the Philippines into three stages of transition based on sociocultural changes: The Huashāng or Traders, the Huáqiáo or Sojourner, and the Huárén or Chinese people/Chinese immigrants.[63] I try to reconcile the different classifications and present my own based on the stories of informants and the present sociocultural constructs.

Richard Chu writes about the life of the Chinese and the Chinese Mestizos of the 1860s to 1930s. Chu employs Frederik Barth's idea of ethnicity. Barth (1969) challenges the fixed notion of ethnicity such as essentialism and focuses instead on the ongoing negotiations of boundaries between groups of people. Chu observes that scholars who study Overseas Chinese tended to see assimilation and integration as the main identity theories along with nation-based metanarratives. He see these approaches as problematic in the sense that ethnicities are often reified and essentialized and "couched in language of inclusion and exclusion."[64]

Following Ong and Nonini's theory of transnationalism, "third cultures," and flexible accumulations, Chu analyzes microhistories—that is, accounts of the everyday life of the Chinese and Chinese Mestizos in that particular period of Philippine history, in order to show how they negotiated, manipulated, and flexed their identities for the sake of survival or profit. He agrees that the study of ethnicity needs to consider how these people view themselves and not just how they are described by others.[65] Chu ends with the question, who is a Tsinoy? He searches for an answer that is not another reification of the Chinese ethnic identity.[66]

---

62. See, "Influx of New Chinese Immigrants," 137–62.
63. See, "Case of the Chinese in the Philippines," 155–56.
64. Chu, *Chinese and Chinese Mestizos of Manila*, 6.
65. Ibid., 8–12.
66. Ibid., 414.

Rosa Shao stresses the importance of family as the foundational social institution for the development of a child. She observes that the traditional Chinese families are "also experiencing swift transformation" from being clannish to a nucleus-centered family; from a male-dominated to equality between genders; and from arranged marriages to personal or individual choice. The fact that the Chinese Filipino adolescents live in two or more cultures complicates their search for self and identity. Her research focuses on the conflict dimension between Chinese Filipino parent-adolescent relationships and how this influence the development of the adolescent's individuated or relational autonomy.[67]

Tracing Chinese identity in view of the Christian faith, Joseph Shao attributes the expansion of the Chinese Protestant churches in the Philippines primarily to the Chinese migrants themselves. With the establishment of independent indigenous Chinese churches, the gospel is spread out to the Chinese Filipinos by fellow Chinese Filipinos. In his essay in *Chapters in Philippine Church History*, Shao chronicles the growth and development of Chinese churches in the archipelago. He mentions that during the Spanish colonization, Protestantism was not permitted in the Philippines.[68]

According to Shao, it was during the American regime that the Chinese churches were established and Protestantism among Chinese migrants grew in numbers. The oldest existing Chinese church was St. Stephen's Church, started by Episcopalian bishop Charles Brent in 1903. Lu Fei Zhong Hua Christian Church, also known in English as the Chinese United Evangelical Church, was established in 1929 by Chinese migrants from Reformed and Presbyterian churches in Xiamen.[69] Today this church is known as United Evangelical Church of the Philippines.

In 1930, another twenty people grouped together for prayer and Bible study. Soon they formed a separate church called the Gospel Church, largely a following of Watchman Nee's Little Flock. Presently, this group is the

---

67. Shao, "Chinese-Filipino Adolescents," 1–7.

68. Shao, "Channel of Blessings," 413. Jean Uayan discovers in her research that there were eleven Chinese Protestants living in Iloilo (1885 to 1892). It is a wonder how they lived since Protestantism was prohibited during the Spanish Period. The Presbyterian missionaries found these believers and started their work among them by 1900. This church was dissolved by the 1920s. Uayan, "Study on the Emergence," 75–77, 88–97.

69. Shao, "Channel of Blessings," 414, 417–19. For more history on the indigenization of Chinese Protestant Churches in Fujian, China, see Cheung, *Christianity in Modern China*, 1–60.

Christian Gospel Church. It has planted many churches in different parts of the Philippines, such as Caloocan City, Quezon City, and Cebu City.[70]

The revival meetings of John Sung and the Bethel Evangelistic Band in the 1930s resulted in significant mission outreaches.[71] Following their example, the Chinese United Evangelical Church created its own Evangelistic Band for its mission outreach programs. This effort gave birth to the many churches in Metro Manila and all over the archipelago. Meanwhile, the first Chinese church in the Visayan Islands was the Cebu Gospel Church (founded 1916) which is the second oldest existing Chinese church. Together with the Davao Evangelical Church (founded in 1951), both were instrumental in the growth and development of the Chinese churches in Visayas and Mindanao.[72]

With new churches and growing number of members, Chinese Christians faced the need to train local leaders for pastoral work. This gave birth to the Bible Institute of the Philippines (presently the Biblical Seminary of the Philippines or BSOP). It was established in 1957. This is the only Chinese seminary in Metro Manila, an institution which provided about 90 percent of the pastors in all the 93 Chinese Protestant churches in the Philippines.[73]

In the chapter "A Descriptive Study of Mission Programs of Selected Philippine-Chinese Churches in Metro Manila: Policies, Motives, and Views of Mission," Chiu Eng Tan classifies the Chinese Filipinos into three groups. First, the Alien Chinese or those born in China and who migrated to the Philippines whether pre- or postwar. Second, the Philippine-born Chinese are those primarily born after the Second World War. Third, the assimilated Chinese are Filipinos with Chinese ancestry extending way back to the Spanish period.[74]

Tan's earlier research in 1996 showed that the Chinese Filipino evangelical Christians practiced what she calls "folk Christianity." She discovered that some Chinese Filipino evangelical Christians remained superstitious and ignorant of the teachings in the Bible. They continued in their adherence to both Christian faith and folk Chinese religions as

70. Shao, "Channel of Blessings," 420.

71. Ka Tong Lim mentions John Sung's impact in the Philippines in his biographical work on Sung's life and ministry. Lim, *Life and Ministry of John Sung*, 172, 183–84, 192–94, 198, 243, and 272.

72. Shao, "Channel of Blessings," 420–23.

73. Based on the information provided by the president of BSOP, Dr. Joseph Shao, dated October 15, 2015, there are at present 93 functioning ethnic Chinese evangelical churches in the country.

74. Tan, "Descriptive Study of Mission Programs," 211–12.

well as fortune and luck. She raises the question how one can reconcile this mixing of beliefs with a monotheistic religion?[75]

In the same way, Jean Uayan believes that the Chinese Filipino worldview is a combination of different elements borrowed from here and there. Different religions like Roman Catholicism, Protestantism, Buddhism, and Daoism are combined with animistic beliefs and practices of Chinese folk religion. She likens the Chinese Filipino worldview to a popular Chinese dish called *chap chay lo mi*. The dish is made of *chap chay* (mixed vegetables) and *lo mi* (thick round noodles). It usually has pork, chicken and other ingredients as well. The Chinese Filipinos are pragmatic people. They desire to establish a harmonious relationship with all people. They are willing to accept Catholicism to please their Filipino friends and at the same time continue to have a carved image of Buddha to identify with their Chinese relatives and friends.[76]

Jose Vidamor Yu is a Roman Catholic priest. He observes that the Chinese Filipinos "form a community of distinct culture mentality." Even with centuries of coexistence with the Filipinos, they have not totally integrated or assimilated into Filipino society. They are not purist in the sense that they are immune from outside influences, but they have somehow managed to preserve their own set of worldviews, rituals, and religious traditions. Having a distinct culture, as Yu mentioned, the Chinese Filipinos are no longer "pure" Chinese in their cultural orientation and yet they were not fully "Filipinized" either. He aims to challenge the Chinese Filipino Catholics to consider priesthood or missionary work to China as well as to tap their resources for the propagation of their faith.[77]

What is lacking in all these literature is an understanding of the ethnic identity of the Chinese in the Philippines in the present era of globalization, the second decade of the third millennium. There is a need to go to the people themselves and discover what they think and what they value. Do they all agree with the classification Tsinoy? Do they all see themselves as Chinese with a Filipino heart or Filipino with a Chinese heart? Do they talk about their Chineseness as if it is a product of primordialism or constructivism? Do they all agree that they are hybrids in some ways or many ways? Or do they insist that they are still "pure" in their cultural orientation and even bloodline? There are books with similar themes on hybridity and homogeneity but I will reserve these for the theoretical framework for conceptual themes.

75. Tan, "Cosmos, Humans, and Gods," 5–6.

76. Uayan, "Chap Chay Lo Mi," 65, 72–77.

77. Yu, *Inculturation*, 3:4–5.

2

Chinese Identities in Philippine History

THE CHINESE TRADED WITH early Filipinos long before the Spaniards came. In succeeding centuries, the Chinese population and enclave were controlled by the Spaniards by placing them within the Parián, a district located just outside the Intramuros or Walled City of the Spaniards.[1] The Americans did the same with policies that contained them within Binondo and controlled their numbers through the Chinese Exclusion Act that was enforced even in the Philippines.[2] Nevertheless, the Chinese managed to spread out all over the country, though most of them concentrate in Metro Manila today. "Their presence and valuable contributions in Philippine economy and culture continued during the American period and up to the present."[3]

The following is a narrative of the history of the Chinese based on the names and labels given to them throughout Philippine history. This section provides the necessary historical backdrop of Chinese identities in the eyes of the Filipinos, Western colonizers, and the Chinese

1. The meaning of "Parián" is rather obscure. Writers have different understandings of its etymology. It could be a Minnanhua word, *pâi-yá-tiàm*, meaning shops or stalls as Phelan recorded in his book. Phelan, *Hispanization of the Philippines*, 11. Wickberg suggests it may come from the word pariah meaning outcast. Wickberg, "Anti-Sinicism," 156–57. Geertz mentioned pariah settlements as referring to ethnic minority groups living as "foreign" traders in newly established states, groups such as the Chinese in Southeast Asia. Geertz, *Interpretation of Cultures*, 268. The Parián was set aside for the Chinese in 1581. See appendix D for more discussion of Parián.

2. Binondo was originally established in 1594 as a Chinese town but became a place for Catholic Chinese. See appendix D for more discussion of Binondo.

3. Uytanlet, "Pride and Prejudice," 57–58. See, "Case of the Chinese in the Philippines," 156.

themselves. This portion does not provide a complete history of Chinese in the Philippines, but a particular history of terms of identity and the role of the Chinese in Philippine history. Table 2 provides an outline of major events and dates in different eras of the Philippine history that affected the Chinese and their identity.

Table 2. Major Events and Dates That Affected the Chinese
and Their Identity in the Philippines*

Major Events	Pre-Hispanic	Spanish	American	Postwar to Present
Labels/Names	Traders Friends	*Sangleys* *Chinos*	Chinamen Coolies Aliens Non-Christian Tribe	**Tsino** **Intsik** **Kabise** Tsinoy Chinese
Trade and Policies of Host Country	Tang Dynasty (618–907) Song Dynasty (960–127) Ming Dynasty (1368)	1565, 1572, 1587, 1869	1899. 1900, 1921, 1935, 1940	1946, 1954, 1955, 1961
Segregation		1581, 1594, 1663	1901, 1902	
Expulsion/ Immigration Ban		1589, 1593, 1690–1700, 1755, 1766	1898, 1902, 1904, 1941	
Resistance against Colonizers		1574, 1593, 1603, 1639, 1762, 1898	1902, 1921	
Massacres		1603, 1639, 1663, 1762		
Hispanization, Conversion, Mixed Marriage		1589, 1594, 1755		
Racial Riots			1919, 1924	
Filipino Citizenship				1975

Major Events	Pre-Hispanic	Spanish	American	Postwar to Present
Integration				1971, 1975, 1987
Overstaying Chinese				1975, 1992
Kidnapping				1990s to present

*The details of these events can be found in this chapter
as well as in appendix D, chapters 4 and 5.

TRADERS AND FRIENDS: CONTACT WITH EARLY FILIPINOS IN THE PRE-HISPANIC PERIOD

Teodoro A. Agoncillo acknowledges the lack of materials about the Pre-Hispanic Period except from what was written by Chinese officials and Muslim scholars. The limited records, nevertheless, present a civilized Philippines that had been engaging in trade with Chinese, Arabs, and neighboring countries in Southeast Asia.[4] Traces of Chinese and Indian cultural influences brought about by trade penetrated into the lives of the early Filipinos as evident in their borrowings of terms into the Filipino (Tagalog) language.[5] Therefore, we cannot know for certain what labels or names the early Filipinos called the Chinese traders. We can only surmise how the Chinese were perceived based on the accounts available.

William Henry Scott acknowledges the rich heritage of the ancient Filipinos before the coming of the Spaniards in *A Critical Study of the Prehispanic Source Materials for the Study of Philippine History*. Scott understands the importance and implication of the thousands of pieces of

4. Agoncillo disagrees with the idea that the Philippines was discovered by Ferdinand Magellan because this implies that the country was unknown to the world until the Spaniards landed on its shores. Agoncillo, *History of the Filipino People*, 20.

5. Tagalog refers to the majority ethnic group in the Philippines. It also refers to their language. Tagalog words like *am* (rice broth), *ate* (older sister), **ingkong** (grandfather), and many others derived from the Chinese Minnanhua. The borrowing of words in Minnanhua showed the predominance of Chinese from Fujian. The words were mostly associated with food or kinship terms. However, words like **bathala** (god), **katha** (story), **ganda** (beautiful), and many others derived from the Indian Sanskrit. Most words borrowed from Sanskrit pertain to deities, moral obligations, numbers, and emotions. Ibid., 28–30.

Chinese porcelains or "chinaware" discovered in Sta. Ana cemetery in Manila during the 1960s. These porcelain pieces were dated to the Song Dynasty (or the Sung Dynasty, 960–1279). Chinese records also show that there was extensive trade on Chinese porcelains throughout Southeast Asia during the Song Dynasty. Further, a large burial jar from a cave in Basilan contained a huge collection of plates dating Chinese imperial reigns from 1530 to 1600. Scott recognizes this as a collection made by a person in one's lifetime. The historian Antonio Pigafetta who visited the Visayan Islands with Ferdinand Magellan in 1521 recorded the elegant porcelain containers used by the locals to store rice grains.[6] This evidence conveyed the presence of Chinese trade among early Filipinos during the Pre-Hispanic Period.

Henry Otley Beyer, on the other hand, writes that the early Filipinos were literate and strongly influenced by Indian social and political dynamics. Their writings were in Old Indian syllabic origin. This cannot be verified because, when Spain conquered the Americas and the Philippines, their fanatical zeal led them to destroy written form and artwork of the natives. They believed these were from the devil. Beyer adds that the Chinese influence was mainly on the economic life.[7]

Chao Ju-Kua 趙汝适 (Zhao Rugua) wrote *Chu-Fan-Chï* 諸蕃志 (Zhu Fan Zhi) "Description of the Barbarous Peoples" in 1225. This book was translated in English and published in 1911 by Friedrich Hirth and W. W. Rockhill. Chao's account was considered as an ethnology, presenting how the Chinese viewed foreign countries, the peoples, and their products used for trade. Chao was a customs inspector and superintendent of trade in Quanzhou, Fujian. He gathered data and stories from merchants who traveled in different parts of the world.[8]

---

6. Scott, *Prehispanic Source Materials*, 13–14, 32, 58. Excavations in different parts of the country have yielded a significant number of Chinese jars, ceramics, vases, and coins of the Tang Dynasty (618–907). Trade between China and the Philippines could have been ongoing even before the Song Dynasty or these were brought by the Arabs and Indians who dominated the Southeast Asia's trade in the tenth century. See, *Tsinoy*, 28.

7. Beyer, "Philippines before Magellan," 861, 865, 892; Agoncillo, *History of the Filipino People*, 28. In 1986, the Laguna Copperplate Inscription was discovered and carbon-dated to AD 900. It is considered as the earliest document found in the Philippines. The inscriptions were mainly in Old Malay but had names in Sanskrit. Abinales and Amoroso, *State and Society*, 37–38.

8. Chao, *Chu-Fan-Chï*, 35–39; See, *Tsinoy*, 20, 24.

Chao mentioned the Chinese engaging in trade with the people of Ma-I (Mindoro) and San-sü (lit. three islands). The Chinese during this period were limited to trading in coastal areas. They did not venture far to sell their goods themselves due to communication and safety issues. Chao says that the people of Ma-I eagerly sought to trade with Chinese as their ships drew near to the shore. He recorded that in San-sü, the Chinese needed to be careful of natives shooting arrows at passersby. They learned to wait in midstream for the natives to approach them to barter instead of going straight to the shore. Lastly, he narrates a case of foreign traders literally holding one or two natives as hostages until the trade and business was all done.[9]

Chao found many similarities with the people in both places although it was not clear what or where San-sü was. He called the natives "fan" 蕃 (lit. barbaric), and "man" 蠻 (savages) because of some observations he had made. First, the people of the islands did not belong to a common jurisdiction, rather, they were scattered as different tribes. Second, their main trading center lacked established places for business. In some places, trade was so dangerous that one could not go ashore until they had secured hostages.[10]

A century later, another Chinese writer named Wang Da-Yan (Wang Ta-Yuan) recorded his explorations among the people of the islands in 1349. He reveals some things about medieval Filipino life. He observes that cultural contacts with India and China produced practices such as the suttee and use of coiffure by both men and women. He mentioned Mintolang (Mindanao) and the Sulu pearls. Wang called the natives barbarians. Wang thought that they were amateurish as traders

---

9. Chao, *Chu-Fan-Chï*, 159–62; Scott, *Prehispanic Source Materials*, 70–71. "Foreign traders were not permitted to land in the Philippine villages, but carried on their business on board ship. Native traders came to the Chinese ship, for example, bringing with them such products as cotton, yellow wax, cloth, coconuts, onions, and fine mats, and they offered these in exchange for goods brought on the visiting ship for sale. The Filipino merchants apparently took some of the Chinese goods on consignment and transported them to other parts of the islands for sale, for the Chinese ships often had to wait in port as long as nine months for the natives to return and pay for the goods which had been entrusted to them." Benitez, *History of the Philippines*, 66–67.

10. Chao, *Chu-Fan-Chï*, 159–62. Chao reserved the term "man" or savage only for cannibals and Negro slaves, people he perceived as primitive and illiterate. As for the word "fan" or barbarian, it can be applied impartially by Chinese to all non-Chinese from hunting cannibals to European monarchs. See Scott, *Prehispanic Source Materials*, 71n18 and 73.

because they did not seem interested in making a profit but more on bodily adornment.[11]

The Chinese people traced their history of civilization to 2100 BC, and they had been proud of their ethnicity and considered their race as the only civilized one. They felt superior over all races with their rich heritage and long history, advanced technological knowledge in many areas, not just sailing and trade. No wonder both Chao and Wang described the early Filipinos as barbarians, for that was how they perceived the rest of the human race.

Two fourteenth-century maps of China showed Taiwan, the Philippines, and Indonesia represented simply by waves in the vast ocean surrounding China. Scott found this puzzling, thinking that either ignorance or lack of interest led the Medieval Chinese to draw the map in such a way. But the fact remains that the Song Dynasty "was literally supported by tariff revenues on overseas trade."[12] Could it be possible that since the Chinese situated China or Zhongguo中國 (Middle Kingdom) as the center of the whole earth or even, the universe, the maps reflected their ethnocentricity by disregarding other countries in the picture even when these were important economic revenues to them?

In 1368, the first emperor of the Ming Dynasty (following the Song Dynasty) declared that maritime trade was a government monopoly. Trade with China was only allowed to countries that were willing to pay tribute to China. There were at least twenty-two places in the Philippines that sent tribute to China. Tribute trade lasted only a century after the death of the first emperor. But during this period, Luzon sent missions in 1372, 1405, and 1410, while Sulu sent six missions from 1370 to 1424. When a Sulu ruler died in the Chinese court while on a visit, the emperor even attended the special funeral for the ruler.[13] This evidence shows that possibly by this time, some Chinese had established centers for trade and even permanent settlements in different parts of the country.

On the other hand, no matter how superior the Chinese might feel about themselves over the natives, they recognized the importance of trade with these people. They valued their relationship with the people and even valued their interests and welfare. Teresita Ang See cites Beyer's work on the Pre-Hispanic Period from stories of early Chinese

---

11. Scott, *Prehispanic Source Materials*, 70–71, 73, 74–76.

12. Ibid., 67.

13. Abinales and Amoroso, *State and Society*, 41.

immigrants. The following are his observations. First, Beyer recorded that the perceptive Chinese traders replaced the Arab and Indian traders on the Philippine shores as they considered the welfare of the whole community and not simply their own profit. The Chinese believed that the prosperity of the community meant good business.[14]

Second, they sold their goods on credit. Purely based on the honor system and trust, the Chinese unloaded their products and let the natives take them to be sold inland. Despite the fact that they could not recognize their faces and that it would take months for the natives to return with the profit, the Chinese seemed sufficiently satisfied with the earnings that they continued such kind of trade without trouble.[15]

Third, Beyer claims that they shared with the natives their knowledge in herbal medicines, agricultural techniques, and skills.[16] Many of the merchants were peasants in China; they also taught the natives the art of domesticating carabaos and training them to plough the fields. They taught them how to extract sugar from sugar cane; masonry; metal tools; textile weaving; dyeing; pottery; carpentry; smith crafting; soap and candle making; and even making chocolates.[17] Based on Beyer's writings, See concludes that the Chinese were not only traders but also friends and teachers, in spite of them calling the natives barbarians and savages.

Established from the above evidences, we can conclude that the Chinese in the Pre-Hispanic Period (1) were primarily traders and merchants, (2) were encouraged by the eagerness of the natives to engage in trade, the trustworthiness of their relationships, and the fact that in Sulu some Filipinos sought the goods more than the profit, (3) felt inhibited from settling or engaging in farming because of the uncertainties of their safety and the restrictions to land in villages during the Song Dynasty, and (4) participated in an exchange of knowledge as well as goods, at least during the Song and Ming dynasties.

14. See, *Chinese in the Philippines*, 1:102.

15. Ibid.

16. Ibid.

17. Ibid., 1:51–52. The early Filipinos learned how to use gongs, umbrellas, lead, and porcelain and even how to manufacture gunpowder from the Chinese. They also copied the Chinese tradition of arranged marriage, including the practice of using a go-between to arrange the marriage. Agoncillo, *History of the Filipino People*, 29–30.

THE SANGLEYS DURING THE SPANISH PERIOD

Ye Yiliang writes that by the fourth to third century BC, Iran was the major link between East and West. "China's silk products had already been introduced to West Asia and East Europe passing through Iran; and glass vessels and art ornaments of the eastern part of the Mediterranean were introduced to China through Iran. Iran was named Anxi 安息 or Bosi 波斯 in Chinese sources.[18] The traditional overland silk route connected Persia or Iran to China, and the route extended to the east of the Mediterranean.[19] Benitez saw the Holy Land or Palestine as a meeting ground for traders among Asia, Africa, and Europe for centuries. After the last crusade in 1272, the desire for Oriental goods exploded as the Europeans "acquired a taste for Eastern luxuries." This led to the growth of trade between Western Europe and the Far East. Oriental products such as spices, fruit, jewels, silks, perfumes, porcelains, precious stones, tapestries, and rugs were exchanged for iron, gold, silver, and woolen cloth.[20]

Benitez, as many other historians, notes the need for new trade routes, as the old ones were controlled by Muslims after the fall of Constantinople (1453) and the expulsion of the Crusaders from the Holy Land (1244).[21] Though the Muslims allowed trade with Europe with fees, the uncertainty and at times monopoly of trade granted to Venice compelled the remaining Western European powers to find new routes to the

18. Ye, "Introductory Essay," 3.

19. Schottenhammer, "Transfer of Xiangyao," 117. Earliest evidences of trade goods on the Silk Road were jade, dated to 1200 BC. China, India, and Iran continued their contact and trade to the first millennium BC. Hansen, *Silk Road*, 235–36.

20. "The Italians made great profits from this trade. They founded banks, which lent money to kings engaged in wars. Cities grew up because of this thriving business. The other European merchants—English, French, Spanish, Portuguese, and Dutch—looked with envy upon the prosperity of their Italian rivals, and thus the ambition of these nations to take part in the Oriental trade was aroused. Indeed, late in the fifteenth century, English merchants began business for themselves in the eastern Mediterranean. By that time all western Europe was deeply stirred over Oriental and Indian trade." Benitez, *History of the Philippines*, 18–19.

21. There were three important trade routes that connected Europe to the East. The first two routes were by sea while the third route was by land. Benitez, *History of the Philippines*, 19. The traditional land route was the most popular one. The maritime silk road was from Persian Gulf via the Indian Ocean to China was of second importance until the late Tang and early Song Dynasties (AD eighth to tenth or eleventh century). By AD tenth century, private merchants preferred to travel by sea than by land due to wars and political unrest thereby making it more unsafe. Schottenhammer, "Transfer of Xiangyao," 117, 120.

East. All these culminated with the maritime explorations and three great geographical discoveries.[22]

The first was Christopher Columbus' search for the shortest route to India by sailing westward in 1492 under the auspices of Spain. He landed in the Americas and called the natives *Indios* or Indians for he thought he was in India.

The second discovery was the route to India by Vasco de Gama in 1498 that destroyed the monopoly of Venice on trade with the East. This also made Portugal powerful both in trade and colonization. Nevertheless, the search for new trade routes continued as Portugal only allowed her own ships to sail in this newfound route.

Spain sponsored Ferdinand Magellan to set sail and find a new route to the East. This marked the third discovery. Magellan's expedition was significant to the world in that it was the first circumnavigation made by sailing westward. In March 16, 1521, Pigafetta chronicled that they sighted the island of Samar which marked the discovery of the Philippines by Magellan for the Western world.[23]

22. During the maritime exploration, Portugal and Spain were competing over conquests of lands. Spanish Pope Alexander VI declared a papal bull *Inter Caetera* of 1493 to preside over the conflict. The Bull put forward a north-south dividing line that gave all the lands 100 leagues (about 320 miles) west of Cape Verde Islands to Spain and all the lands to the east to Portugal. The Pope decided on this dispute with the premise that the two nations would Christianized the countries they subjugated and not merely use them for economic gain. This system was known as the *padroado* (Portuguese) or *patronato* (Spanish). However, in the Treaty of Torsedillas on June 7, 1494, ambassadors from Spain and Portugal moved that line west, thereby allowing Portugal to claim Brazil when it was discovered in 1500. Hill, *History of Christianity*, 277; Jones, *Christian Missions*, 37.

23. Benitez, *History of the Philippines*, 20–21. "Historians generally have conceded to Elcano the honor and distinction of being the first man to sail round the world, but Father Jose Algue, director of the Philippine Weather Bureau, taking into account Magellan's early easterly travels in connection with his last epoch-making voyage, has proved that Magellan himself was to all intents and purposes the first to circumnavigate the earth." Ibid., 22. Magellan, a Portuguese explorer, learned about the vast wealth of Spain and proposed navigation to the east through sailing west of America. Spain sponsored Magellan's exploration with the lure of valuable spices from the East. Magellan continued his explorations under the banner of Spain despite the Portuguese's objections. Interestingly, as Jones noted, Magellan could have known the Philippines even before his first landing to its shore. He had visited the Moluccas before and had in fact acquired a Malay slave who became his interpreter in this voyage. Jones, *Christian Mission*, 37–38; Tuggy, *Philippine Church*, 25. Therefore, the word "discovered" was a misnomer since discovery connotes exposing something hidden or unknown. Constantino and Constantino enclosed the word "discovery" in quotation marks in

John Leddy Phelan, in his *Hispanization of the Philippines*, names
the three objectives of Spanish colonization:

> To secure a share in the lucrative spice trade, which heretofore
> had been a Portuguese monopoly. Another was to establish di-
> rect contacts with China and Japan, which might pave the way
> for their conversion to Christianity. And the third goal was to
> Christianize the inhabitants of the archipelago.[24]

Among the three objectives, the third goal seemed the only one realized. Spain had to wait for many years from Magellan's arrival in 1521
until Miguel Lopez de Legazpi's expedition in 1565 to permanently settle
in the islands and claim sovereignty over the natives. The natives resisted
them. By the 1570s, "an acute rice shortage threatened the new colony.
The sudden descent of two groups of nonproductive consumers—the
Spaniards and in much larger numbers the Chinese—created a severe
food shortage."[25] Hence, the Spaniards recognized three races at this
time in the archipelago: the Spaniards, the natives, and the Chinese.[26]

---

their narration of Magellan's arrival in the Philippines. Constantino and Constantino,
Past Revisited, 14. It is proper then to say instead that Magellan visited the Philippines,
as Osias and Lorenzana aptly put it: "It is such a people [Malay origin] essentially that
Magellan and his companions found when the first Europeans *visited* the Islands in
1521 and took possession of them in the name of Spain (emphasis mine)." Osias and
Lorenzana, *Evangelical Christianity in the Philippines*, 13.

24. Phelan, *Hispanization of the Philippines*, 7.

25. Ibid., 10.

26. Ibid., 11. The natives were called "*indios*" by this time period. The term "Filipino" was not used until the nineteenth century to refer to the *creoles* or *insulares* who
were Spaniards born in the country. Constantino and Constantino, *Past Revisited*, 120.
"The term Filipino which now identifies the native inhabitants of this nation began as
a class concept. It did not originally apply to all the natives, but grew as a concept and
was applied to a greater number of individuals first according to race, later according
to property qualifications, and still later, to social prestige. Only very much later did it
become term of national identification that broke through racial, economic, and social
barriers." Constantino, *Making of a Filipino*, 5. Jose Apolonio Burgos, a *creole* and a
secular priest, entitled his 1864 work as "*Manifesto que a la noble Nación Española
dirigen los leales Filipinos*" (Manifesto Addressed by the Loyal Filipinos to the Noble
Spanish Nation). Burgos was the first to use this term "Filipinos" as identification not
only to the *creoles* and Spanish *mestizos*, but also the Chinese Mestizos, and natives.
The *peninsular* Spaniards and friars sadly continued to refer to the natives as *indios*
until the end of their colonization. Burgos and his camp were fighting for the Filipinization of the clergy which the *penisulares* obviously did not want to happen. The
friars' desire for power and wealth surpassed that of their original calling of service
and preaching; moreover, it blinded them from the possibility of transferring religious
control to the native priests. Corpuz, *Roots of the Filipino Nation*, 2:3–4.

When the Spaniards saw the Chinese in the islands, they called them Sangleys.[27] In trying to understand how the term Sangley is derived, Benedict Anderson "imagined" the first contact between the Iberian colonizer and the non-islander trader. The colonizer asked the non-islander trader, "Who are you?" to which the trader answered, "We are *seng-lí*," meaning merchants.[28] Sangley was said to derive from the Minnanhua word *seng-lí* 生意 meaning business. Kaisa believes that the word Sangley derived from the Minnanhua term *siông lâi* 常來 meaning "one who often comes."[29] I imagined the reenactment will then be like this, "Who are you?" asked the Spaniards. The irate Chinese who had been trading around the area for centuries long before the coming of these Western sailors answered, "We often come." These Minnanhua speakers could have answered in their dialect, "*Goán siông lâi* 我們常來 (We often come)."[30]

The Chinese saw trade as a good opportunity to earn money and they had been engaging in such for centuries. The identification of merchant or traders to Chinese by the Spaniards was not without basis.[31] Nevertheless, the meaning of the term Sangley was not merchant but rather "one who often comes." A Chinese painting dated around 1590 has the title "Sangley" and the Chinese traditional characters 常來 or *siông lâi* in Minnanhua. This painting is found in the collection called the Boxer Codex manuscript dated late sixteenth century. It is held in the library of Indiana University Bloomington. It contains about 270 pages of text with paintings of different people groups. It is probably written by

27. The Spaniards found a settlement of 150 Chinese and 20 Japanese in Manila. They also discovered Chinese trading vessels frequent visits to trade with native products. See, *Tsinoy*, 45. See appendix D.

28. Anderson, *Imagined Communities*, 168.

29. See, *Tsinoy*, 47. Abinales and Amoroso recorded Sangley as "travelling merchant." Abinales and Amoroso, *State and Society*, 65.

30. Uytanlet, "Pride and Prejudice," 58. Based on John Macgowan's Amoy (Minnanhua) dictionary, there is no letter "x" in the Minnanhua alphabet but just "s." Macgowan, *English and Chinese Dictionary*, iv. Therefore, the word Sangley is spelled *siông lâi* in Minnanhua.

31. "The Spaniards took on the role of colonial masters and refused to soil their hands in any kind of occupation. The native Filipinos, on the other hand, still practiced subsistence agriculture. The Chinese thus found the opportunity to quickly fill the vacuum and assumed the role of middlemen and traders . . . They were the vendors, carpenters, bakers, cooks, shoemakers, barbers, tailors, blacksmiths, goldsmiths, artisans, craftsmen, and skilled workers who made life more convenient both for colonizers and the natives." See, *Tsinoy*, 46.

a Spanish and possibly by a Filipino clerk, and drawn by a Chinese since some paintings have Chinese characters.[32]

Figure 1. Picture of Sangleys in the Boxer Codex. Courtesy of Lilly Library, Indiana University, Bloomington, Indiana.

32. Indiana University Bloomington, "Lilly Library Digital Collection: Boxer Codex." Chinese writing is traditionally from top to bottom, left to right columns. Horizontally, it starts from left to right. For this reason, it is very likely that the painter was Chinese, because this person wrote the Chinese characters as corresponding to the Spanish title, from left to right. See figure 1, Picture of Sangleys in the Boxer Codex.

Anderson notices that the term Sangley eventually disappeared and was replaced by Chino in the early nineteenth century.[33] Wickberg observes that by this time, the Chinese population had become diverse and identified more as nationals of China than Chinese merchants. Hence, the term Chino or Tsino replaced the old term Sangley.[34]

In the 1580s, two major developments uplifted the economic situation of the country. Rice production was expanded and was able to meet the demands of the increased population. Second, "the stabilization of the trade with China—the exchange of Chinese silks for Mexican silver—created a solid base of prosperity for the Spanish community."[35] For the next two centuries, the Manila Galleon Trade became the economic lifeline of the Spanish colony in the Philippines.[36]

The continuous great demand for Chinese silks in Europe and equally great demand for Mexican silver in China kept the flow of profits into the pockets of the Spaniards in Manila. At the same time, there was an influx of Chinese immigrants. The Chinese colony became so large that the Spaniards set aside the Parián for the Chinese.[37]

The Chinese success and constant increase in population caused alarm among the Spaniards that led to a number of massacres and the destruction of the Chinese settlements.[38] The resentment and restrictions toward the Chinese resulted in their segregation and concentration in Binondo, population control for centuries, and inevitably, the development and encouragement of the vocation of trade that reinforced the stereotypes.

According to Constantino and Constantino, in *The Philippines: A Past Revisited*, the Chinese trade industry in the archipelago caused some problems among the natives. The people were inclined to buy cloth and

33. Anderson, *Imagined Communities*, 168.

34. Wickberg, "Anti-Sinicism," 166.

35. Phelan, *Hispanization of the Philippines*, 11.

36. "At its peak, the exchange of Spanish silver for Chinese luxury goods created profits that supported the construction of schools, charitable hospitals, and societies and made Manila the 'Pearl of the Orient.' The easy profits of the galleon trade also served as a deterrent to Spaniards who might otherwise have ventured into the Philippine countryside to seek their fortune. Except for a few officials appointed to administer nearby provinces, the bulk of the Spanish civilian population lived contentedly in Manila, borrowing money and speculating on the annual galleon shipment." Rodell, *Culture and Customs*, 11.

37. Phelan, *Hispanization of the Philippines*, 11. See also Mann, *1493*, 157–209.

38. See appendix D.

other produce instead of weaving and planting their own crops. This caused the abandonment of fields and migration to cities for domestic jobs and other services offered by Spaniards. Moreover, the profits from the galleon trade had no effect on the lives of the natives. None of the local products were developed for export, very little of the local produce made their way into the Mexican market. The Spanish economic activity was largely confined in Manila during the first century of their occupation. They were more engaged in the war with the Dutch and Portuguese. Conversely, the Chinese penetrated the interior towns with their goods and bartered with the Filipinos. This resulted in the development of sugar, abaca, and resin industry in other parts of the Philippines.[39]

Throughout the period of Spanish colonization, the oppression of the natives was usually the main cause for uprisings. Unfortunately, none of these uprisings was truly successful. Still, these were evidence of the cries of the natives for justice, liberty, and equality. The beginnings of the nineteenth century set the stage for further fanning the flame of liberalism and nationalism among the natives. With the fall of Napoleon Bonaparte and the rise of liberal views in Europe, especially Spain, the indios, and Chinese Mestizos were also swept away with these ideas of Enlightenment. The opening of the Suez Canal in 1869 brought about easier trade and more students traveling to Spain.[40]

By this time, the social structure of the Philippines had also undergone transformation. From the Pre-Hispanic **barangay** structure of aristocrat, freeman, and commoner, five principal social classes had emerged. The *peninsulares* were Spaniards who came from Spain and held important offices in the government. The friars belonged to this class. Second was the *creoles* or *insulares* who were Spaniards born in the country; they were the first to be called "Filipinos" in this time period. The Spanish Mestizos were also considered to be part of this group. They perceived themselves as superior to the natives. Third were the Chinese Mestizos who were products of inter-ethnic marriages between Chinese and Filipino. Fourth were the natives who were called *indios*. The fifth and lowest class belonged to the Chinese.[41]

In summary, the Spaniards had their goals set for the Chinese in the Philippines: segregation, Hispanization, or expulsion. They had been

39. Constantino and Constantino, *Past Revisited*, 55–58, 110–11, 120, 139.
40. Ibid., 129.
41. Ibid., 120, 139.

successful in segregating the Chinese from the Filipinos. The Parián and Binondo were visual and physical markers of segregation. Segregation was the Spaniards' way of management and control of the Chinese, especially after the Lim A-Hong incident in 1574 that resulted in the 1581 forced containment within the Parián. Segregation became a weapon against the Chinese in times of crisis and suspicion. Segregation made the Chinese vulnerable targets for massacres, expulsion, restrictions, and population control. On the bright side, it further developed the Chineseness of the Chinese people, uniting them as one in times of crisis and trouble. It also aided in the development of communities, contacts, and commerce.

Second, the Spaniards were not successful in Hispanizing the Chinese in the sense of Christianizing them. Hispanization meant Christianizing more than assimilating them into the Spanish community or even into the Philippines as a whole. The Intramuros and the Parián were clear indications of difference, distrust, and discrimination. The physical reality was that the cannons on top of the massive walls of Intramuros pointed toward the Parián. The restrictions on Chinese traveling within the country also exposed the Spaniard's fear of them monopolizing trade or inciting revolts with the natives. Further, when the Chinese became Roman Catholics or intermarried with native women, they were again contained within Binondo. Their status as Chinese Mestizos might have given them an edge as the Dominicans desired to train them to be missionaries to China, yet still they were considered lower than the *peninsulares* or *insulares*.[42]

The fact that most Chinese considered themselves as Sojourners, assimilating in Spanish Philippine society was not a priority or a goal. Moreover, the ill-treatment by the Spaniards of the Chinese throughout the Spanish colonization prevented them from assimilating into the Spanish community, and did not impress them to accept Christianity. Some Chinese might have assimilated into the local community by interethnic marriage, birth as Chinese Mestizos, or conversion into Roman Catholics. But the majority of the Chinese remained as non-Catholic Chinese. Their Chineseness was what made them distinct and different from the other two races in the country.

Third, the Spaniards were successful in controlling the Chinese population by expelling or banning them from the country. Massacres

42. See appendix D specifically on years 1589, 1598, eighteenth century, 1755, 1800, and 1855 for discussion on Hispanization and Chinese Mestizos.

were also employed for control and elimination. The Spaniards' distrust and suspicion toward the Chinese had led to a series of revolts and massacres, such as in the years 1593, 1603, 1639, 1663, and 1762. These revolts and massacres invoked restrictions and expulsions as in the years 1589, 1593, 1755, 1766, and 1778.

The Spaniards saw the Chinese mainly as Sangleys or traders and merchants who were important agents of the Philippine economy. They needed them for their own convenience and financial gain; at the same time they also saw them as competitors. Looking back, the restrictions and repressions led the Chinese to focus on one vocation that would have immediate profit since their tenure in the country was not secured. Their concentration in business enabled them to become experts in that area. But since the meaning of Sangley was "one who often comes," the Chinese should not be labeled as traders and merchants only. Many of them came as artisans, craftsmen, skilled workers, and laborers. Their perseverance in the midst of massacres, expulsions, and oppressions paid off as their existence continued in the islands to the present. Their presence had cultural and economic impacts among the Filipinos and Spaniards. Further, throughout the centuries, many intermarried and settled in the country, thereby producing the Chinese Mestizos.

THE CHINESE AS ALIENS IN THE AMERICAN PERIOD

The Filipino revolutionaries had already contained the Spaniards in Manila even before the arrival of American soldiers in June and July of 1898. As early as May 31, 1898, the Philippine forces had been laying siege on Manila. Three times, Emilio Aguinaldo demanded the surrender of the Spanish troops and even offered them generous terms. The Spaniards simply ignored him and entered into secret negotiations with the United States. The two colonial powers staged a mock battle in Manila that forbade the Filipino troops to enter the city. Immediately, this was followed by the surrender of Spaniards to US troops. The Filipino soldiers who fought on the side of the Americans were completely unaware that they had been sold out.[43]

43. The Spaniards preferred to surrender to the Americans rather than to the Filipinos. On August 13, 1898, Americans occupied Manila and restricted the Filipino soldiers from that area. It is unfortunate that the Filipino soldiers who once were allies with the Americans were now labeled as rebels with the American occupation of the Philippines. Tuggy, *Philippine Church*, 82. And on December 10 that same year, the Treaty of Paris resulted in Spain ceding the Philippines, along with Guam and

Many Chinese Mestizos and Chinese were involved in the revolution. In fact, many of the leaders like Jose Rizal, Emilio Aguinaldo, and Apolinario Mabini were Chinese Mestizos. One of Aguinaldo's generals was a Chinese named Jose Ignacio Paua. Paua was a full-blooded Chinese from Lao-na, Fujian. He came to the Philippines with his uncle in 1890. He served as an apprentice blacksmith on Jaboneros Street. His skill eventually led him to be an important player in the making and repair of cannons, and the production of ammunitions and gunpowder for the revolution. He was able to raise an astounding amount of 386,000 pesos in Bicolandia alone for the newly established Republic. The funds came mostly from the Chinese. He also fought against the Americans in the Philippine-American War.[44]

Another important Chinese patriot who supported the revolutionaries was Roman T. Ongpin. He was born on Nueva Street in Binondo, Manila on February 28, 1847. See notes that

> Ongpin furnished the revolutionists with funds, foodstuff, and other supplies; his store became an outlet for propaganda materials. He gave, as his contribution to Aguinaldo, 90 percent of the indemnity paid by an insurance firm after his store was burned on February 6, 1898.[45]

He was imprisoned at Fort Bonifacio on December 6, 1900, when the Americans discovered his revolutionary activities. He was released on March 23, 1901. He became bitter toward the Americans and never sold

---

Puerto Rico, to the United States for the amount of $20,000,000. Even though Spain was already losing the war to Filipino revolutionaries, she still sold the Philippines to the United States. The action of the United States, however, also caused distrust and resentment on the part of the Filipinos. Aguinaldo trusted the Americans when they told him that they would aid Philippine independence. These promises were not written down, but for Filipinos who value *palabra de honor* or word of honor (something inherited from Spain), they considered their oral declarations as good as the written contract. Constantino and Constantino, *Past Revisited*, 208–9. To their dismay, the United States forgot their promises. See also Uytanlet, "Pride and Prejudice," 61–62.

44. Paua cut off his queue (pigtail) on June 12, 1898, when Aguinaldo proclaimed Philippine independence in Kawit, Cavite. His comrades teased him, but Paua replied, "Now that you are free from your foreign master, I am also freed from my queue." The queue, for the Chinese, is a sign of humiliation and subjugation because it was imposed on them by the Manchu rulers of the Qing Dynasty. The Chinese revolutionaries in China cut off their queues to signal their uprising against the Manchu government which ended the Qing Dynasty. See, "Jose Ignacio Paua," 90–93; See, *Chinese in the Philippines*, 3:110–12; Catindig, "Gen. Jose Paua."

45. See, *Chinese in the Philippines*, 3:112.

anything to them. He even insisted his children not to receive a single centavo from them. Other financiers of the revolution against Spain and the United States were Mariano Limjap, Flaviano Yenko, Telesforo Chuidian, and Teodoro Yangco.[46] Therefore, the Chinese community identified with the Filipinos as the wars ended.

Unfortunately, the Chinese suffered greatly in the hands of the Filipino revolutionaries throughout the revolutionary period against Spain and the United States. Wong Kwok-Chu cites John R. M. Taylor's *The Philippine Insurrection*, noting that the Chinese were abused, killed, robbed, and properties confiscated in spite of Aguinaldo's prohibition. In 1899, the number of Chinese in the Philippines was 40,000. During the Philippine-American War, the Americans hired hundreds of Chinese in the absence of the Filipinos to provide the supplies needed by the troops. They were given a monthly salary and ration in exchange for their labor. However in middle of 1900, the Chinese were replaced by the Filipinos.[47]

The Chinese during the American Period were called Chinamen. They were also called Coolie for they were known to have provided Coolie Labor or cheap labor.[48] Yet a report by the United States Philippine Commission in 1904 showed the disapproval over hiring of Chinamen though they were more skillful and might expedite the building of infrastructure in the country.[49] Amid complaints from Americans and foreign businessmen that they had difficulty finding skilled laborers in the country, the commission recommended employment of Filipino laborers. The commission added that they might not be as good as the

46. Ibid., 3:112–13; See, "Roman Ongpin," 145.

47. Wong, *Chinese in the Philippine Economy*, 23–24. For more discussion on Philippine-American War, see Uytanlet, "Pride and Prejudice," 61–62.

48. See chapter 4 for more discussion on Coolie Labor.

49. The Coolies in the Philippines were known to have helped build the Kennon Road in 1902–1905. It was for many years the main access to Baguio City, the summer capital of the Philippines. Go Bon Juan proudly presents new evidence on Coolies building the Kennon Road in the Beijing national archives through the efforts of Kaisa. One document dated 1905 recorded the abuses the Coolies suffered during the American Period. There were 1,000 Chinese laborers distributed in ten working stations. Go writes that when the Chinese Exclusion Act was extended to the Philippines on April 29, 1902, all the Chinese in the Philippines were required to register with the government. Unfortunately, many of these Coolies who worked on Kennon Road were not able to register since they were not allowed to leave their post. They were deported back to China. This is why only a small number of those who built Kennon Road stayed behind and lived in Baguio City or in this country. Go, "Kennon Road's Chinese Laborers," 122–23.

Americans or Chinamen but better than admitting the Chinamen freely into the country.[50]

The "yellow peril" scare of the early 1900s in the United States was transported into the Philippines.[51] Clark Alejandrino explains that the Chinese Exclusion Act of 1902 not only affected the Chinese but the Filipinos as well. The exclusion law was originally enacted in 1882 to ban Chinese immigrants into the United States for ten years and renewed for another ten years in 1892. It was also applied in the Philippines upon American colonization in 1898. In less than a month after the arrival of the American military, General Elwell Otis extended the exclusion laws to the Philippines on September 26, 1898. The "Otis Order" was a temporary answer to the Chinese immigration issue in the country until the official policy in 1902.[52]

When General Arthur MacArthur succeeded Otis as military commander in 1899, he believed that the Chinese presence in the country was a threat to American economic interests as well as a hindrance in pacifying the Filipino insurgents. However, this same law also signified that the Americans considered it necessary for them to protect the Filipinos whom they considered too indolent and lazy and incapable of governing their own country.[53]

In 1901, the Bureau of Non-Christian Tribes was created as a new state agency to understand ethnoracial diversity in the Philippines. When a census was taken in 1903, the term "Filipino" was reserved for those who were Christians, which included the Spanish, Filipinos, Chinese Mestizos, and Catholic Chinese. The rest were classified as pagans and Muslims. This eliminated the Spanish Filipinos and Chinese Mestizos classifications. Abinales and Amoroso view that the "American racial classification and state structures perpetuated the outsider status of the

---

50. The Commission used the Atlantic, Gulp and Pacific Company's experience with Filipino laborers as an example of how the Filipinos could also be good laborers. United States Philippine Commission, *Report of the United States Philippine Commission*, 54–55.

51. The "yellow peril" referred to the anti-Chinese sentiments of the white people in the United States in 1870s as the economy lagged and labor became uncertain. Zhou, *Contemporary Chinese America*, 44.

52. Alejandrino, *1902 Chinese Exclusion Act*, 10–13, 34, 49. See also Wong, *Chinese in the Philippine Economy*, 28.

53. Ibid., 13–15, 34, 49.

Muslims and other non-Christians."[54] The Chinese at this point became known as an ethnic minority.

Chu concisely explained that the people in the Philippines were basically classified into two groups, Filipinos or non-Filipinos (also called aliens). The term Filipinos was used to classify all Filipinos and Chinese Mestizos. Interestingly, the Chinese Mestizos born to Chinese fathers were still Chinese citizens or aliens until they reached the age of maturity and could apply for Filipino citizenship.[55]

This classification is still in effect as the current Philippine government retains the classification made by the former colonizer. One is either Filipino or Alien. The Chinese who did not have Filipino citizenships but are legal residents must have an identification card as imposed in 2007 by the Philippine government called Alien Certificate of Registration Identification Card or ACR I-Card. "This is a microchip-based credit card-sized identification card issued to registered alien [sic] replacing the paper-based ACR. It has an embedded computer chip with biometric security features capable of data management and can be updated electronically."[56]

The term "Alien" sounds strange and derogatory in nature as a description or classification. It seems to connote something totally far-off and even extremely odd as though they were from outer space. Why did the American government choose this term instead of foreign, international, outsider, or simply non-Filipinos? And why was this classification retained by the Filipinos? Was there an underlying prejudice for such classification?

Wickberg believes that the term "Alien" connotes both national and cultural identities that reflected "the marginal political status of this non-citizen group and the cultural alienness of a group that did not share the dreams and new values of the majority."[57] The introduction of this term, in Wickberg's observation, redefined Chinese identity as opposed to Filipino from a religious standpoint during Spanish period, when Roman Catholicism was so important, to that one based on the values and understanding of modern nationhood. Thus, under the new colonial rule, the Chinese and their Chineseness were seen as opposing values as

54. Abinales and Amoroso, *State and Society*, 124.
55. Chu, *Chinese and Chinese Mestizos of Manila*, 251.
56. Bureau of Immigration, "ACR I-Card."
57. Wickberg, "Anti-Sinicism," 166.

Filipinos sought nationalism and came under the tutelage of the American government in preparation for self-governance.[58]

See describes the American occupation as "divide and rule." Employing the same strategy as the Spaniards in terms of segregation toward the Chinese, the American liberal policy opened the way for Chinese to establish their own hospitals, restaurants, associations, charities, schools, drugstores, and cemeteries. Yet in exchange, "the long-term effect is even more insidious than the legacy of the Spanish policies." See observes,

> Under the liberal policy of the Americans, the Chinese prospered. Economic growth of this ethnic group was unprecedented. However, having a separate existence from the mainstream, the economic prosperity of the Chinese again became the source of envy and hostility which sporadically broke out into racial riots like what happened in 1919 and 1924.[59]

See's accounts seemingly contradict the idea that the American regime was anti-Sinicism with the liberal policies that prospered the Chinese. Indeed, the Chinese Exclusion Act of 1902 placed restrictions on Chinese immigration to the Philippines which presented anti-Sinicism but Wickberg points out that this law was loosely enforced. Evidences show that the Chinese during the 1930s continued to grow steadily that its population reached to 117,000 by 1939. The percentile of the Chinese has always been around 2 percent of the total Philippine population. At times in Manila, it might have risen to 5 or even 10 percent.[60]

During the Commonwealth period, the nationalization policies sought to reserve the development of natural resources and operation of public utilities to Filipinos, not immigrants. The nationalism for future

58. The Overseas Chinese were then concerned with the political developments in China. They were divided in their alliances whether pro-GMD (Guomindang or Kuomintang 國民黨) or pro-Mao (Mao Zedong 毛澤東 or pro-Communism). Ibid., 166.

59. See, *Chinese in the Philippines*, 2:37. The Philippines had a rice shortage in 1919 "due to drought, poor farm management, and shortfall in imports . . . As the shortage became more acute, Chinese millers and distributors became the convenient scapegoats for the government's failure to avert the crisis in the first place." Violence erupted against Chinese storekeepers in the provinces and the government did little to stop such anti-Chinese sentiments. Another anti-Chinese riot happened in October 1924 when rumors about the Chinese wildly spread among Filipinos such as Chinese declaring war against Filipinos, Chinese poisoning Filipinos, or Chinese killing Filipinos in Shanghai. See, *Tsinoy*, 136–37.

60. Wickberg, "Anti-Sinicism," 164.

independent governance extended to economic control. The elimination of Chinese control over business and trade was evident in legislation such as nationalizing the public market stalls, leaving the Chinese to wholesale and distribution.[61] This was history repeated as seen in the "self-sufficiency" Bourbon Reforms of the Spanish government.[62]

Abinales and Amoroso stated that the Chinese residents were once again considered outcasts in this period. With the American exclusion laws extended into the Philippines, legal Chinese immigration was halted until 1941, when the Commonwealth government allowed an annual number of five hundred only per nationality into the country. During the immigration ban, the Chinese men were forced to find wives within the community instead of going to China to find a Chinese bride.[63]

In 1898, the ratio of Chinese women to men was 1:40.[64] Wong argues that the sojourning nature of the Chinese led to predominantly male immigrants. Also, Chinese women were discouraged from leaving the homeland. The ratio of Chinese women to men in 1903 was 1:78. The increase in men could probably be attributed to the Coolie Labor.[65] By 1918, the ratio had improved to 1:13. By 1939, it had reached a more balanced 1:3.[66] A careful look at the numbers provided by Wong reveals that the ratio of marriageable Chinese women and men under the age 20 to 34 was still 1:5. The sociological implication of such a sex ratio was that many Chinese men had to be bachelors, intermarry with Filipinas, or wait for many years before they could find women of marriageable age.[67]

61. See, *Chinese in the Philippine*, 2:37. See also See, *Tsinoy*, 134–35, 140, on Chinese protests against the Exclusion Act (1902), Bookkeeping Law (1921), and Commonwealth Era.

62. In the middle of the eighteenth century, the Spanish government sought to establish self-sufficiency in the country with the Bourbon Reforms. They believed it was necessary to expel all Chinese to achieve this goal. They believed that the Chinese controlled the wholesale and retail trade that made them rich leaving the Spaniards and the Filipinos nothing to gain. They believed that when the Chinese were gone, they could take over and could even put in new industries to add revenues for the new self-sufficient colony. Sugaya, "Expulsion of Non-Christian Chinese," 111.

63. Abinales and Amoroso, *State and Society*, 159.

64. See, *Chinese in the Philippines*, 3:124.

65. The Chinese Exclusion Act of 1902 placed restrictions on Chinese immigration to the Philippines, but Wickberg points out that this law was loosely enforced. Wickberg, "Anti-Sinicism," 163.

66. Wong, *Chinese in Philippine Economy*, 18–19.

67. If those under the 10 to 19 age range were included with the 20 to 34 age range, the ratio between male and female would still be 1:5. Ibid., 20. The bachelor society

This immigration ban fostered cohesive unity among the Chinese people in the community. Further, the Chinese by this time shifted into domestic retail instead of export trade due to a protected US market for Philippine exports that favored Filipino elites. The Chinese then came to dominate the groceries and hardware stores.[68]

To recapitulate, the Chinese in the American period were segregated from the Filipinos primarily because of race or ethnicity not religion as the division Filipinos and Non-Christian Tribes indicated. They were called Aliens or non-Filipinos, grouping them along with the Muslims and other tribal groups. They were encouraged to maintain their ethnicity as they built their own schools, hospitals, cemeteries, shops, restaurants, charities, fire departments, and others. They were mostly confined in Binondo, Sta. Cruz, and Tondo.

Their "Alien" status had social, political, cultural, and psychological consequences. Centuries of segregation and exclusion further developed their ethnicity as a community and as a group of people that made them foreign and strange to the Filipinos. Thus, the Chinese alienated themselves from the mainstream Filipino communities with the newfound liberal policy in this period. Second, alienation and foreignness naturally became the norm; suspicion and distrust were hardly avoidable especially in times of crisis and chaos. Finally, suspicion and distrust bred indifference, hostility, and oppression.

Their numbers were controlled as immigration was banned. From 1940 onward, the American administration in the Philippines outlawed immigration from China except in cases where people came as investors, retirees, or students.[69] Their business ventures were also controlled as the Filipino elites were given export trade priorities, aid in the development of industries, and control over public utility corporations. But the Chinese entrepreneurial spirit enabled them to face the new challenges with determination to succeed.

---

situation was not unique in the Philippines, Zhao Xiaojian also reported the same situation in the early twentieth century United States. Zhao, *New Chinese America*, 19.

68. Abinales and Amoroso, *State and Society*, 159.

69. See, "Influx of New Chinese Immigrants," 137–38.

THE *INTSIK* WHO IS ALSO THE *KABISE* IN POSTWAR PHILIPPINES TO PRESENT

The Chinese in the Philippines are usually referred to as **Intsik** by the Filipinos. **Intsik** comes from the Minnanhua *lín tsek* (your uncle). They are also called **kabise** or boss. **Kabise** derives from the Spanish word *cabeza* or head. The **Intsik** is usually perceived as **kabise** because of their dominance in retail and wholesale businesses. However, not all **Intsik** are **kabise** just as not all **kabise** in the country are **Intsik**. The animosity between the Chinese and the Filipinos can be traced to the Pre-Hispanic Period with the Chinese's prejudices against the local people. This was further encouraged and developed in the colonial periods. Worse, as nationalism burned in the hearts of the Filipinos with their newfound independence and autonomy by 1946, this concurred with the division of the ethnic Chinese between pro-China and pro-Taiwan. The prejudices remained strong between the two ethnicities.[70]

Interestingly, both Filipinos and Chinese suffered much during the Second World War. They collaborated in their fight against the Japanese. They even worked hand in hand trying to rebuild their lives in the aftermath of war. Both were looking forward for a brighter future. On July 4, 1946, the Philippines obtained its independence and full autonomy from the United States of America. Following immediately was legislation that forbade Chinese to occupy professional occupations such as doctors, dentists, ophthalmologists, chemists, pharmacists, engineers, architects, accountants, nurses, and lawyers. Chinese teachers were banned from teaching history, sociology, and political science.[71]

Further, the Nationalization of the Public Markets, Retail Trade Nationalization Act, and Nationalization of Rice and Corn Industries Act were passed in order to ensure that Filipinos would control the economy. Amusingly, Caroline Hau noted that the Retail Trade Nationalization Act exempted the "citizens and juridical entities of the United States" revealing the government's double standard and distrust toward the Chinese.[72]

---

70. The Chinese Filipinos during the twentieth century mostly pro-Taiwan and supportive of the Nationalist Party or Kuomintang or Guomindang (GMD). Those who were pro-China were not necessarily pro-Mao.

71. See, *Chinese in the Philippines*, 2:37–38.

72. Abinales and Amoroso, *State and Society*, 188. Agoncillo writes that the Philippine economy suffered gravely due to the aftermath of war and the alien control of domestic trade. The establishment of the newly independent nation led to implementation of policies such as Market Stalls Act (1946), Retail Trade Nationalization

The adoption of the Filipino First policy in 1961 gave natural-born citizens priority in various economic activities as opposed to those who were naturalized citizens.

The reality is that obtaining Filipino citizenship as an immigrant was very difficult prior to 1975.[73] The Chinese who acquired Filipino citizenships were naturalized. Therefore, they have to wait for the next generation to acquire the benefits and privileges for natural-born citizens. Hence, a large number of alien Chinese resided in the country, but not alien by their own choice. If the Philippines had not established diplomatic ties with China in 1975, it is probable that President Ferdinand Marcos would not have thought of granting mass naturalization to the "alien" Chinese.[74]

In the 1980s, Marcos issued a presidential decree to open the Philippines to foreign investors from communist and socialist countries such as China, just as China was opening its doors again. Following these two acts, there were waves of new immigrants from China who, however, mostly entered the Philippines illegally.[75] In 1992, amnesty was given to all overstaying Chinese or illegal residents who entered the country prior to 1975. In March of 1997, Senator Nikki Coseteng, who was a Chinese Filipino, exposed the Bureau of Immigration anomaly. Reports were made that showed that bribes ranging from $4,800 to $8,000 (₱120,000–₱200,000) were given in order to obtain Filipino citizenship among Chinese residents.[76] Even today, obtaining national citizenship is not easy for the Chinese. It involves a long process where bribery is a temptation and sometimes an expectation at every step.

Law (1954), Filipino Retailer's Fund Act (1955), NAMARCO Act (1955) to ensure Filipino not alien control over economy. Agoncillo, *History of the Filipino People*, 503. Tan writes that only the Chinese were affected from anti-alien control. The Americans continued to enjoy exemptions and privileges. Tan, *History of the Philippines*, 78.

73. For the Chinese immigrants to obtain citizenship in the 1950s, they needed to pay five thousand pesos or approximately two thousand five hundred dollars as application fee. Abinales and Amoroso note that this process was used by politicians for their own gain. A business license was sold for fifty thousand pesos or twenty-five thousand dollars. Abinales and Amoroso, *State and Society*, 253.

74. Suryadinata, "Government Policies," 72–73.

75. "Chinese who have permanent residency numbered about 120,000 before 1975. In 1985, this number was drastically reduced to just about 25,000. Nearly 96,000 Chinese obtained Filipino citizenship through presidential decree from 1976 to 1985 . . . Today, the number of alien Chinese have gone back to the pre-1975 figures of about 100,000." See, "Influx of New Chinese Immigrants," 141.

76. Ibid., 145.

The stereotyping of Chinese Filipinos as **Intsik** and **kabise** led to labeling all of them as owners of businesses and therefore rich. Furthermore, they were perceived as the minority who control the Philippine economy. The Chinese Filipino businessmen used this to their advantage as investors are willing to collaborate with them. But this labeling and spreading of myth have their undesirable and nightmarish consequences.

Go Bon Juan wrote *Myths about the Ethnic Chinese "Economic Miracle"* in 1996 in response to the growing interest in the economic progress of Chinese people in relation to their cultural practices. He emphasizes that the myth that the Chinese in general can turn stone into gold with superhuman abilities must not be perpetuated. It is true that the six rich businessmen he mentions produced new money and not simply possessed old wealth. However, Go claims that only Lucio Tan has "truly cultivated considerable knowledge on Chinese culture."[77] The rest of the five, namely, Alfonso Yuchengco, John Gokongwei, Andrew Gotianum, George Ty, and Henry Sy, are more Westernized than Sinicized.

Go argues that there are also many unsuccessful Chinese Filipino businessmen, either big or small. He does not negate the successes of these outstanding Chinese taipans but he discourages using them as describing all Chinese across the board.[78]

In 1997, the Manila became known in the media as "Asia's kidnapping capital." From 1993 to 1997, the number of kidnap victims within the Chinese community numbered 179 to 286 per year with the yearly ransom money growing from $2.5 million to $10.4 million.[79] This meant there were 15 to 24 victims per month, as though one victim every other day. See reported in the Philippine Center for Investigative Journalism's 2004 *Yearender* magazine that there was a dramatic drop of kidnapping cases in 2004 to 154 cases, reducing to 12 cases per month.[80]

The then vice-president, Erap Estrada, was assigned to head the Presidential Anti-Crime Commission (PACC). Most of the victims were ethnic Chinese and none were from affluent Filipino or Spanish Mestizos community even when they were wealthier than those being kidnapped.

77. Go, *Myths about the Ethnic Chinese*, 13.
78. Ibid., 28.
79. Abinales and Amoroso, *State and Society*, 254–55.
80. See, "Long Wait."

Politicians, police, and military were believed to be involved in this "business."[81]

Hope Ngo, a CNN correspondent, interviewed See on kidnapping of Chinese Filipinos back in 2001. See then stated that the Chinese Filipinos own 20 to 22 percent of the country's wealth. See debunked the claim that the Chinese control the Philippine economy but she admitted that the Chinese economic contribution is enough to make a significant difference in the country's economic development and recovery. With this, See hopes the government will be able to solve the problem of kidnappings in the country.[82]

The kidnapping of many Chinese Filipinos was and remains a beleaguering dilemma. Many Chinese households during the height of the kidnapping in the 1990s to early 2000s feared for their safety and many Chinese businesses closed their shops earlier than the usual time. Manila Chinatown became like a ghost town after six in the evening when it used to be festive and busy even at night time. The Chinese Filipinos were at a loss as rumors circulated that police and high officials were involved in the kidnappings. They could not trust the authorities. This is one incident that shows how stereotyping can lead to disastrous consequences.

In summary, the postwar era continued to bring about restrictions to the Chinese Filipinos with regard to professions and commerce. This evidently was continuity from the Spanish and American Periods. The distrust of the colonizers toward the Chinese people was adopted into the mindset of the Filipino people. Gone were the days when the Chinese and Filipinos trusted each other as they conducted trade with one another. From depriving citizenship to limiting business activities to present kidnappings, these seem to be the genealogy of the racial problem.

However, the mass naturalization of 1975 and amnesties for overstaying immigrants in 1975 and 1992 led to the Chinese's opportunity to be permanent residents, acquire citizenship, venture into different professions, and purchase properties. The administration of President Benigno "Noynoy" Aquino looks promising as he spearheads the fight against corruption in the government. This partly restores the trust, not only of the Chinese Filipinos, but even Filipinos in the government. Further, the institution of Kaisa has helped improve the relations of the two

81. Mydans, "Kidnapping of Ethnic Chinese."
82. Ngo, "Kidnapping on the rise."

ethnic groups through dissemination of information with their publication and through their many charity projects.

CONCLUSION

In Rizal's magnum opus, *Noli me Tangere*, a novel that addresses the ills of the Spanish government, the Chinese were mentioned many times all throughout the novel. They were depicted as water peddlers, vendors, traders, storekeepers, waxmakers, infidels, and rebels. In the beginning chapter, there was even a debate among the guests of Kapitan Tiago on who really invented gunpowder. Father Damaso insisted that a certain Franciscan priest invented gunpowder and not the Chinese.

Rizal presented how the *indios* and the Spaniards perceived the Chinese in chapter 13. Crisostomo Ibarra was looking for his father's gravesite. The gravedigger informed him that his father's remains were exhumed to be transferred to the Chinese cemetery for he was deemed an infidel by the head parish priest. In an attempt to excuse himself, the gravedigger told Ibarra that he did not bury Don Rafael in the Chinese cemetery. He believed that it was better for one to be drown than to be with the Chinese. Henceforth, the gravedigger threw the body in the water. This angered Ibarra even more.

In chapter 32, Father Damaso was giving his sermon. Father Damaso was a Franciscan priest who abused his power as a friar. He symbolized corruption and immorality in the church and country. In his sermon, he admonished the people to learn by heart the Holy Scriptures and the life of the holy saints. He added that in this way, they will not live lives such as the Protestants and the heretics or worse, the pagan Chinese. Rizal continued narrating how one Chinaman named Carlos responded irritably toward the priest's sermon. In Carlos's broken Filipino or in this translation in broken English, he said, "Whatsa matta that Pale[83] Damaso!"[84]

The Spaniards and the *indios* saw the Chinese primarily as Sangleys, traders, and merchants. Moreover, they saw the Chinese as pagans and infidels. The Americans recognized them as an ethnic minority and aliens of this country. They were the Chinamen, Coolies, and cheap labor force. The postwar Filipinos saw them as **kabise** or bosses and at the same

---

83. The word "Pale" is supposed to be *Padre* or Father, the title given to priest. The Chinese in the Philippines were perceived to have difficulty pronouncing the letter "R" since the Minnanhua or Amoy does not have the consonant "R."

84. Rizal, *Noli me Tángere*, 10–11, 22, 33, 36, 56, 61, 73, 186, 208, and 366.

time, they disliked the presence of these **Intsik**. Conversely, the present Filipinos have recognized the contributions of the Chinese particularly to the Philippine economy. Many Chinese Filipinos have Filipino citizenships. However, these Chinese remained liked and disliked, welcomed and unwelcomed. The perception of others about them have affected how they were treated and interrelated. People's perceptions on a particular ethnic group are usually not equivalent to who they really are. Consequently, the stories from this ethnographic research will help us discover who they say they are.

3

Cultural Hybridity among Postcolonial Philippine Chinese

Theories on Ethnic Identity and Hybridity

I WITNESSED THE CHINESE Filipinos patronizing many Hong Kong movies back in the 1970s until the early 1990s. Many of these movies were in Cantonese and had subtitles in Putonghua and English. The golden years of Hong Kong cinemas had made Jackie Chan a household name worldwide. In Manila, young Chinese women would buy the magazine 姊妹 Jiemei (Sisters) to find the latest fashion trends and gossip about movie stars. When Betamax and VHS were introduced in the Philippines, Chinese Filipinos would flock to the video shops in Manila Chinatown to rent the latest Hong Kong drama series or movies.

Chinese Filipinos during this time also tended to identify with Taiwan (Republic of China) more than mainland China (People's Republic of China). They were afraid to be identified with Communism during the Cold War. Philippine Chinese schools employed the Taiwan educational system and relied on Taiwanese teachers. The socio-political and cultural situations led to their construction of complex multiple identities and hybrid culture. Many of these Chinese Filipinos sought to find a place and a country they could call their own and where they could belong.

In the movie *God of Gamblers Returns* (1994), one particular scene vividly showed how Chinese were capable of switching identities and negotiating their Chineseness.[1] The following brief narrative candidly encapsulated the idea of multiple identities and cultural hybridity.

---

1. Chow Yun-Fat starred in the movie *God of Gamblers* Dǔ Shén 賭神, which had

56

Ko Chun and his friends were from Hong Kong and got into trouble while in China. They captured the police chief as hostage and got into Condor's boat to escape. While on the boat, Condor revealed his secret identity as an undercover spy for the Taiwan government. He burst into tears as he ripped his jacket to reveal a shirt with Taiwan flag. He shared how he missed his homeland while working in China for the past eighteen years. Condor then attacked the police chief and pointed his gun at Ko's friends. Ko fought Condor to rescue his friends and overcame him.

During the chaos, the police chief grabbed one of Ko's friends as his hostage. Suddenly, there were loud sirens blasting in the air. The police chief laughingly announced that that was the warning sound coming from the mainland Chinese ships. They will all be caught and be brought back to China. He started singing China's national anthem and shouting for his comrades. Ko and his friends disagreed with him and hushed him to quiet down. They pointed to him the Taiwanese flag waving on top of the ship. It was a Taiwanese patrol boat after all.

The police chief was shaken and Ko's friend freed herself. Ko and his friend beat him up till he passed out. The Taiwanese patrol boat approached Condor's boat for the police thought they heard someone singing China's national anthem. When they got near the boat, they heard Ko and his friends singing the Taiwanese patriotic song Plum Blossom or *Méi Huā* 梅花 with their hands up waving in the air. The Taiwanese police were convinced that they were mistaken and left them.[2]

ETHNICITY AND IDENTITY THEORIES

The Chinese in mainland China and those in Hong Kong and those in Taiwan cannot simply be classified as Chinese and presumed to have the same language and culture. Those in Hong Kong speak Cantonese and are influenced by their former British colonizer. Those in Taiwan use Taiwanese or Minnanhua, though at present, the younger generation prefers Putonghua. Taiwan's script is the traditional version with Chinese phonetics to aid in pronunciation. Taiwan was once colonized by Japan. China's script, however, is the simplified version employing Pinyin alphabet to aid in pronunciation and easy learning of the language. Those

---

three sequels and a prequel. The movie and its succeeding sequels were box office hits in Hong Kong and other Asian countries back in the late 1980s and 1990s. Chow played the main character Ko Chun who was a master gambler.

2. *God of Gamblers Returns* (1994).

in the mainland also have many other languages and dialects. China went through big changes with Communism and the Cultural Revolution. These Chinese from three different places represent different kinds of Chinese in the sense that they have different languages and cultures. There may be traces of Confucian values or elements of Daoism and Buddhism in varying degrees in all of them, yet they have constructed their unique beliefs, practices, and traditions with years of influences inside and outside their borders.

In the same way, the Chinese scattered in Southeast Asia cannot be clumped together as one. Each of them has been influenced by their respective host countries as was the case of the Chinese in the Philippines. This chapter suggests the theory or theories which will be most helpful and suitable in understanding and analyzing the Chinese Filipino identity and cultural hybridity.

Hutchinson and Smith's Ethnie Definition

John Hutchinson and Anthony D. Smith acknowledge that the term ethnicity is recent but the concept of kinship, group solidarity, and common culture is as old as history. The word "ethnicity" first appears in the English language around the 1950s, but ethnos or ethnie has been around since classical Greek times. Ethnicity is often associated with conflicts and power struggle. Still, there are ethnic communities living side by side with each other in peace and harmony. The authors also talk about the variations within ethnicity. There are even paradoxes in ethnicity. They see ethnic groups that are durable through the years and yet there are new ethnic groups rising. There are existing ethnic groups that have undergone transformation and shifting of identities.[3]

Hutchinson and Smith refine Richard Schermerhorn's ethnie definition and state it as a "named human population with myths of common ancestry, shared historical memories, one or more elements of common culture, a link with a homeland and a sense of solidarity among at least some of its members."[4] The authors emphasize that there are varying degrees of display for these six features in every ethnicity. Some features may be stronger while some weaker. The authors use the word "myth" of common ancestry rather than "fact" to stress the fictive kinship shared by the people in the group. Consequently, the authors use ethnie inter-

3. Hutchinson and Smith, *Ethnicity*, 3–7.
4. Ibid., 6.

changeably with ethnic or ethnicity.[5] For this dissertation, I will utilize the words ethnic and ethnicity and this definition to explain how the Chinese Filipinos are an ethnie or ethnic group in the Philippines.

The Chinese in the Philippines are identified as Chinese since most of them or their ancestors came from China. They shared a "myth" of common ancestry and that is of the Han Chinese. They share the same historical past with the Filipinos from the Pre-Hispanic period to colonial periods to Philippine independence and to the present. Throughout history, many of the Chinese were traders and merchants from the Pre-Hispanic past to the present. By virtue of interest, opportunity, colonial policies, and government laws, the Chinese were molded and encouraged in such occupations. Upholding Confucian values, using the Minnan language, and practicing endogamy are some of the common elements within their culture.

They have a link to a homeland, but it must be noted, however, that immigrants from Fujian speak Minnanhua, from Guangdong speak Cantonese, and that many of the New Immigrants speak Putonghua. Moreover, having a link to a homeland for the Chinese Filipinos may mean home country or cultural roots. The Chinese also organized associations to protect themselves and also help each other. The Kaisa is, to this day, the most influential and outspoken Chinese Filipino organization that seeks to unite the Chinese and the Filipinos in solidarity and seeks to retain their ethnic cultural heritage.

Rynkiewich's Sociocultural Constructs as Dynamic Elements of Interaction

Michael A. Rynkiewich defines anthropology as "the study of the ways of mankind, the different ways in which humans perceive, evaluate, and respond to the world round them."[6] Academic anthropology has four fields—namely, physical, archaeology, linguistic, and cultural or sociocultural. This study narrowed the scope to sociocultural anthropology since the research primarily examined people's cultures, identity, and ethnicity. No Chinese in the Philippines can assume that they understand all the Chinese in the country just because they are Chinese themselves, including the author. With culture being contingent, contested, and constructed, change is always in process. Therefore, the Chinese and their

5. Ibid., 6–7.

6. Rynkiewich, *Soul, Self, and Society*, 14–15.

culture have been subjected to change throughout history due to the social and cultural factors around them. Rynkiewich proposes:

> Against the background of the "standard anthropological model" for teaching missionary candidates, we need to consider the model of culture as contingent, constructed, and contested. As it turns out, our own deeply rooted assumptions about life, persons, and cultures, something like a folk theory of society, tend to pervade our thinking so much that we miss any possibility for locally understood sociology to be different. We need to understand how culture is contingent on regional and global flows, how culture is constructed from materials brought into the present over historic and geographic distances, and how culture is constantly being contested in daily life. If we do not have such an understanding, we fail to grasp the missionary situation and to communicate the gospel properly.[7]

I believe that the sociocultural constructs are the dynamic elements for interaction between the Chinese and their environment that lead to changes whether unexpected, expected, or accepted. This is the primary framework in which this study dwelt.

Primordialism or Constructivism as Ethnic Identity Theory

Aletta J. Norval concedes that the theorization of ethnicity, multiculturalism, and the politics of identity and/or difference are real in our present world and have "long and difficult trajectories."[8] She posits that the history of the theorization of ethnicity "is not a progressive and cumulative one" but instead "intimately bound up with political concerns and normative judgments."[9] Hence, she concludes that a genealogical form is needed to attempt to reconstruct its trajectory. It has to start from where we are, from our current concerns, and present commitments. It is impossible to attain a complete account of this complex genealogy. Rather it will be helpful to be reminded of the limits of this trajectory. She lays out three different views of ethnicity: primordialism, instrumentalism, and constructivism. In constructivism, she proposes poststructuralist as oppose to linguistic monism[10] since the markers for race are "not in any

7. Rynkiewich, "World in My Parish," 16.

8. Norval, "Politics of Ethnicity and Identity," 272.

9. Ibid.

10. Linguistic monism is "where linguistic construction is taken to be generative and deterministic through instrumentalist accounts." There are three difficulties

sense natural or given," but are "historically evolving, culturally variegated" yet nevertheless have "a powerful structuring influence on individual experience."[11]

Ted Lewellen believes that primordialism is "no longer considered valid by anyone." He defines constructivism as "flatly reject[ing] primordialism," and that ethnicity is constructed situationally and thus is constantly changing. He breaks down constructivism into four approaches, namely, (1) instrumentalism, in which the common goal is the prime motive for group formation; (2) cultural, where "culture" binds people together as they seek a sense of belonging; (3) political, when ethnicities result from exclusion and marginalization; and (4) radical historicism, a Marxist approach which focuses on class struggle, labor, and class consciousness.[12]

Caroline Brettell simplifies constructivism into two approaches. The instrumentalist approach focuses on ethnicity as a political strategy that is pursued for pragmatic interests. The situational approach, emerging from the theoretical work of Barth, emphasizes the fluidity and contingency of ethnic identity, which is constructed in specific historical and social contexts.[13] These approaches are not mutually exclusive, but are more like different perspectives on the construction of ethnicity and the production of culture.

Norval views primordialism as "a mask deployed strategically to advance group interests that are often economic in character."[14] It is ethnic identity stemming from social givens such as those defined by Geertz. Geertz defines primordial theory or primordial attachments as people joining together by virtue of "givens" like blood ties or kinship, race, language, customs, or religions.[15] The primordialist thesis is first discussed by Edward Shils in 1957 but popularized by Geertz in the '60s. Despite its criticisms, Norval believes this view was and is still influential in the study of ethnicity as evident in the works of Smith. She analyzes Smith's work as one that emphasizes the symbolic dimension of identity and still

---

arising from this form: verbal limitations, reinforcement of a top-down view of ethnicity, and disregarding the force of ethnic identification on the people. Ibid., 275.

11. Ibid., 277.

12. Lewellen, *Anthropology of Globalization*, 106, 108.

13. Brettell, *Anthropology and Migration*, 106.

14. Norval, "Politics of Ethnicity and Identity," 272.

15. Geertz, *Interpretation of Cultures*, 259.

retains emphasis on the "enduring, and even premodern, character of ethnicity."[16]

In contrast, Lewellen and Brettell believe that primordialism is passé and no longer popular or even valid due to its fixity and unchanging nature.[17] In studying marriage, family and kinship, Rynkiewich discusses the primordialist view as a given or "it was there from the beginning" while constructivism as constantly negotiated or "it was made up on the spot." He sees that both are needed to help explain people's behavior.[18] Talking about the resurgence of ethnicity, he poses the question,

> Is ethnicity linked to primordial (built-in and deep-seated) attributes of persons in groups, or is ethnicity continually constructed and reconstructed to meet political and economic challenges in society? Those who argue that ethnicity is primordial point to enduring attributes of some groups; things like language, customs, and beliefs. Those who argue that ethnicity is a construct point to the shifting set of attributes that define groups and to the continual emergence of new groups, each replete with a freshly minted tradition.
>
> Others sidestep the issue, noting instead that it takes two to play the ethnicity game. That is, ethnicity is about a relationship negotiated with a dominant cultural group and shared with other "minorities" in a given society.[19]

Tong observes that the Chinese in the Philippines are still primordial while See has a constructivist notion with the coining of Tsinoy. Interestingly though, the goal of Kaisa is to foster unity and progress between Chinese and Filipinos and thereby enabling the Chinese to be integrated into the Filipino society without losing their cultural heritage. Elements of both primordial and constructivism seem to be present with such a vision and ideal. Is Kaisa primordialist with the reification of Chineseness or constructivist with the understanding of hybridity and changes among Tsinoys today? As Robert C. Young contends that multiculturalism is another way of reifying individuality and differentness, he observes that

16. Norval, "Politics of Ethnicity and Identity," 272–73.

17. Ibid., 272. See also Lewellen, *Anthropology of Globalization*, 106; Brettell, *Anthropology and Migration*, 106.

18. Rynkiewich, *Soul, Self, and Society*, 78–79.

19. Ibid., 164.

little attention has been given to the "mechanics of the intricate processes of cultural contact, intrusion, fusion and disjunction."[20]

I struggled with the inescapable fact that ethnicities persist in spite of globalization and even thrive in a regime of globalization. Over against this multi-ethnicity or multiculturalism there was the idea of homogenization or standardization of all humans. Riding the subway in New York, one could not avoid the multicultural atmosphere inside the train. One heard people speaking in Spanish, Russian, Indian, or Putonghua. One saw people of diverse race and culture. Upon arriving at Canal Station, a unique characteristic unfolded as numerous Chinese waited for their turn to ride the subway when most stations had more varied groups of people. A New Yorker informed me that the only white people you would see in Chinatown were tourists. To one's surprise, the place was indeed packed with Asians and predominantly Chinese. In 2010, half a million, or 15 percent of the total Chinese population in the United States, lived in the state of New York.[21]

This reality brought us to the fact that people would tend to group with those that they perceived to be their own kind. There was a sense of camaraderie, comfort, and familiarity for someone newly arrived at a place with people of his/her own kind. These Chinese were a good example of Michael Novak's "unmeltable ethnics."[22] Despite years of assimilation, many ethnic groups in the United States continue to persist and remain distinctively their own kind. Yet these ethnic groups cannot escape the fact that one way or another, they are also influenced by other cultures.

Similarly, the Chinese in the Philippines have been influenced by Filipino culture and the constant changes brought about by technological advances and the tremendous flow of people and ideas here and there. These affected the "purity" of one's culture. I am also convinced that ethnicities evolve, develop, or improve yet without losing their main or "essential" elements that distinguish them from others. As culture is being constructed, it accepts or rejects elements that will help shape its own identity and uniqueness. For my dissertation research on Chinese Filipino identity in the early twenty-first century, I have been open in using both primordialist and constructivist approaches. I want to discover

20. Young, *Colonial Desire*, 4–5.

21. Hoeffel et al., "Asian Population 2010," 15, 18. The Chinese was the largest Asian group in the United States with 4 million who described themselves as Chinese alone-or-in-any-combination. The Chinese alone numbered 3.3 million.

22. Novak, *Unmeltable Ethnics*, xliv, 82.

whether the people see themselves as "purist" or "hybrid." The next part lays out the different hybridity theories to explain the possible kind of mixing the Chinese experienced in the Philippines.

HYBRIDITY: DEFINITION, CLASSIFICATION, AND THEORIES

Robert C. Young traces the history of the word hybridity. Hybridity was defined by Webster in 1828 as "a mongrel or mule; an animal or plant, produced from the mixture of two species."[23] Tracing its development from biological and botanical origins, in Latin it meant product of a tame sow and a wild boar. The *Oxford English Dictionary* defined it in 1861 as "of human parents of different races, half-breed"[24] and adding that this word had occurred early in the seventeenth century but more so in the nineteenth century. Young indicates that nineteenth-century hybridity connoted a physiological phenomenon while in the twentieth century it connoted a cultural one.[25] Throughout history, hybridity involved many issues such as the phenomenon of diminishing fertility, monogenesis (one species) or polygenesis (many species); extinction or amalgamation; miscegenation; progressivist or degenerationist.[26] A hybrid then can have negative (bastard) and positive (hybrid vigor) meanings.

Hybridity Defined

Jan Nederveen Pieterse measures hybridity based on its context. Hybridity is about the mixture of phenomena such as religious syncretism or cross-category mixing such as fairs or carnivals where the exotic and familiar come together. Hybridity, as an idea, can also be applied to cultures, nations, ethnicities, status groups, classes, and genres. He adds that "hybridity by its very nature blurs the distinctions among them."[27] He defines hybridity as a concept that "carries different meanings in different cultures, among different circles within cultures and at different periods . . . Hybridity is entirely contextual and relational."[28] He challenges,

---

23. Young, *Colonial Desire*, 6.
24. Ibid.
25. Ibid.
26. Ibid., 6–19, 46–47.
27. Nederveen Pieterse, *Globalization and Culture*, 72.
28. Ibid., 72, 106.

A theory of hybridity would be attractive. We are so used to theories that are concerned with establishing boundaries and demarcations among phenomena—units or processes that are as neatly as possible set apart from other units or processes— that a theory instead would focus on fuzziness and melánge, cut'n'mix, crisscross and crossover, might well be a relief in itself. Yet, ironically, of course, it would have to prove itself by giving as neat as possible a version of messiness, or an unhybrid categories of hybridities.[29]

For this study, I utilized Nederveen Pieterse's categorization of hybridity as my definition and classification. Hybridity then is defined in this study as the result of the mixing of "blood" or mixing of cultures and/or cultural elements within a culture. The mixing of "blood" pertains to the Chinese Mestizos. The mixing of cultures is about being a bicultural or multicultural. In the mixing of cultures, it can be a mix of one or more cultural elements in varying degree of influence like languages, religions, traditions, customs, and stories within a culture or cultures. Likewise, I use this definition in classifying the different kinds of mixing.

Hybridity Classified

Based on personal experience and research conducted, I classify hybridity among the Chinese in the Philippines on the basis of mixing of "blood," as a local concept, which produced the Chinese Mestizos; and the mixing of cultures (Chinese, Filipino, Spanish, American) including cultural elements (language, religion, tradition).

MIXING OF "BLOOD"

The issue of Chinese Mestizos in the Philippines dates back to the Spanish period. Assimilation of the Chinese happened mostly during the eighteenth century of the Spanish Period when expulsions of Chinese people constantly posed a threat that led to inter-ethnic marriage with the Filipinos to gain the right to stay in the country. This resulted in the Chinese Mestizo "race" or group. The Spaniards referred them as *mestizos* (half bred) or Chinese Mestizos as distinguished from the Spanish Mestizos.[30]

29. Ibid., 72.

30. Sugaya, "Expulsion of Non-Christian Chinese," 111–14; Caoili, *Origins of Metropolitan Manila*, 37.

There were still inter-ethnic marriages between the Chinese and Filipinos after the Spanish Period and even to this day which produced the current Chinese Mestizos. The Chinese Mestizos will either be more Chinese or more Filipino depending on the dominant culture. It can be that the father or the mother exercise more influence and power which affects the kind of cultural adherence in terms of the language spoken, religion accepted, practices and traditions applied.

In the past, animosity was present between some Chinese and some Filipinos. The Chinese Mestizos were also looked down as "not pure or not full-blooded." Nonetheless, this present generation witnessed the gradual diminishing of these offensive classification or name calling. Endogamy is still widely practiced but Chinese parents today are more lenient in allowing inter-ethnic marriages with Filipinos or other ethnicities.

Mixing of Cultures or Cultural Elements

The issue of a mixed Chinese culture in today's generation was unavoidable. The Chinese Filipinos today are no longer "pure" Chinese in their cultural orientation in the sense that it is exactly the same as that of China, Hong Kong, or Taiwan or even of other Chinese in diaspora. Interestingly they are not fully "Filipinized" either. They have constructed a culture that is uniquely their own, a "third culture" or a "third way."[31] They cannot deny the fact that they have been influenced by the host country and the former Western colonizers. The issues of language and religion were integral to one's identity and ethnicity. However, various customs and traditions, as well as food and clothing are also indications of cultural mixing.

The younger generation Chinese Filipinos mixed Minnanhua with Filipino and English words as they converse with their peers. They can be fluent in all three languages. They can communicate perfectly with their parents in Minnanhua at home, in Filipino with Filipinos, and in English in classrooms. But somehow, the mixing of the three languages is the best way to communicate from the heart. An example is *"Di be chia* hamburger for **merienda** *bo*? (Would you like hamburger for snack?)"

---

31. Gessner and Schade employs John Useem's definition of third culture as, "not merely a mutual accommodation or amalgamation of two separate, parallel cultures, but the birth of something new as far as behaviours, lifestyles, world views, etc. are concerned." Gessner and Schade, "Conflict of Culture," 260.

David Cheung calls this generation the EnRAWGen or English Reading and Writing Generation.[32]

With regard to religion, the syncretistic folk Christianity among the 85 percent Chinese Filipinos is a reality that See, Tan, and Uayan have observed.[33] The pragmatic business-minded Chinese fostered good relations with others by accommodating even different faiths. This research further discovered what categories, pure or hybrid, are operative now in Tsinoy society.

Hybridity Theories

As hybridity was properly defined and classified into mixing of "blood" and mixing of cultures or cultural elements, the following hybridity theories were used in understanding the different kinds of mixing among them.

Robbins's "Mixed yet Unmixed"

Joel Robbins believes that hybridity has been theorized in different perspectives, but it will be best theorized in the context of culture. He seeks to understand cultural hybridity from the standpoint of "interaction" as a way of mixing that still produces a clear view of each component's distinctiveness rather than hybridity as a synthesis that cannot tell one from the other. His theory of cultural hybridity opens the possibility of mixing yet not really mixed together. It is like the Urapmin Christians who live in two distinctive cultural logics.[34]

To reconcile this hybridity without real mixing or remaining distinctive separate cultures, I believe that the Urapmin experience is an "enhanced culture" with the influence of Christianity. It may or may not

32. Cheung, "EnRAWGen Ministry," 1.

33. Jaime Bulatao coined the term "split-level Christianity" to describe the folk Roman Catholicism practiced among Filipinos. Bulatao, *Split-Level Christianity*, 2.

34. Robbins contends that the Urapmin are moral and lawful people. They see the law as a gift from the colonizers and a relational construct. He argues that these people accept Christianity in its entirety and yet remain very much Urapmin in their culture. Christianity is adopted as a whole new culture with little assimilation of the new into the old. Christianity is a cultural phenomenon among the Urapmin. He observes that there is no Western influence in their practice of Christianity. He sees the individuality of Christianity and the relational culture of the Urapmin as being at odds with each other. In his conclusion, Robbins suggests a cultural theory of hybridity as a way of solving the issue of these two conflicting desires of the Urapmin. Robbins, *Becoming Sinners*, 3, 34, 58, 75, 311, 327–33.

necessarily follow that they are living in two separate cultures at the same time. But they have created an all new and improved culture, a reconstructed culture. They are Urapmin Christians that still retain much of their Urapmin cultures yet upholding Christian values and teachings. It is a hybrid of two cultures mixed together yet distinctly recognizable from one to the other. It is a hybrid of two cultures that has been mixed together without clashing and fighting against each other. They are combined to produce a blend that further enhances the Urapmin culture toward a better understanding of the world and God though not necessarily gaining development and progress in the economic sense.

The Urapmin's culture may not necessarily be one big culture or one mixed culture. It may be that they acquire the ability to operate in categorically separate cultures on different days. This can also be understood as "compartmentalization." Lewellen describes compartmentalization as the ability to selectively use different cultures in different settings. In his view, it may not necessarily mean a real "mixing" of cultures occur. Paul G. Hiebert defines it as adapting to the culture we are in but separating these different cultures in our minds.[35]

Cultural hybridity, for the Chinese in the Philippines, seems to result to their advantage. They have acquired knowledge of different cultures and languages. They became multilinguists and multiculturalists. They speak their ethnic language in the home and switch to English in school. They switch to Filipino when interacting with Filipinos. Mastery of the languages enable them to switch from one language to another. They can also respond through appropriate cultural behavior without losing or mixing one's culture with another. This hybridity can be the ability to switch from one culture to another yet maintaining one's natural or core identity and culture. This research proposed the possibility of finding three categories of Chinese Filipino culture: (1) Pure; (2) Hybrid Mixed, meaning "enhanced culture" or third culture as by product of mixing two or more cultures; and (3) Hybrid Multiple: that is, Multiple "Selfs" or Multiple Identities. Multiple "selfs" may be understood as cultural competency or compartmentalization rather than cultural fusion.

35. Lewellen admits the popularity of the word hybrid even in instances wherein compartmentalization may be more the case than real mixing. Lewellen, *Anthropology of Globalization*, 54, 99. See also Hiebert, *Anthropological Insights*, 106–7. However, since compartmentalization is employing appropriately acquired knowledge of different cultures in different situations, this can be a form of hybridity like Robbins's mixed yet unmixed theory. Henceforth, this study views Robbins's mixed yet unmixed theory and compartmentalization as forms of cultural hybridity.

Bhabha's "Unhomed"

The first-generation immigrants and even the second-generation local-born Chinese had sentiments of being "unhomed" in the Philippines. They did not see China or Taiwan as their home and yet they could not feel at home in the Philippines due to immigration laws and discrimination. Their state was similar to Homi Bhabha's discussion of the "unhomed" in *The Location of Cultures*.

For Bhabha, "To be unhomed is not to be homeless, nor can the 'unhomely' be easily accommodated in that familiar division of social life into private and public spheres." The unhomely marks deeper historical displacement. Bhabha cites examples like the unhomely world of the apartheid and the unhomely dead daughter named *Beloved*. He focuses a significant portion of his writing on Toni Morrison's book *Beloved*. He sees the return of the dead daughter as a ghost to liberate herself by loving and hating her mother. Her mother, Sethe, murders her as a child to free her from slavery. The murderous love of her mother is to liberate her daughter from the evil and pain she has experienced as a slave.[36] Such historical backdrop will help understand the unhomed slaves in the United States and the unhomed ghost who seeks love and affirmation.

Bhabha proposes a "third space" theory for the postcolonial diaspora discourse that I find fitting for these Chinese in the Philippines who find themselves unfit and unsettled in the land they hope to plant their roots. This "third space" theory is to help deconstruct the issue of the unhomed and reconstruct their identity based on their circumstances.

Barth's "Situational Approach"

Barth's introduction on *Ethnic Groups and Boundaries* challenges the primordialist approach and brings out the need to study the interactions between ethnic groups and how that affects the development of ethnic identities. He sums up the findings of the essays in the book in two important discoveries. First, ethnicity does not depend on the "absence of mobility, contact and information" to remain as exclusive. Second, ethnicity persists "despite inter-ethnic contact and interdependence."[37] Realizing that ethnicities are not boxed and immune from outside influences, there's a need to evaluate and study ethnicities from this constructivist point of view against the essentialist approach.

36. Bhabha, *Location of Cultures*, 9–17.
37. Barth, *Ethnic Groups and Boundaries*, 9–10.

This new definition leads to development of concepts like migration; transnationalism by Nina Glick Schiller, Linda Basch, and Cristina Szanton Blanc; flexible citizenships and third cultures by Aihwa Ong where negotiations, manipulations, accommodations, adaptations, and adoptions happen along the way for survival and/or for profit. Nevertheless, the fact that ethnicity persists in this global age led us to reconsider how essentialism could help enlighten this quest for ethnic identity.

CONCLUSION

The Chinese Filipinos are an ethnic minority in the Philippines. They are essentially Chinese in ethnicity as they share a common ancestry, history, link with a homeland, and a sense of solidarity. Nevertheless their language and culture have gone through a series of transformations with influences from here and there and in different time periods. Cultural hybridity is a very interesting topic that I find refuge in for the identity of the present Chinese in the Philippines. These theories have guided this research in its quest for understanding the Chinese Filipino ethnic identity.

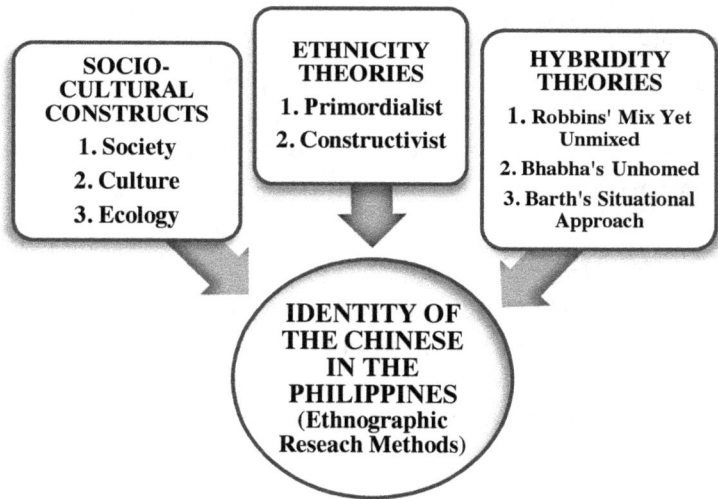

Figure 2. Theoretical Framework of the Study

It is my aim to provide a balanced and objective presentation, being aware that I am a Chinese Filipino who has my own personal biases. It is my desire that my research will help discover whether the present

Chinese Filipinos are homogenous or hybrids in terms of cultural practices. The discovery of their cultural orientation will aid in how this affects their understanding of their identity and how they go about other aspects of their lives.

4

Reconstructing Identities:
Who Are the Tsinoys Today?

ONE SATURDAY MORNING, I was having breakfast at McDonald's in Banawe, Quezon City. As I sipped my coffee, loud noises behind me interrupted my quiet morning. I turned around and saw a group of Chinese elderly adults gathering together for breakfast. They were so into their conversation that their voices reached up the ceiling. For a second, I thought I was in one of the Chinese restaurants in Manila Chinatown. But no, I was in Quezon City. They were speaking in Minnanhua and talked as though they were at home. I observed that they loved to talk and share their stories of long ago. Similarly, my late father enjoyed ceaseless conversations with his friends over tea or just sitting outside our store. There was something about speaking and exchanging stories. It was through these activities that realities of everyday life were constructed. The past was relived and culture was reinforced. As a word was uttered, a thought conveyed, or a story shared, connections were being made and camaraderie strengthened. Speaking with your native tongue, the language of the heart, added the depth of connection and the joy of speaking. I guessed maybe that was why in Minnanhua, we liked to use the word *lanlâng* 咱人 to refer to Chinese. *Lanlâng* meant our people or our own. As *lan e lâng* (our people), we loved to gather together to share our stories and our past.

Lewellen observes the complexity of understanding people or how they identify themselves. Identity is defined as (1) how one perceives himself/herself, (2) how he/she is popularly perceived, and (3) how the social scientists perceive him/her. Let me add another, (4) how missionaries,

72

missiologists, and mission agencies perceive him/her. Identity is a complex concept and usually the way people perceive themselves is not what others see and understand.[1]

There are popular sketches of the Chinese in the Philippines. Names or labels were given to them in different colonial and postwar periods, and even until the present. The Spaniards called them *Sangleys* then *Chinos*. The Americans called them Chinamen and Coolies. They were also classified as Non-Christian Tribe and Aliens. The Filipinos called them **Tsino, Kabise, Tsekwa, Intsik, Beho, Barok, Bulol, Butsekik, Singkit** or **Singkot, Tsinito** or **Tsinita**, Chinky-eyed, Chinks, Tsinoy, or Chinoy.

The social scientists categorized them as Huáshāng 華商 or merchants, Huágōng 華工 or Coolies, Huáqiáo 華僑 or Overseas Chinese, Jìjū 寄居 or Sojourners, Huárén 華人 or Chinese people in diaspora, and Huá-yì 華裔 or of Chinese descent. They were also labeled as Jews of the East, immigrants, transnationals, essential outsiders, market-dominant minorities, flexible identities, cosmopolitans, cosmopolitan capitalists, or global cosmopolitans.

Missionaries and missiologists have referred to them at different times as heathens, pagans, unbelievers, EnRAWGen, split-level Christians, syncretistic, folk evangelical Christians, or *chap chay lomi* (mixed belief system). In academics, proper reference to the Chinese in the Philippines has evolved as well from mere "Chinese" to "Philippine Chinese" to "Filipino-Chinese" to "ethnic Chinese" to "Chinese-Filipino" to "Chinese Filipino," dropping the hyphen.

The Chinese Filipinos referred to themselves in Minnanhua as *lan-lâng, Tiong Kok lâng, Banlam lâng, Hua-din, Hua-è*, Chinese, Tsinoy, or Chinoy. There were those who called other Chinese or even themselves *hoan-á*.[2]

Cultures as broad linguistic groups are diminishing in the present age, yet identities are ever increasing in the form of ethnicities, nations, religious cults, local and international clubs, political parties, transnational associations, and digital villages. The globalizing nature of our world today produces global flows of people, ideas, and products that detach, dislocate, and relocate people, language, and culture in complex mosaics of sociality. Constant migration also fosters changes and "mixing" of one

1. Lewellen, *Anthropology of Globalization*, 92–93.
2. See appendix E.

culture with another thereby producing a hybrid of cultures.[3] Migration has been a major factor for changes in one's culture and redefining one's identity as in the case of the Chinese in the Philippines.

Rynkiewich is convinced that in understanding people, one must study them through the lenses of culture, society, ecology, and history. Further, even though this group of people belongs to a specific local system, that local system is part of the larger system or multiple systems.[4] For the Chinese Filipinos, the realities of their past and even present histories intersect with the ever changing society and environment in this global age lead to a continuing construction or reconstruction of their cultural identity or identities.

This chapter attempts to present a profile of contemporary Chinese Filipinos by classifying them into six groups. This classification is based on the interviews, data gathered, and the present understanding of most Chinese Filipinos, taking into consideration the specific time periods including historical, political, and sociological significance. My classification may not necessarily reflect the opinions of all Chinese Filipinos. It may not even be congruent with the classification of specialists like Cheung, See, Tan, or Wickberg.[5] Nonetheless, this presentation is the product of my analysis and investigation based on literature review and ethnographic research methodology.

Discussion of the six groups is divided into three parts. Part 1 discusses the sojourning experiences of the Old Immigrants and the New Immigrants (henceforth, OI or OIs and NI or NIs, respectively). The sojourning nature may lead to settling or continued sojourning as transnationals. Part 2 explores the Tsinoy identity and their "unhomely" nature as Chinese living in the Philippines with Chinese citizenships and

---

3. Lewellen, *Anthropology of Globalization*, 92–101.

4. Ecology or cultural ecology in this context refers to how the people perceive their environment; how they see the things around them; how they value these; and/or how they produce these. Rynkiewich, *Soul, Self, and Society*, 64–65, 77.

5. See chapter 1 on Review of Relevant Literature for the classifications made by See, Tan, and Wickberg. David Cheung classifies the Chinese into three groups: (1) Alien—are legal and illegal residents but not citizens; (2) Ethnic—are residents or citizens and consider themselves Chinese in culture and identity; (3) Assimilated—are residents or citizens but no longer Chinese in culture and identity. Based on the research made by Chinese Congress on World Evangelism Fellowship Philippines in September of 1993, the Chinese population in the Philippines comprises 947,590 with only 8,235 active believers in 72 Chinese churches. Cheung, "Chinese-Filipino Profile," 2, 6, 9.

as Overseas Chinese Filipino Workers (OCFW). They are situated in an in-between space, a third space that is "unhomely" and ambivalent. Part 3 presents the issues of Sinicization or Filipinization among the spouses in inter-ethnic marriages between Chinese and Filipinos and their off-spring, the Chinese Mestizos (CM or CMs). This portion tackles the issue of marriage and family.

PART 1: OLD AND NEW IMMIGRANTS, FROM SOJOURNERS TO SETTLERS

In *Sojourners and Settlers*, Wang Gungwu defines a "sojourner" as one who visits a place briefly with the intention of returning home. Wang argues that the word "sojourner" is not limited to the Chinese case. It is applicable to the migratory situations of other ethnicities or groups as well. It is not limited to the past but is still relevant in the present global phenomenon.[6]

The OIs were Sojourners because their initial purpose was simply to earn money to send or bring home. They were also called Overseas Chinese or Huáqiáo 華僑 (Putonghua) or *Huakiao* (Minnanhua).[7] For this study, I will use Huáqiáo. The Huáqiáo were the first to migrate to the Philippines, whether as individuals or with their families. Throughout the centuries, some stayed behind either by choice or forced by circum-stances. These OIs inadvertently turned into settlers.

Wang argues that the term "Huáqiáo" is no longer suitable for Southeast Asian Chinese who have decided to stay in their adopted coun-try because their loyalty resides in their current host country. The term is politically suggestive encouraging continuous loyalty and patriotism to China.[8] He suggests the use of the expression "Chinese Overseas" or what he calls the hyphenated Chinese (e.g., Chinese-American, Sino-Thai, and Chinese-Filipino) to refer to the Huáqiáo. He admits that the term Hǎiwài Huárén 海外華人 or Huárén still causes confusion because it literally means "Overseas Chinese." Leo Suryadinata prefers ethnic Chinese and

6. Wang, "Sojourning," 1–3. He also discovers that the word "sojourner" is not included in the lexicon of migration studies.

7. Huá 華 means "China" or "Chinese," qiáo 僑 means "one who lives abroad."

8. Wang, "Sojourning," 1–3. Since the revolution against the Qing Dynasty, the GMD and CCP (China Communist Party, also known as Communist Party of China or CPC) were eyeing the support of the Overseas Chinese. After 1949, when China mainland became communist, the GMD and CCP continued to seek the patronage of these Huáqiáo. Wickberg, "Anti-Sinicism," 169.

this term has recently gained acceptance in most scholarly writings.[9] For this research, I will use Chinese Filipino without the hyphen to broadly refer to all Chinese in the Philippines including non-citizens and New Immigrants since most of those interviewed refer the Philippines as their country.

Wang is correct to say that Huáqiáo is no longer a valid term for the present Chinese in diaspora. Nevertheless, for the sake of popular notion and a "neat fit" in classifying the different Chinese groups, the term Huáqiáo will still be used to refer to the OI and NI categories.[10] The term "Sojourner" is still applicable for the Chinese scattered in different parts of the world in this global and migratory period. Sojourner aptly describes these Chinese Filipinos who might decide to migrate to another country in the future. Their transient nature and unsettled disposition mark their sojourning character.

There are two types of Immigrants or Sojourners or Huáqiáo for this study: (1) Old Immigrants or Jiùqiáo 舊僑 or *Kukiao* who entered from 1898 to 1975 and (2) New Immigrants or Xinqiáo 新僑 or *Sinkiao* from 1976 to the present.

The OI's timeframe for this study marks the start of American Period in 1898 and ends with President Ferdinand Marcos' Naturalization Act of 1975.[11] The two historical periods brought about significant social

9. Wang clarifies that the Chinese in Taiwan and Hong Kong must not be classified as "Overseas Chinese" or Huáqiáo even though they are not situated in the mainland. The Taipei government totally rejected the idea of calling their people Huáqiáo. The term Huáqiáo can be traced back to the first decade of the twentieth century when it referred to Chinese citizens residing outside China territories, under foreign governments or "regarded by a series of Chinese governments." People in Hong Kong and Macau may have been under foreign rule but they do not see themselves as Huáqiáo. The People's Republic of China employed the term Tóngbāo 同胞 or compatriots to people in Hong Kong, Macau, and Taiwan. Wang, "Dilemmas of Place and Practice," 120–21.

10. The OIs' migration to the Philippines is traced back to the Pre-Hispanic and Spanish Period. There will always be NIs as opposed to the OIs. The OIs will always see themselves as old-timers as new migrants arrive. The new influx of immigrants will eventually become "old" immigrants as time goes by and as newer immigrants continue to enter the country. See chapter 2 on Chinese Identities in Philippine History.

11. After Marcos established diplomatic ties with China in 1975, he granted mass naturalization to the Chinese Filipinos who wished to have Filipino citizenship to ensure their loyalty to the Philippines and not to China. The Chinese in the country, based on the interviews with the OIs, were mostly pro-GMD than pro-Mao. Consequently, most OIs and Tsinoys with Chinese citizenship today have Taiwan passports not China passports. Kaisa argues that the government had a false understanding.

changes in the lives of the local Chinese. The first date marked the start of a new hegemony while the second date marked the law that liberated them from their identity as aliens and strangers. These former strangers and aliens now had the opportunity to apply for citizenship which entailed many privileges and rights. They could now buy houses and own lands. Many moved out of the crowded Chinatown and into the suburbs.[12] Integration and assimilation became possibilities and realities.

The NIs are those immigrants who entered the Philippines from 1976 onward. They are considered NIs for this study even though they may have been living in the country for a few decades already.[13] Most of the NIs interviewed were from Fujian, one from Macao, one from Taiwan, one from Hong Kong, and one from Inner Mongolia. Seven of them were interviewed individually and four youth in a focus group. All of them are residents of Metro Manila.

Old Immigrants

Four people were interviewed individually for the OI category aside from the two focus groups of elderlies, namely, Focus Group A-OI with five people and Focus Group B-OI with seven people. This category has a total of fourteen informants. All of them are presently residing in the Philippines.

The local Chinese were actually capitalist and not pro-Mao. Further, most of the local Chinese were already native born and grew up in the country. If anything held them back from being fully Filipinos it was citizenship. See, *Tsinoy*, 194–95; "Ethnic Chinese as Filipinos," 163–66. Marcos and his administration may have remembered the fateful event of the MV Karagatan in 1972. The Karagatan set sail from China to Isabela to supply arms to the New People's Army which is the communist party of the Philippines. This was thwarted by the military that led to a bloody end and confiscation of the arms. Severino, "Pagbalik sa Karagatan." Nonetheless, this fear led to a positive outcome for the local Chinese which was the opportunity to acquire Filipino citizenships.

12. After acquiring Filipino citizenships, the wealthy Chinese Filipinos helped in the development of suburbs as they were able to buy lands and created subdivisions and little Chinese villages for their security and convenience. Guéguen, "Moving from Binondo," 124–25.

13. Marcos had hoped that the diplomatic ties with China would attract more Chinese investors into the country. Unfortunately, most of those who entered in the seventies and eighties were not big investors. Many were actually relatives of the OIs. Those who entered in the nineties were not necessarily reconnecting with families or relatives. See, "Influx of New Chinese Immigrants," 137–38.

FINDING GREENER PASTURES

> "Life in China was hard. It was difficult to earn money to place food on the table. We heard about people going overseas and so we followed them here." —Jimmy[14]

Jimmy's grandfather, Meng, was one of the thousands of Chinese who sought a greener pasture outside China because of the political instability, wars, and famines at the end of the Qing Dynasty. Meng was in his thirties in the early 1900s when he boarded a ship to the Philippines. He left his wife and children behind. Upon arrival, he worked as a *thiao du* or porter, a work that required much strength and stamina.[15] Life was not easy in the new country; but like many Chinese hoping to find a better future, he was not deterred by hardship.[16]

Jimmy recounted that his grandfather came to the Philippines to work as a Coolie.[17] Coolie was the transliteration of the Putonghua kǔlì 苦力, or "bitter strength." This speaks volumes of the laborers' hardships. Coolies became a popular term synonymous to Chinese by the late nineteenth to early twentieth century. They were called Coolies by their foreign employers because of their menial jobs as cooks or house helpers.[18] Some, like Meng, saw themselves as Coolies because of the nature of their work.

Meng continued to toil. He eventually saved enough to do business along sidewalks by spreading a **banig** (mat) to sell slippers. Together with a friend, he established a **hopia** store.[19] In the 1920s, his three sons came to the Philippines to help him in their business. Meng left the business to his sons upon reaching his sixties and returned to China for good.

---

14. Jimmy, OI individual interview by author, 4 July 2012.

15. Wickberg writes that in the nineteenth century, the Chinese Coolies quickly replaced the *indios* (or Filipinos) in warehouses as stevedores and labor in public works projects. Wickberg, "Early Chinese Economic Influence," 284.

16. See appendices F and G.

17. The word "Coolie" originally refers to an aboriginal Gujarat tribe of India, and stretches to mean migrant laborer or hireling. It later refers to Chinese contract laborers. Pan, *Sons of the Yellow Emperor*, 45; Watt, *Chinese Bondage in Peru*, 16. Coolie means cheap Chinese labor. Alejandrino, *Chinese Exclusion Act*, 8. See appendix G.

18. Pan, *Sons of the Yellow Emperor*, 45.

19. Hopia is a sweet mung bean biscuit. It is called *lék tāu piá* 綠豆餅 in Minnanhua. The Filipinos call it **hopia**. Ho (好) meant good. Piá (餅) meant biscuit/cookies. Chan-Yap, "Hokkien Chinese Loanwords," 31.

Not all Chinese who emigrated were Coolies, or merchants and traders. Some were sent abroad by family members; some emigrated voluntarily by using their own savings, or help from family, relatives, kinfolks, or friends.[20] Some considered themselves as Coolies because of the nature of their work. Others were forced to leave a comfortable life in China because of wars.

AT HOME IN FUJIAN, CHINA

"We have a big house, a big courtyard. What fun we have back then. Life was comfortable." —Un-Tién[21]

Most of the local Chinese in the Philippines trace their ancestry to the southern Fujian province, particularly the Minnan 閩南 or *Banlam* region.[22] Minnan means "South of the Min," namely, the Min River. Fújiàn 福建 and Hokkien (or Fukien or Fookien) refer to the same place. Fujian is the Putonghua rendition while Hokkien in Minnanhua. The expression can refer to the province of Fujian, the language spoken by the people, or the people themselves. An alternative term use by the Chinese Filipinos for the spoken language, namely, *Banlam ōe* or Minnanhua 閩南話.[23] To avoid confusion, the term Hokkien will be used to refer to the people from Fujian and Minnanhua to the language spoken in this work.

Many Chinese in the Philippines originated from Jinjiang 晉江 County or *Chin-kang*. Research shows that 90 percent of the Chinese in the country traced their origin from Fujian while 10 percent from Guangdong. More than 60 percent of those from Fujian were specifically

---

20. Da Chen, "Chinese Migrations," 13–15. Min Zhou writes that in the colonial era, Huágōng or Coolies had two main means of migration: credit-ticket system or labor contracts. Merchants and traders served as brokers and agents. Provision for their tickets were either advanced or through labor contracts. Chu notes that in the credit-ticket system, the facilitator or credit provider initially paid for the Coolie's passenger ticket and living expenses. The Coolie would then have to deduct part of their wages to pay back the loan. This system had led to underpaid laborers and more debts to the benefit of the rich Chinese Coolie brokers. Zhou, *Contemporary Chinese America*, 32; Chu, *Chinese and Chinese Mestizos*, 110–11; appendix F.

21. Un-Tién, OI individual interview by author, 15 July 2012.

22. *Banlam* is the Minnanhua version of Minnan.

23. The language spoken by the people living in Minnan region such are the cities of Zhangzhou 漳州, Quanzhou 泉州, and Xiamen 廈門 is called Minnanhua. Chu, *Chinese and Chinese Mestizos of Manila*, 25. Amoy is the English transliteration for Xiàmén 廈門 or *Ēmn̂g* in Minnanhua.

from Jinjiang.[24] Jinjiang is close to the hearts of many OIs because it reminds them of childhood and family, their roots, their ancestors, and their country.

Un-Tién was born in 1927 in Jinjiang, China. She recalled her childhood with enthusiasm, vividly remembering the images of the South China Sea, the stone houses, the white sands, and the children playing on the beach. She had a big family. She recalled living in a huge house made of bricks and stones with many rooms. It proudly stood side by side with houses of their relatives forming a cemented courtyard in the middle. She remembered seeing peanuts, sweet potatoes or other crops. Their house was the only one with electricity and indoor plumbing in all Jinjiang at that time. They had an indoor bath room and a toilet with running water. Her father's ingenuity and interest in machines made this possible.

The story of Un-Tién contrasts with those of the Coolies. Her family emigrated, not because life was difficult, but because of fear of wars. This is one of the main reasons for the sojourning and later settling of many OIs.

ESCAPING WARS AND PLANTING ROOTS

"Which war are you referring to? Even at present, wars never end." —Mr. Lim[25]

I was surrounded by several esteemed elderly Chinese intellectuals who met weekly over coffee discussing current events and politics. When I asked whether any of them had come to the Philippines after the war? Mr. Lim immediately asked me to which war am I referring. Everyone roared with laughter. Sheepishly I realized I should have specified that I am referring to the Second World War. After Japan surrendered in 1945, civil wars between the two political parties continued in China until 1949. Communism took over China, and Jiang Jieshi with his two million GMD supporters fled to Taiwan in December of 1949.[26] China had a long history characterized by ceaseless wars and many atrocities. Many OIs

24. See, *Chinese in the Philippines*, 3:196–201; appendix H.

25. Mr. Lim, Focus Group B-OI by author, 11 July 2012.

26. Roberts, *Concise History of China*, 249–55. Jiang Jieshi or Chiang Kai Shek was the leader of the Nationalist (GMD) Party after Sun Yat Sen died in 1925. He was not able to win the support of the Communist Party, instead the two camps engaged in civil war. The defeat of Jiang Jieshi led him to retreat to Taiwan in 1949 and established his government there.

who have firsthand experiences of wars can attest to the brutalities and
haunting fear of wars. Mr. Cheng volunteered to summarize the history
of the Chinese in the Philippines.

> Let me explain why we came here in the simplest way. Ages
> ago, definitely many did not wish to leave their family but life
> in China was really hard. It was difficult to earn money. Espe-
> cially in our *Banlam* province, there were much lands and many
> mountains, but they were not arable. *Ták-ê tióh khì goā kháu
> thàn tsiáh* (Everyone should leave home to earn a living). There
> were wars and corrupt officials. So our ancestors had arrived
> here long time ago. 90 percent who came wanted to earn some
> money, *beh tò khi tn̂g soa* 唐山(they want to return back to
> China) and retire there. After the Second World War, *bōe tit tò
> khì lo kò, lau le chhia lò* (they could not go home and so they
> stayed here). Then there was the civil war in China . . . many *bōe
> tit tò khì* (they cannot go home). They decided to stay and adapt
> to this country.[27]

Un-Tién left China at age eleven in July of 1938 to escape the Second
Sino-Japanese War. She arrived in Manila with her relatives. Upon arrival, Un-Tién still remembers their passports and papers being checked.
Their bodies and stools were examined before they were permitted to
enter the country. Her grandmother was actually detained for a while at
San Lazaro Hospital.[28] They settled in Binondo.[29] When the Japanese
invaded the Philippines, she and her family hid in the province and returned to Binondo after the war. They had three stores selling shoes along

27. Mr. Cheng, Focus Group B-OI by author, 11 July 2012. China is also referred
as *tn̂g soa* 唐山 (Tang Mountain) aside from *Taidiok* 大陸 (Mainland) and *Tiong Kok*
中國 (Middle Kingdom) by the Hokkien people.

28. San Lazaro Hospital was established in 1577 by the Spanish government as a
dispensary clinic. It was originally located in Intramuros but moved to present site in
Quiricada Street, Sta. Cruz in 1784. The Americans turned it into a contagious disease
hospital in 1898. In 1918, the Filipinos took over the operations of the institution.
Gannett et al., *Census of the Philippine Islands*, 408–9.

29. Her father's shoe business enabled him to bring his family over. Some of
their relatives were adopted as her father's children in order to obtain passage into the
country. Her father also helped some *bóe toā jī* (to buy "paper names" or immigrant
papers). Buying "paper names" or immigrant papers became popular with tight immigration laws. Many came as sons or daughters of relatives or friends. This led to
confusing last names. The Chinese last names used by most Chinese Filipinos were
their real last names to trace their lineage.

Gandara Street.[30] In 1949, she got married and had children. She now considered the Philippines as her home and no longer wanted to return to China because her children are also in the country. She is so *kuí sì* (used to) living in the Philippines.

Ahbi was born in Manila in 1936. His father was able to come to the Philippines by using the surname of his father-in-law and declaring himself as the latter's son in his documents. Ahbi's family, except two elder brothers, returned to China in 1946. When Communism took over, the war reached *Hok-tsiu* 福州 (or Fuzhou) and Xiamen. By 1949, his father sent him and his sister back to the Philippines so that they would not lose their immigrant status.[31] Unfortunately, they lost communication with their parents and their youngest sister until he got married in 1965. "*Goán kiet hun e sî tsun, thau tsáu jíp khì* (After we got married, we secretly entered China.)."[32] Ahbi at present is a retired Chinese school teacher.

Jimmy was born in 1936 in Jinjiang, China. He also lost communication with his father Yuan after Communism took over China in 1949.[33] After six years (1955), he and his mother were able to go to Hong Kong. His father was able to visit them, but for Jimmy, "the Philippines was the final destination." Another six years passed (1961), he finally came to the Philippines. Jimmy has been writing articles for a Chinese daily since 1988. As an OI, he longs to see a better Philippines with a strong economy and less corruption. He continued,

> That [returning to China] is my grandfather and father's thinking. But because there are changes ... Majority of the family members are here ... Transition from a visitor to become a resident to a citizen ... Chinese need to integrate into mainstream

30. Her family lived *tiàm lāi téng bīn* (above their store). She learned Tagalog (Filipino) through their house helper. She remembered seeing Henry Sy hanging around their store as a shoe salesman. Henry Sy is a Chinese Filipino businessman who presently owns the chain of SM or Shoe Mart Department Stores all over the Philippines.

31. According to Ahbi, failure to return to the Philippines within three years, one would forfeit the immigration Huáqiáo status.

32. Ahbi secretly entered China for fear that he would be branded a Communist. GMD was very strong in Manila. If one spoke against them or visit one's parents in China, one would immediately be branded a communist. As a teacher, one could forfeit the license to teach. Ahbi, OI individual interview by author, 1 August 2012.

33. His father had been going to the Philippines since the 1920s, replacing his grandfather Meng. Since Yuan could not return to China, Jimmy and his mother tried to go to the Philippines instead.

so you can do business, you can live here as a citizen. Now Fil-ipino-Chinese consider Philippines their home already . . . I do not think China as my home. China is about relatives. Maybe we come from there. We might want to visit to know what is hap-pening in China. But China is China, Philippines is Philippines. Philippines is my home. I am quite old but this is my thinking, even the younger generation, **lalong ganyan** (moreso).[34]

Bee-Hua, an only child of her parents, remembered how they trea-sured her as their *kam pó pó* (precious one). She grew up in *Kolongsu* or Gǔlàngyǔ 鼓浪嶼, Fujian.[35] During the Second Sino-Japanese War, her father feared for her safety so he left his business and moved his family out of the island. They moved once again when the Civil War began. In her last year in high school, she met her husband. Her face blushed as she shared her story.

Goán mister (my husband) was born in the Philippines . . . His grandmother was Spanish, his grandfather was Chinese so his mother was a—what we call *chhut-sì-á* (Chinese Mestiza). His mother married a Chinese from China . . . My husband be-longed to three countries. [Laughter in the room] He joined the resistance to fight against the Japanese. He was captured and the enemy cut off one of his fingers. After the war, he took the first boat sailing back to China . . . Then once, he saw my picture that my father gave to his friend. He insisted to meet me . . . And so we were wed . . . Communism came by the time I gave birth to our first born in China who now lives in Hong Kong . . . My in-laws thought it was best we went to the Philippines . . . That time, *iá kín tiu, ták-ê lâng beh tsáu* (everyone was in a hurry, everyone wanted to run and leave). *Goán* mister (my husband) wanted me to go with him but I could not read English. So I left all the paperwork to them. We only have one English class every week so my English was not good. My *hoan-á ta-ke* (Filipina mother-in-law) did all my paperwork. I became her daughter born in China so I could go to Philippines with them. I became my husband's sister in the documents . . . I could not bring my son with me, so I had to leave my son in China with my other mother-in-law.[36]

34. Jimmy, OI individual interview by author, 4 July 2012.

35. Gulangyu Island is a car-free island off the coast of Xiamen. It became an in-ternational settlement in 1913. The Japanese took control of the place in 1941. Brown, *Amoy Magic*, 17–18, and 72.

36. Bee-Hua's father-in-law had two wives. One was in China and one in the

From these stories, we see that the Chinese were Sojourners who became settlers; from visiting or staying for a while to living permanently. In most cases, they suddenly had to choose between China and the Philippines, family or freedom, survival or death.

TRAPPED CHINESE: UNHOMED IN THE PHILIPPINES

> "As a stranger in the land of others, losing the strong support from our homeland, it was not difficult to imagine how miserable the situation would be. At that time, we could not be employed, could not get married. We were like the most pathetic parasites in the Chinese society. Some of us who could not bear this kind of heavy stress anymore chose to finish their own lives. There were also many who had gone astray . . . However, since we always hoped that one day we would gain legal residence, we continued the fight for our lives." —Luther[37]

Luther was nineteen when he took a plane to Manila in January of 1948. He entered the Philippines alone with the help of his brother-in-law who got him a student visa.[38] He enrolled in Tiong Se Academy's English night school but later transferred to a Filipino high school. He was forced to stay in the Philippines when China became Communist. He kept renewing his student visa in order to extend his stay. Hence, he finished two bachelor degrees and one graduate degree.

Like Luther, many Chinese sought to escape the political instability of their motherland leading them to migrate to the Philippines, a nation that had just acquired its independence. These OIs felt unwelcomed, unhomed, and unwanted. They were rejected and many were deported.

Luther lamented that many Chinese who came with missionary, tourist, temporary, or student visas between 1946 and 1953 became "overstaying Chinese" or what he preferred to call in English "trapped Chinese." Overstaying was a violation of the immigration laws. Tragically,

---

Philippines. The Chinese Mestiza mother-in-law in the Philippines was the mother of her husband. Interestingly, she calls her *hoan-á ta-ke* (Filipina mother-in-law). Bee-Hua was forced to leave her firstborn son. Her China mother-in-law had *pák-kha* or bound feet. She diligently looked after Bee-Hua's little one. Her own mother also helped take care of her son. Bee-Hua, Focus Group A-OI by author, 14 June 2012.

37. Luther, OI individual interview by author, 1 August 2012.

38. Luther adds that at that time, the Philippines followed the American's Chinese Exclusion Law. Only five hundred immigrants per year were permitted unless you entered with a missionary, tourist, student, or temporary visa. See Abinales and Amoroso, *State and Society*, 159.

they were trapped because of China's political situations. Unless one was fortunate to get an immigrant visa, which was allotted to only fifty persons for any given nationality yearly, one remained an overstaying Chinese.[39] To be in such a state was to be in constant dilemma and anxiety. Unless one received permanent residency, the possibility of being ejected out of the country and sent back to nowhere was frightening.

Luther also remarked,

> After Communism took over China in 1949, we could not return to China. Everyone had to stay here. We become a political football. The Philippine government wanted to deport two thousand seven hundred Chinese to Taiwan. Taiwan refused to admit them since their point of origin was not Taiwan. *Beh tsu na kiò Tâi-oân tsiap siu* (How would you expect Taiwan to accept all these Chinese)? They did not come from Taiwan anyway. They must be returned to where they originally come from, which was China. But the Philippine government did not have diplomatic ties with China and so we became "overstaying Chinese." This was a big problem, a big history. "Overstaying Chinese" was part of Philippine history.[40]

According to Luther, as early as 1971, President Ferdinand Marcos called the president of the Federation of Filipino-Chinese Chambers of Commerce & Industry, Inc. 菲華商聯總會 (FFCCCII or Federation) to solve the problem of overstaying Chinese. Every overstaying Chinese would be required to pay ₱15,000, against which the Federation disagreed.[41] As the Federation sought for help, someone recommended Luther, who they also claimed to be an *aktibista* (activist). Hence, he helped the overstaying Chinese attain permanent resident status. Ferdinand

39. Quota immigrants must not exceed fifty per nationality or without nationality annually while the non-quota immigrants may be admitted without numerical limitations. Bureau of Immigration, "Immigrant Visa." Luther explains that there were four waves of Chinese immigrants after the Second World War. The first wave of immigrants were those who entered from 1946 to 1953. After 1948, the immigration allotted five hundred per nationality but reverted back to fifty from 1950 to 1971. The second wave of immigrants were mostly from Hong Kong from 1954 to 1960. The third wave was from 1961 to 1981. He recalled that during Martial Law, the immigration was the most lax. A Chinese immigrant could enter the country by paying approximately ninety pesos for a visa fee. The fourth wave was from 1981 onward, after the Martial Law era. These were mostly the New Immigrants or Xinqiáo.

40. Luther, OI individual interview by author, 1 August 2012.

41. The amount ₱15,000 is roughly $2,143 with the exchange rate then of $1 to ₱7. Daquila, *Economies of Southeast Asia*, 24.

Marcos revised the Presidential Decree concerning the overstaying Chinese three times from 1971 to 1975 before he granted them amnesty. In April of 1975, Marcos granted mass naturalization to all Chinese who applied for Filipino citizenship as his gesture of diplomatic ties with China.[42]

CONCLUSION

The OIs were situated in a time and space when both China and the Philippines were going through rapid political, economic, and social changes. Many were forced to leave their homeland because of hardship, wars, and famines. They became Huáqiáo or Sojourners who intended to return to China someday. They embodied the identity and function of Coolies as they entered in different eras of colonial rule in the late nineteenth and early twentieth century. They witnessed the change of political climate in China and their visions of going back dimmed.

Their stories show that they are unhomed during their sojourning. They became "trapped Chinese," "overstaying Chinese," and unwanted aliens caught in the tumultuous politics of their time. Nevertheless, they planted their roots in the Philippines. They settled down, built families, and started businesses in this new land. As Wang observes,

> When conditions were favourable, many such people finally made a decision not to return home. In that context, sojourning was a prelude to eventual migration. Whether it is a variant form of migration—that is, something that might be called experimental migration over long periods of time or migration with extended options—needs closer study. I have argued elsewhere that, if we examine early forms of migration closely, sojourning was pervasive in Asia and elsewhere for centuries. It was only following the rise of the modern nation-state, and its demands on migrants to settle and identify with it, that the idea of residing temporarily, without any prior commitment to settle, came to be considered suspect and not to be acknowledged, least of all encouraged.[43]

---

42. Luther notes that many Chinese took this opportunity to apply for Filipino citizenships. Unfortunately, as to his knowledge, there are still Chinese whose papers have not yet finished processing since their application back in 1976. After amnesty was granted for these "overstaying Chinese" in 1975, there was another amnesty in 1992. See also See, "Influx of New Chinese Immigrants," 141–45.

43. Wang, "Sojourning," 2.

New Immigrants: In Transit Nationals

Go Bon Juan tries to explain the conflict and differences between the OIs and the NIs in the Philippine context. The OIs had to leave China due to hardship and wars, but the current migrants, the NIs are leaving a progressive and economically powerful China. The OIs were mostly illiterate, but the NIs are mostly educated. At the same time, the NIs are deemed ill-mannered by established Chinese Filipinos.[44] Since China became Communist in 1949, the OIs were not able to return to China and have mingled among themselves. As years went by, the Chinese in China and the OIs may have shared the same origin but not necessarily the same values and practices.

From the perspective of the OIs, the NIs are giving the Chinese in the Philippines a bad name because some are involved in illegal activities and crimes. Their shrewd way of doing business is resented by the OIs. Go justifies that even though many of the OIs have come with bought "paper names," they are at least genuine documents.[45] Additionally, social and political circumstances forced them to do such. Some NIs, however, "deliberately used illegal means" to enter and overstay in the country. They used fake passports and other documents. Go muses that just when the problems and issues of the OIs have been largely solved toward the end of the past century, these issues resurface in new forms with the new influx of immigrants.[46]

See calls these Huáqiáo as *Sinkiao* or Xinqiáo 新僑 (New Immigrants). China calls them Xinyinmin 新移民 (new immigrants). The

44. The old immigrants mostly came alone while the new immigrants came with wives and families. The former helped their relatives to come, to assist in their businesses as well as to earn money to send back to China. The latter also help their relatives to come and aid in their businesses. Go, "Old and New Immigrants from China," 311–12, 314.

45. "Paper names" are bought genuine documents for entry into the Philippines. They are illegal in the sense that some claim to be sons or daughters of so and so to gain access into the tight immigration laws.

46. Ibid., 312–18. Newspaper reports do indicate that there are NIs involved in illegal activities in the country. Then again, we need to be careful of generalizing all NIs. Hostility divides the two groups of Huáqiáo at the end of the twentieth century and even at the turn of the twenty-first century. Generally, the Filipinos cannot distinguish OIs from NIs. Some of the illegal practices are entry with illegal papers, overstaying in the country, selling and manufacturing of illegal drugs, distributing and making pirated DVDs, unfair and unethical trade practices, bribery, and involvement in kidnapping fellow Chinese. Consequently, the crimes of some reflect negatively on the Chinese Filipino community as a whole.

Chinese Filipinos call them *Taidiok-á* (mainlanders) or TDK for short.[47] See classifies these NIs as those who came from China and entered the country from late 1970s to the present. Most of the NIs are also from Fujian province. However, some came from Liaoning, Shandong, Jiangsu, and other places.[48]

Within three decades since 1976, many NIs acquired Filipino citizenship or permanent residency. They have also integrated into the Philippine society like the OIs. Therefore, the NIs in this research include (1) Filipino citizens; (2) immigrant status or permanent residents; (3) nonpermanent visa holders like students, tourists, businesspeople, employed, or retired; and (4) illegal aliens both overstaying and undocumented. In my interview with See in 2012, she estimates that the number of NIs may have increased to 100,000.[49]

Among the six adults interviewed for this category, four acquired retirement visas to enter and stay in the country.[50] One of the five young NIs is already a Filipino citizen. A total of eleven NIs were interviewed; one came in 1976, four came in the late 1990s, and six came after 2000.

Luther assesses that the NIs were first of all predominantly from Fujian and therefore, Minnanhua speakers. This is because Minnanhua remains the language used by most businessmen in the country. Second, most NIs were born during the Cultural Revolution. This significantly affected their way of thinking and even culture. Lastly, he observed that most of them came to visit and reconnect with families and relatives.[51]

Considering the economic progress that Taiwan, Hong Kong, and China are experiencing at present, one wonders why many NIs still

47. *Taidiok/Tailiok* or Dàlù 大陸 means "mainland" as opposed to Hong Kong or Taiwan. Nèidì 內地 also means "mainland." There are also immigrants from Hong Kong and Taiwan but they do not want to be associated or be referred as from *Taidiok*. *Taidiok-á* also signifies someone whose citizenship is specifically of the People's Republic of China.

48. See, "Influx of New Chinese Immigrants," 138, 140.

49. The 100,000 include the illegal and undocumented immigrants. Teresita Ang See, individual interview by author, 29 July 2012. See explains that there is a difference between illegal immigrants and undocumented immigrants. There are NIs who employ illegal means to enter the country and there are those who abide by the law. See, "Influx of New Chinese Immigrants," 139–40.

50. Any foreign national or former Filipinos aged 35 years and above can be eligible to apply for a retirement visa. They can bring their families with them. Philippine Retirement Authority, "Special Resident Retiree's Visa."

51. Luther, OI individual interview by author, 1 August 2012.

choose to migrate to the Philippines. See's article on "Influx of New Chinese Immigrants" sheds some light on this: (1) some use the Philippines as a transit point to the United States; (2) with China's one-child policy, some married couples want more children; (3) some want to be with their family or relatives from whom they have been separated; (4) some found the Philippines a suitable place to conduct their illegal activities; (5) some simply want to open a business in the Philippines; (6) some want their children to learn English; and (7) some just prefer to reside in the Philippines.[52] What follows are the stories of some NIs that both exemplify and add reasons to See's list.

Following Their Ancestors to Fortune, Luck, and Prosperity

> "My ancestors came to this place to prosper . . . It's hard for me
> to say I will stay in this country and not return back to China. If
> I prosper, I may stay. If I fail, there is no reason to stay." —Ping[53]

Ping (b. 1962) is a native of Jinjiang, Fujian. He came to the Philippines in 2009 with his wife, but their two daughters came two years earlier and really liked living here. His ancestors have been coming to the country since the Qing Dynasty for business purposes. Ping claimed he wanted to try his luck in the Philippines. If he succeeds, he wanted to stay here like his grandfather.

Ping's great grandfather and grandfather came together during the Spanish Period. His great grandfather even sent his grandfather to study under the Spaniards. His grandfather was fluent in Putonghua, English, Spanish, and Filipino, aside from his native language Minnanhua. His grandfather returned to China to marry and returned to the Philippines. He came and went. He had five children. The last time his grandfather visited China was in 1947 after the Second World War. He only stayed for a month. Since then, he never had the chance to go back. He died in the country in 1975.

> When *an-kong* (grandfather) was still alive, he told my father
> to go to the Philippines. My father refused to go because he is
> a Communist and he is a teacher . . . My *ahpeh* (father's eldest
> brother) came here in the Philippines. *A-ko* (father's eldest sister) also came but she now lives in United States. My two other
> aunts are in Hong Kong. Only my father stays in China . . . My

52. See, "Influx of New Chinese Immigrants," 137–50.
53. Ping, NI individual interview by author, 25 July 2012.

>*thàikong* (great grandfather) advised my grandfather to remarry
>and find a wife in the Philippines . . . I do not know whether he
>marries a Chinese or a Filipina, my father did not tell me. *Bô su
>iao kò khì tsai* (No need to know).[54]

Like Ping's grandfather, many Chinese who work or have businesses overseas left their wives and families back home in China. After Communism took over, many of these men were not able to return. Years and decades of separation led to remarriages for some men.

Women in colonial times were banned from leaving China. They were left behind at times immediately after wedding, giving birth, or conceiving a child. The men were prone to find local wives in the Philippines to meet their needs.[55] At times, the wives and children back in China were neglected because of their husbands' new families in the Philippines. But in most instances, the men did not fail in their obligation to send money back home. Many tried to bring their wives and family to the country.[56]

Another informant, Li (b. 1964) is also from Fujian. He applied for a retirement visa and brought his wife and daughter with him in 2011. His eldest son stayed in China to finish college.[57] He wanted his daughter to learn English and so her education was the primary reason for their coming to the country. Like Ping, Li's grandfather stayed in the Philippines since 1935 and never returned to China. His grandfather also died in the country. Li's grandfather was a teacher by profession at Tiong Se Academy.[58]

54. Since Ping's grandfather was not able to return to his family in China, he remarried in the Philippines. Ping, NI individual interview by author, 25 July 2012.

55. My father, Lee Loh, used to recite a poem that goes something like this, "Let the Chinese work hard and earn money to send back home. But when a pretty Filipina sticks a flower behind her ear; home is forgotten and the money disappear."

56. The Americans allowed the Chinese to bring their wife and family to the Philippines as long as they were merchants or sons of merchants. See, *Chinese in the Philippines*, 3:124–27. The low percentile of Chinese women as compared to Chinese men has led to a "bachelor society," inter-ethnic marriages, and marrying younger Chinese women. See also chapter 2 on American Period.

57. Li's eldest son was born in 1989. He exceeds the age limit of 21 years old to be qualified as a dependent.

58. Li's grandfather came with his *ahpeh* (uncle) who married a local-born Chinese and stayed in the country. His *a-má* (grandmother) tried to live in the Philippines, but decided to return to China. She complained that the weather was too hot. His father remained in China. However, back in 1998, he and his father came to the country for the first time to clean his grandfather's tomb. Eventually, they continued to visit the

Li opened a noodle shop in Manila Chinatown, and occasionally, he would meet customers who were his grandfather's former students. These former students, now elderly folks, would share stories on how his grandfather inspired them. Through their stories, Li learned about the grandfather he had never known. He turned melancholic as he talked about the day they received news about his grandfather's death in 1975.

> I don't know my grandfather, I've never seen him . . . *Goán ti Taidiok, goán an-kong kè sin, goán bōe sai tì-i kháo le* (We were in China when grandpa died in the Philippines, we cannot mourn). During the Cultural Revolution, if the government finds out you have relatives overseas, they will suspect you or your family as spies. *In e ka di chhiau ke* (They will search your home). I remember I was thirteen years old then. It was like that back then. We receive the news through a telegram from our relatives in Hong Kong. Back then, there are no diplomatic ties between China and the Philippines. That is why my relatives in the Philippines made a long distance phone call to Hong Kong and from Hong Kong send a telegram to China . . . Mother told us not to cry. *An-kong sí bōe sai khao e, bōe sai ho tsèng hu tsai iá* (Grandpa is dead but we cannot mourn. We cannot let the government know about this). I still remember. I was thirteen years old then . . . (After Communism took over China) we have no communication with grandfather and *ahpeh*. We cannot communicate with them.[59]

Both the OIs and the NIs suffered from separation and loss of communication with loved ones after 1949. Nevertheless, the NIs today have the option to bring their families. Out of the eleven NI informants, eight came with their families, and three came alone but one of the three got married in the country and another has relatives in the country. In short, only one out of the eleven is without a family or relative.

Some NIs have unpleasant experiences as well. Two informants shared how they were cheated as they came to the country. Kerri (b. 1962) was just fourteen when her parents decided to migrate to the Philippines in 1976.[60] Someone promised to help them with the processing of their

---

Philippines until Li decided to live in the country.

59. Li, NI individual interview by author, 24 July 2012.

60. Kerri's father wanted to return to the Philippines and to do business again. Her grandfather and father had been in the Philippines decades earlier. However, after her father got married, the new couple decided to live in Hong Kong since Kerri's mother back then could not get an immigrant visa to the Philippines.

documents and assured them they could acquire Filipino citizenship. Kerri remembers that she and her siblings were filled with excitement. They could not wait to dip into the big blue sea, lie on the white sand beach, and enjoy the beautiful sunset. To their disappointment, they were cheated and did not get Filipino citizenship. To make matters worse, she and her siblings were stunned to see slums and garbage instead of the beautiful postcard pictures they saw in Hong Kong. The first few years were very difficult for the whole family.[61]

Another informant, Peter (b. 1959) is originally from Inner Mongolia of Northern China. His Hokkien friends introduced him to the Philippines in 1997. Initially, he came as a tourist to see the place. He enjoyed his visit and wanted to stay. He also wanted to avoid the revolution happening in his hometown.[62] He especially liked the weather of the Philippines because Inner Mongolia is cold and there are occasional sand storms. Someone offered to help him with his paperwork but that person turned out to be a swindler.[63]

Based on the interviews, all of them were hoping that the Philippines would be a greener pasture and provide more opportunities whether in business, education, or other careers in spite of the fact that China is now more progressive. Out of the six adults interviewed, four were businessmen while the other two had other occupations. Among the five young people, four were students and one was a teacher.

---

61. Kerri's parents were busy with their business, they lived with their nagging aunt, and they could not speak Filipino. They were adjusting to new school and new environment. Though they were Hokkien, having grown up in Hong Kong caused them to speak Minnanhua with a Cantonese accent. The students in school laughed at them. She was called "*intsik*" and was told it means insect. After three years, they adjusted. She admitted that her faith in God helped her overcome all the challenges at that time. She is presently married and has three children.

62. Inner Mongolia is an autonomous region, but already it consists more predominantly of Han Chinese than of ethnic Mongolians. There are series of revolutions seeking independence from China.

63. As a reporter, Peter revealed that there were many local Chinese from the mainland who used falsified documents to cheat their way into the country. They also bribed immigration people. He discovered that when people applied for authentic documents, the documents were reproduced by the swindlers, who would then sell them to innocent victims.

LOVING THE PHILIPPINES

> "There are so many good things in the Philippines way incomparable to China. China is better economically but in terms of culture and relationships, I find the Philippine Chinese is better than China." —Li[64]

Li found the Philippines a very good place to live. He has many relatives in Manila. His family lived just beside the Chinese school his daughter attends. In the beginning, he had difficulty adjusting to life in the Philippines, but in his opinion, the Philippines is better than China as far as culture and education are concerned. For this reason, he believes the Philippines is a very good place to raise children.

> I find Chinese Filipino children more obedient to their parents and virtuous than children in China. Children in China are so spoiled after the one child policy . . . Papa and mama, grandpa and grandma of both sides, all six people are focused on one child. I hope as my daughter studies here, she will be influenced to be courteous and polite not like those children in China *bô límào* 沒有禮貌 (impolite) . . . *Taidiok gín-ná tsin tsōe si sim-míh lé* (Children in Mainland is like this) . . . [Then switching to Putonghua] 不知道呼出, 父母親給他們的都是應該的. (They don't know how to give sacrificially, whatever their parents give to them is what must be given to them.) . . . 沒有什麼感恩. (They don't know what it means to be thankful.) . . . Most of the Chinese Filipinos are very respectful to their parents. This is how they tremendously differ. 大陸的孩子, 現在是父母親要讓了他們. (For the children in the Mainland, the parents today must give in to whatever they want.) The children here are very respectful and obedient to parents. It is incomparable to China, incomparable indeed. Culture must probably have something to do with all this. With the one child policy in China, the children are spoiled by parents.[65]

64. Li, NI individual interview by author, 24 July 2012.

65. Li observes, "The way parents raise their children is wrong. For example, when a child falls down, he just has to get up and everything is okay. It is natural for a child to fall or trip or hit something. But Chinese parents will tell the child, 'Do not cry. Do not cry. I will strike the ground for causing you to fall.' Parents will blame the ground and scold the ground . . . In this way, falling which is the child's fault becomes the ground's fault. Kids then grow up thinking others always have the problem not them. My own eyes have witnessed these kinds of children. How can these kids grow up to be respectful?" Li, NI individual interview by author, 24 July 2012.

Mr. Chia (b. 1949) had been visiting the Philippines since the nineties looking for business opportunities. He exports *jít-ēng phin* 日用品 (household products) to the Philippines from China, so he frequently travels back and forth to oversee his businesses in the two countries. He is an example of a transnational and a cosmopolitan capitalist.[66] All his children were in China. His wife had recently joined him in the country.

> Our business is exporting China products to the Philippines. During Mao times, China was poorer than the Philippines (*pi Huilípin khah lok hio*). Our goods were not many. After Deng Xiao Ping's economic revolution, China's economy improved. Products multiply . . . Even if you wanted to come decades ago, you won't find any business opportunities. [Laughter] *Taidiok* (mainland) earlier had no products to sell. There were more products from the Philippines exported to China. Nowadays, after economic revolution, products in China are way too many. We cannot consume them all (*Ēng bōe liáu*) and even cheaper (*kho khah siók*). Earlier you do not have anything to sell. [Pause] Now we have business to do. [Laughter][67]

Mr. Chia likes the Philippines very much. He likes the weather, the living environment, and the local Chinese. He finds them friendly and helpful.

> The local Chinese treat us Huáqiáo very well. The Chinese people in general are friendly. The old immigrants help us in our transition and adjustment. *In tsin thià sioh tsoē Sinkiao* (They value our presence). They know that the new immigrants are not used to life here especially with the language, immigration, and culture. Like English, *goa tsiu* put tōng 不通 *lo* (I don't understand English). They help us in all these.[68]

---

66. A transnational is someone who juggles between two countries, an ethnic minority in one and a national in another. Basch et al., *Nations Unbound*, 4–5. A cosmopolitan capitalist is based on the research on Hong Kong and Hongkongers at the late twentieth century. The premise is that capitalism is viewed as organized economic activities as oppose to national economies. Capitalism is fluid and goes beyond borders. These Hongkongers have maintained their connection at home and spread their assets abroad. They are global cosmopolitans who find economic opportunities outside their borders. They can live as Hongkongers in another country. Hamilton, *Cosmopolitan Capitalists*, 3–10.

67. Mr. Chia, NI individual interview by author, 27 July 2012.

68. Mr. Chia, NI individual interview by author, 27 July 2012. Most of the NIs have good opinions about the OIs. They even praised their kindness, hospitality, help, and support in their transition to this country. Either they were using *khè khí ōe* (polite

Carla was born in Fujian in 1987. She came to the Philippines in 2006 to help her sister who has a store in 168 Shopping Mall. She confessed that she does not have any days off. She works every day, except holidays, from eight in the morning to seven in the evening. Even after work, she has to go home, wash her own clothes, and help with house chores. And yet, she loves to live in the Philippines. In fact, her friends back home call her *hoan-á* because they observed she has become just like the Filipinos. Her mother also calls her *hoan-á*. Carla reasoned that the word *hoan-á* simply means having a happy disposition, without worries.

> *Hoan-á* is not a bad word. It does not have a bad meaning. Early on, the Filipinos were called *hoan-á*. *Hoan-á* means *lok kuan sim thai* (someone having a happy disposition in life). It is having no worries in life, always happy . . . When I went home for vacation, my friends observed that I have acquired this happy disposition in life. That is why they call me *hoan-á*. Living among them, I have become like them.[69]

Kerri admitted that she was no longer comfortable living in Hong Kong. She noticed the people there speak so fast and can be impolite. She already feels at home in the Philippines. Her Filipino may not be perfect and people may still laugh at her. She will just tell them *"**pasensiya**"* (have patience) if they cannot understand her.

Peter said for now he is considering not going back to China. In 2004, he married a Filipina who gave birth to a daughter in 2007. He brought his wife and daughter once to Inner Mongolia to visit his family. He observes that the Chinese in the Philippines are more conservative and traditional. He claims that they preserve the Chinese culture better than the Chinese in China.

Everyone interviewed for this category expressed a positive outlook on the Philippines. They acknowledged that the country is not perfect and has its ills. They still have reservations whether they will really stay

---

words) or they truly did not find anything bad to say. But most of the OIs perceived the NIs negatively. They saw them as too aggressive in doing business and not abiding the law; wanting to get rich immediately; loving *lâu diet* (to be festive); *ay tì miâ* (want honor) to show off; and *ta ge be ài tsōe thâu* (everyone wants to be the leader). Nevertheless, these elderly OIs helplessly admitted that the present young Tsinoys were not capable of preserving the Chinese language and culture without the help of these NIs. Further, the NIs are said to be generous contributors to the needs and projects for the Chinese community and the Filipino community.

69. Carla, NI individual interview by author, 20 June 2012.

due to the uncertainties of their businesses and future. Nevertheless, all of the six adults would like to settle in the Philippines.

THE YOUNG AND THE RESTLESS NEW IMMIGRANTS

The younger NI that I interviewed, people like Mina, Abraham, Francis, and Alan, are here to study. Mina and her younger brother are both taking dentistry. Her family came from Taiwan in 1997 when she was seven. They live in San Juan. Abraham arrived in the country in 2006 while Francis arrived in 2010. Abraham and Francis have come with their respective families. Both of their parents have their businesses in the country. Both attend the same Chinese high school in Manila. Both admit that they have more lessons to study back home. Schooling in China is very competitive they say. Francis finds it easy to learn English but has difficulty with Filipino. Abraham is very good in Filipino but very poor in English.

Alan is a college student from Macao. He came on his own with a student visa in 2010. He lives with his relatives. His family recommends that he finishes his college in the Philippines. His brother preceded him a decade ago. Janice also came by herself using a professional visa. She was sent by the Chinese government to teach Putonghua in the Philippines. She has taught for a school year in 2011. She likes the Philippines and has renewed her contract to teach another year in 2012.[70]

All five informants from China prefer to return to China. They have their attachments in China that they are not yet willing to cut. All five informants hope to migrate to other countries. Moreover, in their accounts, they experienced unhomely situations and feelings as they tried to fit in this new country. Being young, they are not ashamed to share their first impressions about the country.

Abraham sees the country as ***madumi at mabaho*** (very dirty and smelly). Janice quickly defended claiming that the streets were dirty but inside the houses were clean. Francis realized schooling in the Philippines was easier. Abraham added that he used to have after school programs in China and went home by eight in the evening. Janice explained that because China had such a big population, the competition was really stiff and tough. You had to be better than the other.

70. Janice is included in the NI Youth category because she was in her early twenties when interviewed and was part of the Focus Group NI Youth. "China began in 2004 to recruit volunteers to teach Chinese overseas in an attempt to meet the global demand to learn the language." Xinhua, "China to send 119 language teachers."

Abraham has difficulty making new friends in the Philippines. His Minnanhua is not good but his Putonghua is. The local Chinese his age can speak Minnanhua but are very poor in Putonghua, so language becomes a barrier. He cited one incident wherein he was glad to find a Chinese classmate but when he realized they could not communicate, his heart was broken. In his words, "It felt like I lost a friend." In the beginning, he confessed that he was being bullied in school because he could not speak and understand Filipino. They cursed him in Filipino so he did not understand what they were saying.[71] But after two years, he mastered Filipino. Probably because of this unfortunate incident, he tried very hard to learn the language. Nowadays, his Filipino is flawless though his accent still betrays him. He is a senior in high school for Chinese classes but sixth grade for the English classes.

Francis is also a senior in high school in Chinese classes but he is a sophomore for English classes. His situation is similar to Abraham's. He narrated,

> In my class, I am the only Chinese. I mean, they are Chinese but cannot speak Chinese. They always speak to me in Filipino but I cannot understand. Some of my friends or classmates talk to me in English. It is okay at least I can speak in English. In my Chinese class, they can speak Chinese (Putonghua).[72]

Alan observes that his professors at times will suddenly speak in Filipino and he has difficulty understanding what they mean. Janice conversely enjoys her teaching stint. She is happy to teach Putonghua and in turn learn Filipino from her students. Mina likes the Philippines but she is hoping to work and migrate to the United States. The sojourning disposition seemed to best describe them. They can be likened to nationals in transit or in transition. The grass is always greener on the other side.

Conclusion

The limited sampling of informants for this research did not fully reflect the descriptions made by Go, See, and Luther regarding the NIs. However, certain points they raised were confirmed, such as that the NIs are predominantly from Fujian and can speak Minnanhua; were born during

71. It is really sad that Abraham has to experience being bullied in a Chinese school and by Chinese Filipino classmates. They may all look alike as Chinese people but they are not all alike in terms of language and culture.

72. Francis, Focus Group C-NI Youth by author, 13 July 2012.

the Cultural Revolution; have been affected by the one-child policy in terms of filial piety; arrive with families as evident among eight out of eleven informants; left behind a progressive China; may be using the Philippines as a transit point to another destination; are learning English like the young NI and the children of Ping and Peter; are at work opening businesses like Mr. Chia, Li, Ping, and Carla; are trying to find their fortunes; and intentionally have chosen to reside in the Philippines.

The OIs and NIs interviewed share some similar situations but under different circumstances and subject to different issues. There are six observations to conclude this part. First, both are Sojourners. However, the OIs left a chaotic and poor China. Further the OIs were forced by circumstances to settle in the country with Communism taking over China in 1949. The NIs conversely intentionally choose to live or open businesses in the Philippines. The NIs are not so much running away from China as they are searching for new business and educational opportunities.

Second, both are settlers or potential settlers. The difference is that the OIs had gone through much difficulty to finally attain legal and permanent residency and eventually citizenships. The NIs have less trouble acquiring immigrant visas with the Special Resident Retiree's Visa being promoted by the Philippine government. Moreover, the OIs had to start from scratch while the NIs have experienced a better transition with an established Chinese community, Chinese schools, and other organizations.

Third, both are Chinese culture-centered. The OI and the NI informants are very much concerned with the Chinese culture and language being preserved and propagated within the Philippine Chinese community. The NIs see the OIs as very traditionalist but not the second and third generations. The OIs see the NIs as the solution to the present problem of diminishing Chinese language and culture in the country. The NIs desire the Confucian-structured culture that they might perceive was lost with the Cultural Revolution. The OIs desire the reinforcement of Minnanhua and Putonghua with the coming of the NIs.

Fourth, both are catching up on their losses. Both OIs and NIs suffered loss of communication with fathers, families, relatives, and loved ones when China closed its doors in 1949. Both are reconnecting with families here and back home with China reopening its doors under the regime of Deng Xiao Ping.

Fifth, both have unhomely experiences with their transitions and adjustments. Their identities as Sojourners add to their unsettling disposition and unhomed nature. The OIs' desire to return to China or to be "at home" was a dream. This somehow became a reality with amnesty for overstaying and citizenship granted by the Philippine government in 1975. Most considered the Philippines their home already though not all of them had Filipino citizenship. The NIs' sojourning experience is not yet clear. They are transnationals who may decide to stay if circumstances here are more favorable than back home in China. They may return to China or migrate elsewhere as they continue their search for greener pastures and better opportunities for better futures for their families.

Sixth, both do not have the same China pictured in their minds. The NIs can always go back to China if things do not turn out the way they want. But for the OIs, they have no China to return to. For more than half a century, they have planted their roots deep in the Philippine soil, and the China they knew has changed. Uprooting them will be very difficult and painful.

PART 2: THE UNHOMELY TSINOYS

Bhabha defines the unhomed as one who is not necessarily homeless but is "unhomely" or is not easily at home in his/her private and public social spheres. Using the stairwell, he illustrates the liminal space, the in-between space of the unhomely.

> The stairwell as liminal space, in-between the designations of identity, becomes the process of symbolic interaction, the connective tissue that constructs the difference between upper and lower, black and white. The hither and thither of the stairwell, the temporal movement and passage that it allows, prevents identities at either end of it from settling into primordial polarities. This interstitial passage between fixed identifications opens up the possibility of a cultural hybridity that entertains difference without an assumed or imposed hierarchy.[73]

Bhabha warns that one must not be hasty in concluding difference as "pre-given ethnic or cultural traits set in the fixed tablet of tradition."[74] The minority's perspective on social difference is complex and an "ongoing negotiation that seeks to authorize cultural hybridities that emerge in moments of historical transformations."[75] The stairwell or liminal stage

73. Bhabha, *Location of Culture*, 5.
74. Ibid., 3.
75. Ibid.

is the border of engagements where cultures meet and may result in a product beyond the original identity or received tradition. He reminds his readers that he is not out to glorify the margins or peripheries but to make known the realities of surviving as a minority.[76]

The second part of this chapter will focus on the unhomely nature of the Tsinoys being both Chinese and Filipino, not necessarily because of "bloodline" but because of culture. They have an ambivalent disposition that marked their cultural hybridity as Chinese in diaspora. They struggled in their desire to understand their identity and belongingness. I will first present the Tsinoys in general, then this portion will focus on the minority among the minority who are the Chinese citizens and the Overseas Chinese Filipino Workers.

Tsinoys

The word "Tsinoy" is an ethnic label for the Chinese in the Philippines who sought integration, not assimilation. They wanted to retain their cultural heritage and expressed their loyalty to their host country. Retaining one's culture may not necessarily mean ethnocentrism. It is a celebration and acknowledgment of one's cultural heritage.[77] At the same time, retaining one's culture may not necessarily mean immunity from outside influences. Often it is a question of which culture may eventually become more dominant in practice. As culture continually evolves, people accept or reject different cultural elements, and one may emerge as more Filipino, more Chinese, in between, or in some cases, more Western.

Hence, the word "Tsinoy" signifies cultural hybridity, an in-between space, a cultural cross breed, a Chinese and a Filipino, cannot be one without the other. Tsinoy is a third space with unhomely experiences. Tsinoy is a third culture, a product of mixing two or more cultures. The Tsinoy can also be influenced by other cultures aside from the Chinese and Filipino cultures.

See stresses that the Chinese Filipinos included those with Chinese and Filipino citizenship. She classifies them this way:

76. Ibid., xi, 3–5.

77. "We are Filipinos of Chinese descent and ancestry, tracing our past and recognizing our origins in Chinese history. We pride ourselves as inheritors of this rich cultural heritage and acknowledge the debts of loyalty and the allegiance we owe the Filipino nation." Kaisa, "Declaration of Principles."

Sociologically accepted definition, they must have a measurable degree of Chinese parentage; they have a working knowledge of Chinese language and education; they have gone through some form of education in Chinese schools; they have retained some Chinese practices; and the fifth is enough to call themselves or be called by neighbors as ethnic Chinese or Tsinoys.[78]

The Tsinoys in this category are local-born Chinese of immigrant parents or having immigrant grandparent/s, who have retained Chinese practices in education and language or in marriage and family, regardless of citizenship. The Chinese Mestizos are also included in the Tsinoy category.[79] Those interviewed are second-, third-, fourth-, and even fifth-generation Chinese. The age ranges from thirteen to seventy-one years old. Out of the seventeen individuals interviewed and one focus group in this category, most of them have accepted the term Tsinoy to refer to themselves and the Chinese in the Philippines. There are a number who did not like the term Tsinoy and preferred Fil-Chi or Filipino-Chinese, Chinese Filipino, or simply Chinese.

AT HOME BUT NOT IN CHINA

"I visited China because I joined our *tóng hiong hōe* (hometown association). That's how I am able to go to China. But when I was there, nobody knew me so I came back [Laughing]." —Milo[80]

Milo (b. 1950) is a second-generation Chinese whose parents are both immigrants from China. His parents never returned to China, but he had the chance to join a tour to China organized by their hometown association. He visited his *hiu di* or village, unfortunately, no one knew him. He felt like a stranger in his "hometown." He returned to the Philippines disappointed.

Some Tsinoys visited China as children, but returned soon because of the Second Sino-Japanese War or the Civil War. Such is the case of second-generation Tsinoys like Ahbi, Patty, and Martha. Ahbi went to China at age ten after Japan surrendered in 1946. He returned to the Philippines in 1949 because China became a communist country. Patty (b. 1930) was two years old when her parents brought her and her siblings

---

78. Teresita Ang See, individual interview by author, 29 July 2012.

79. This particular Tsinoy category consist mostly of "pure" Chinese informants than Chinese Mestizos. See appendix A.

80. Milo, Tsinoy individual interview by author, 23, June 2012.

to China to attend the funeral of her *an-kong* (grandfather). They stayed there for five years before returning permanently to the Philippines in 1937. Martha was born in Manila, left with her family for China from 1946 to 1949 before coming back for good.

Mr. John is a second-generation Tsinoy businessman. He has been visiting China since 1986. Today, he frequently visits as a representative of *Siong Chóng* (Federation of Filipino-Chinese Chamber of Commerce and Industry, Inc.). He observes that China is very different now. He claims that, in today's socialist-capitalist China, all the people can think of is how to make money. They are very aggressive in doing business unlike the local Chinese in the Philippines and Southeast Asia who are more conservative.

Jonathan (b. 1987) is a third-generation Chinese in the Philippines. He joined a China study tour in the summer of 2008 for six weeks.[81] He shared, "When I went to China to study Putonghua, my teacher asked if I am a Filipino. When I entered college in UP (University of the Philippines), my teacher asked if I am a Chinese."[82]

The elderly gentlemen in the Focus Group B-OI complain that study tours are useless. They claim that such tours do not really help the students learn Putonghua since the students are cloistered together all the time. They continued to speak Filipino among themselves. They believe that sending each of the students alone to China for a year would force them to learn Chinese. Mr. Ang shared that his friend's grandson actually joined a study tour. When he asked him what he had learned in the study tour, the young man replied that he learned a few Putonghua words, "I learned Màidāngláo 麥當勞 (McDonalds), Xīngbākè 星巴克 (Starbucks), and Kěntǎjī 肯德基 (Kentucky Fried Chicken)."

China was not home for these Tsinoys, although they consider it as the home of their ancestors and relatives. They see China as a destination for tourists, or perhaps a place to study. It can also be a land of opportunities for employment or business ventures.[83] China is a strange land that

81. At present, some Chinese schools in Metro Manila offer short-term Putonghua courses as refresher for those who had Chinese education, advanced classes for those who wanted to learn more, or basic classes for beginners. As China has reemerged in the world economic arena in the last two decades, the popularity of learning Putonghua has also increased.

82. Jonathan, Focus Group D-T3 by author, 17 June 2012.

83. As the OIs and NIs sought greener pasture in the Philippines, the present Tsinoys also look to China as possible greener pasture.

they heard so much about from their parents or grandparents. Out of the thirty-four respondents, less than ten had been to China.

THERE'S NO PLACE LIKE THE PHILIPPINES

> "We are so used to life in the Philippines. If we have enough money to use, enough money to buy what we want, the Philippines is a good place to live. If you want to go to Hong Kong, you cannot speak their language. When you reach there, you are useless. In Taiwan, you have to have money. If you have no money, you are like a beggar. It means you have to work (even when one is old) . . . In the Philippines, if you have some extra money, you can live a good life. You only need lots of money if you love to go to Shanghai, Beijing, or follow after those who love to travel and tour." —Martha[84]

All her life, Martha (b. 1946) lived in Binondo. Her husband is fourteen years her senior and an immigrant who registered as someone else's son. He later acquired Filipino citizenship. She is not a citizen but she considers the Philippines her home. She has no problems making friends with Filipinos but sees herself as a Chinese.

Nellie (b. 1946) has a son living in the United States who provides for her, which allows her to travel abroad. The son also wants her to move to the United States, but she prefers to live in the Philippines.[85] She sees herself as a Chinese who happens to have Filipino citizenship. She does not like to be called a Tsinoy, saying that the term *"thia khi lâi tsin bōe sóng* (not so good to her ears)." Like Martha, she considered the Philippines her home.

Milo, who is still a Chinese citizen, announced, "If someone asks what I am? I will say, *goá si tsiá lanlâng* (I am a genuine Chinese)." His father opted not to apply for naturalization because of his principle, yong yuen shi Zhong Guo ren 永遠是中國人 (forever a Chinese, or could also mean, forever a citizen of China). Milo did not bother to change his citizenship as he reasoned that he did not own a business.[86] However, he

---

84. Martha, Tsinoy individual interview by author, 29, June 2012.

85. Once, Nellie lived in New York City for six months. She worked as a nanny and enjoyed her stay there. But when her son moved to Ohio and Kentucky, she did not want to stay with him because she could not drive. She felt trapped and could not go anywhere. She tried to learn driving but she had difficulty learning to *atras* or drive in reverse. She believes she was too old to learn.

86. After their family's vegetable farm was closed down during the Macapagal

did not consider himself a stranger in this country. In fact, he felt like a stranger when he visited China. All his life, he has been living in this country. He has many friends and relatives here. He can speak Filipino and enjoys Filipino food. The Philippines is home for him.

All of the Tsinoys interviewed consider the Philippines as their home. They no longer see themselves as strangers in this country but part of it.

LABELS AND NAME CALLING

> Mr. Ang: What is **Intsik**?
>
> Mr. Lim: It's not a bad word. It's not a bad word. It means *lín tsek* (your uncle).
>
> Mr. Go: It's the Chinese fooling the Filipino. [Laughter] I heard this is so. The Chinese *tiâu kang* (deliberately) made that up.
>
> [More laughter in the room][87]

> "Maybe it's because of my facial features. Sometimes, as I walk down the street, Filipino bystanders will stare at me. There are those who will pass by and say, 'Ching, ching, chong, chang.' I felt bad and alienated." —Jacob[88]

Jacob is a second-generation Chinese, speaks Minnanhua at home and finished high school in a Chinese institution. Although he lives in Quezon City, he is often surrounded by Chinese family and friends.[89] While growing up, his Chinese facial features combined with his Chinese-accented Filipino have invited some unpleasant experiences. At times, he still feels estranged. He said that when he went to Hong Kong, he immediately felt at home since all the people looked like him. Yet at the same time, he also felt not at home since he could not speak Cantonese. He realized that home was where his family and friends were, and that is the Philippines.

---

administration and his Christian background had taught him not to love money, Milo was content with a simple life. Candidly, he added that in Buddhism, it was okay to *thàn tsin tsōe tsî* (make a lot of money).

87. Mr. Ang, Mr. Go, and Mr. Lim, Focus Group B-OI by author, 11, July 2012.

88. Jacob, Focus Group D-T3 by author, 17 June 2012. Quezon City.

89. Quezon City is the largest city in Metro Manila. It is considered *chhi gua* (outside Manila) as opposed to *chhi lâi* (inside Manila). Manila is still considered as more "Chinese" than other cities in Metro Manila by the elderly gentlemen of Focus Group B-OI.

I hosted a focus group of college students and young professionals, all of them were third-generation Tsinoys. Four out of thirteen experienced being discriminated against for being ethnic Chinese (whether because of facial features, Chinese last names, or having a different accent). When asked whether any of them had been called "rich" just because they are Chinese, only a couple did not raise their hands.

Benjie vehemently denied that all Chinese Filipinos were rich. He cried, "**Bakit kami** (Why are we not rich?)"[90] Benjie, a third-generation Tsinoy, grew up in the Caloocan area speaking Cantonese and Filipino. He did not finish college because he fell in with bad **barkada** (friends). He is in his early thirties, works as a dishwasher in a restaurant, and has remained single since he thinks that his salary is not enough to provide for a family.

Benjie recalled getting into a fight one time with a Filipino classmate because he was called "**Singkit**" or chinky-eyed. Now that he is older, when his Filipino coworkers call him "**Singkit**," he simply replies, "**Naiwan na lang sa lahi** (That is all that is left of my ancestral genes)." He was glad that his skin is darker and his last name sounds Filipino. He tries to hide his Chinese identity to avoid being discriminated against. He also rails against the myth that Chinese are **kuripot** (stingy). He used to work in a hotel where Americans gave the biggest tips. But the Chinese, he observed, were not that bad either. If he greeted them "ni hao 你好 (hello)," he usually received one hundred pesos.

Milo observed that racial discrimination has decreased. He believed that it is because the Philippines became poorer as compared to the 1960s when it was a rich country. Consequently, the people also became humbler and treated the Chinese better.[91] Mr. Ang also had similar observation,

> In the past, the Chinese who came to the Philippines were not so educated. The Filipinos always looked down on them. Nowadays, most of the Chinese in the Philippines are no longer

90. Benjie, Tsinoy individual interview by author, 21, July 2012.

91. "*Kha tsa u* (Used to be) *Hoan-á tui lanlâng ia phai* (Filipinos maltreated the Chinese) . . . *Hoan-á ia phai si* (The Filipinos were unkind). They will curse the Chinese when they see one. When I was a child, I was persecuted just because I am a Chinese. I fought with them. I was not afraid because we know how to speak Tagalog. That time *hoan-á bo huan hiong* (the Filipinos were not that vicious), we fight **mano mano** (using bare hands). Those days, police would even remove their hats when they see a lady passing by. Nowadays, they will **pito** (whistles). [Laughter]" Milo, Tsinoy individual interview by author, 23 June 2012.

looked down. Why? Because they are now educated. Before, when I was a young man, the Filipinos on the street will call me *intsik beho kain lugaw* (the Chinese in loose half pants eats porridge).[92] Have you heard of *intsik beho kain lugaw*? Those days, Chinese experienced those kinds of name-calling. Today, we do not see or hear that much anymore.[93]

Animosity was stronger in the past. The Chinese called the Filipinos *hoan-á* (barbarians). The Filipinos called the Chinese *tsekwa* or *intsik beho tulo laway kain lugaw*. Some Chinese also showed contempt for fellow Chinese who cannot speak fluent Minnanhua. They were referred as *hoan-á* (barbarians), *hoan-á gong* (stupid barbarians), *hoan-á kúy* (barbaric like), or *hoan-á thé* (barbaric lifestyle). If a Chinese person is educated and lived in *chhi gua* (outside Manila), he/she is sometimes described as *kha siōng hoan thé* (live like classy barbarians), *kha sai hong* (more Westernized), *kha ko siōng* (more classy), or *ia u hak bun* (very educated).

The *chhi lâi* (literally, "within city limits," referring to downtown Manila) Chinese, were also called Binondo Chinese or Chinatown Chinese. The younger and more Filipinized Chinese jeered the more conservative ones by calling them "GI" or Genuine *Intsik*. The Chinese Mestizos were not exempted from derision. They were called *chhut-sì-á* (born local, but the *á* added as suffix is what makes the word a condescension) as opposed to *tsiá lanlâng* (genuine or pure Chinese person).[94] Worse, the Chinese Mestizos were once called *poà tháng sái* (literally means pail half full of dung). The NIs were called *Taidiok á* (from China, again the suffix *á*) by the local Chinese. Conversely, the NIs viewed the local Chinese

---

92. *Intsik* is a label used to refer to the Chinese. *Beho* pertains to the loose half pants the Chinese wear. Rose recounts that the Chinese in the past will make their own pants using *katsa* (sack cloth) or plain cloth to save money. The pants are usually loose pants above or just below the knee in length. The pants help them to move around easily and comfortably while working. Rose, Tsinoy individual interview by author, 18 June 2012. *Tulo laway* means saliva trickling on the side of the mouth which can happen as one falls asleep due to tiredness. *Kain lugaw* means eat rice porridge. The Filipinos back then have stereotyped the Chinese as always eating rice porridge. This is actually true. The Chinese of older generation love to eat rice porridge with sweet potatoes (*han tsû bé*) for supper so that it will be easily digested.

93. Mr. Ang, Focus Group B-OI by author, 11 July 2012.

94. The local-born Chinese of Chinese parentage will call themselves *pun tuey chhut sì* (locally born) while those of mixed parentage *chhut-sì-á*.

as *hoan-á* and *chhut-sì-á*. Nonetheless, this present generation witnessed the gradual diminishing of these offensive name calling.

ENDOGAMY AND *KÀI SIĀU*

> "Choose a Chinese to marry because race matters, that's what my mom says." —Ellis[95]

Endogamy is still practiced and encouraged by many Chinese parents today. The second-generation Tsinoys are mostly prohibited to inter-marry. Paolo shared how his mother threatened him, *"Tiòh chhē lanlang.* ***Pag*** *chhē hoan-á-po, li that chhu khì* (You have to find a Chinese wife. If you marry a Filipina, you will be kicked out of the house)." Even the third, fourth, and fifth generations have been strongly encouraged to find a Chinese spouse. In case they insist on marrying a non-Chinese, their parents cannot prevent them. Martha observed that the present genera-tion Chinese are given more freedom to choose their partner, something earlier generations did not enjoy.[96]

Mrs. Chan, a second-generation Tsinoy, is married to a Chinese. She observed:

> Personally, *goa bo tsan sēng* (I am against) mixed marriages. Not that I look down on the Filipinos or that the Filipinos are bad. There are many good Filipinos and there are many bad Chinese. The problem lies in the different upbringing and cultures. As *pêng iú* (friends) okay, marriage is a different story. Not just the two people tie the knot. The two families are also married together. ***Di ba*** (Isn't it)? Initially, okay but in the end they will have many problems as culture clashes. *Būn tĕ chhut hiān* (Prob-lems will surface) . . . Nowadays, there are so many mixed mar-riages. At the same time, many marriages in general *tsin kín tiau tit* (end in a short time) . . . You have to remember that marriage is not just the two people, it also involves two families. Usually, husband and wife *bo tāi tsi* (no problems), usually it is the in-laws *i tì* ***gulo***, *i tì* ***gulo*** (who keep on disrupting). ***Pero bô hoat rin***, *bô hoat* ***iwas*** (But we can do nothing about it, we cannot avoid that). Of course we want them to find Chinese spouses,

---

95. Ellis is a fifth-generation Tsinoy and yet Chinese culture is still practiced in his home. Ellis, Tsinoy individual interview by author, 11, June 2012.

96. See also part 3 of chapter 4 on the Conclusion of Hybrid Partnerships.

however, if they really want to marry a Filipino, *lan ma si bô hoat* (we cannot do anything).[97]

Nellie echoed Mrs. Chan's sentiments,

Times are changing. Mixed marriage is very common today. My friends, their children marry Filipinos. The children want to, *bô pan hoat lāu e* (the old people cannot do anything).[98]

In discussing marriage, the Tsinoy could not evade the issue of *kài siāu* (literally, "introduce," a practice wherein a matchmaker "introduces" a potential partner)[99] versus *ka kī liao* (literally, "courting by oneself" or by one's choice). Un Tién shared that she met her husband through *kài siāu*, their *hm lâng* (matchmaker) also became their godfather. She and her husband dated briefly before getting married. Jimmy, who met his wife through *kài siāu*, did not see any difference between *kài siāu* and *ka kī liao*. He pointed out the reality that present-day Tsinoys also find their partners through their friends' referrals. That was also *kài siāu* in his opinion.

Kài siāu in my days is *tsin pho piēn* (very common) ... *Tse si ka kī khi pat e lo, in ma si thong kè pêng iú kài siāu tsa ka kī khi develop.* (Nowadays, people find their own partners. However, they also meet their partners through introduction of their friends and then they develop further the relationship.) *Kasi* traditionally women in the past do not have many friends like women today. Therefore, it is hard for them to find their partners. A third party is needed to introduce possible male partners to them for marriage.[100]

Most of the OIs find their partners through *kài siāu*. Among the nine second-generation Tsinoys interviewed individually, five claimed to *ka kī liao* their future partner, and four found their respective partners through *kài siāu*. Among the eight third- and fourth-generation Tsinoys, only one was married and through *ka kī liao*.

97. Mrs. Chan, individual interview by author, 7 July 2012.

98. Nellie, Tsinoys individual interview author, 28 June 2012.

99. The matchmaker is usually a family friend or relative who usually receives *ti-kha* (pork leg) as a gift from the couple when they get married. Many Tsinoys do not prefer *kài siāu* since it tends to imply arranged marriage. They want to have the freedom to choose their spouses.

100. Jimmy, OI individual interview by author, 4 July 2012.

Marriage and family are central values in the Chinese culture, so marrying in the group is a way of preserving the culture. A second major value is the well-being of the children by ensuring a good spouse to have a good future. Parents would explore the background of the suitor and that tended to create the wrong impression. This concern is often interpreted by their children as meddling although the parents had the long-term interests of the family in mind.

EnRAWGen and Beyond

> "I agree with that term (EnRAWGen)[101] but that should change. *Kumbaga para sa akin* (in a sense, for me), we need to upgrade ourselves. We should not stay that way ... We should really learn the (Putonghua) language *eh*. That is fall in love with the language. There's really much pressure for the Chinoy but we have to overcome that pressure. *Iba talaga tayo eh* (We are really different), from the start we learn three languages. As we grow up, we're expected to know and develop them ... *Kasama sa* (It comes with) identity *yan* (that which is language) of a Chinoy ... We have to be excellent. *Huwag tayo magpapatalo* (We should not be defeated) ... During the time of my *lolo* (grandfather), *pinagtatatawanan siya* (he is laughed at) because of broken Tagalog. During the time of my Dad, my Dad was really excellent trilingual. So *sa panahon natin dapat ganun din tayo* (So in our generation, we ought to be the same)." —Nolan, prefers Chinoy over Tsinoy[102]

In the early 1990s, Cheung popularized the term EnRAWGen (English Reading and Writing Generation) among the Chinese Filipino churches to describe the younger generation Chinese. They prefer to read and write in English, but usually mix two or three languages in their conversation, such as Minnanhua, English, and Filipino.[103] This mixture produces a variety of mixed conversational languages such as ChiLish (Chinese and English), TagLish (Tagalog and English), ChiLog (Chinese and Tagalog), and EngChiLog (English, Chinese, and Tagalog) or EngChiFil (English, Chinese, and Filipino).

101. EnRAWGen means English Reading and Writing Generation.

102. Nolan, Tsinoy individual interview by author, 25 June 2012.

103. Cheung is the former director of the Chinese Congress on World Evangelism Fellowship-Philippines (CCOWEF-Philippines) from 1991 to 1996. Cheung, "En-RAWGen Ministry," 1.

The third- and fourth-generation Tsinoys confessed that they used EngChiLog at home with their parents. Even though most of them could speak fluent Minnanhua or English or Filipino, they prefer to combine the three languages to best express their thoughts in conversation, especially with their peers. The OIs, as well as the second-generation Tsinoys, at times also use some Filipino words and expressions. Milo saw the need to do so because some words do not have an exact equivalent in another language, so there is a need to loan words. Adding to this, I see the failure of transmission or mastery of the language which leads to incomplete vocabularies that leads to borrowing from another language. This phenomenon is an example of cultural hybridity.[104]

The elderly gentlemen group described the younger generation as *ke kóng hoan-á ōe* (Filipino speakers). Mr. Ang and Mr. Lim debated as to who is to blame for such a disgrace (a Chinese who cannot speak Minnanhua and/or Putonghua). Mr. Ang believed that the generation after his grandchildren will eventually lose the Minnanhua. He argued that external factors are overwhelming. He mentioned his own grandson who lived in Canada who used to speak Minnanhua as a child. Whenever his grandson spoke in English to his wife, she would tell him to speak Minnanhua for she could not understand English. Now that he is grown up, he just speaks in English. With China growing strong economically, Mr. Ang believed that the Chinese in the Philippines will relearn or put more importance on Putonghua than Minnanhua.

Mr. Lim, on the other hand, believed that the parents were responsible for teaching their children the language. He admitted that the grandparents were important agents in enhancing the learning and speaking of Minnanhua. He remembered hearing his grandchildren speaking Filipino all the time since they were left to the *yaya* (nannies). He reprimanded his sons to teach Minnanhua to their children. Henceforth, his grandchildren were forced to learn Minnanhua.

The OIs and the second-generation Tsinoys expressed their disappointment with the lack of interest and enthusiasm of the younger generation to speak fluent Minnanhua, more so, Putonghua. They all agreed

104. Since the medium of instruction in the Philippines is English, the Chinese are educated with the English language. The Filipino language is the language of the majority while the Minnanhua or Cantonese is the language at home. Putonghua is also learned through the Chinese classes they attended but in most cases, it remains a foreign language. They do *si thák* (rote memorization). Furthermore, they do not use it and so the language dies eventually. With China becoming a global power, the need to learn or relearn Putonghua also increases.

that the younger generation changed dramatically in their culture as evident in their preference for Filipino more than Minnanhua, or English over Minnanhua in some families.

Martha saw those who prefer English *kha ko siōng* (are more sophisticated) but some Tsinoys believed it was more important for their children to be fluent in English than Minnanhua. And yet, there were those like Nolan, a fourth-generation Chinese, who believed that it was about time for the Tsinoys to take up the challenge to learn and master as many languages as possible to be able to compete in our current global scenario.

Conclusion

Rynkiewich proposes that postmodern culture is contingent as people take what is available around them. Culture is constructed in that people pick and choose what elements to use on a regular basis. Culture is contested when it is challenged by other people within the family or community.[105] In line with a constructivist view of culture, is there a pure untainted culture or an original culture? What is Chinese culture? What is Filipino culture? Or, have we always had hybrid cultures, and now they are even more mixed up? Marvin Harris explains that there are two fundamental processes that have shaped cultural differences and similarities: independent invention and diffusion. The former is the development of certain ideas or practices that are unique to the group. The latter is a product of spreading culture(s) from an origin to near or far places. "Migration, conquest, trade, and inter-ethnic marriage are some of the more common modes of diffusion."[106]

Culture develops as a group of people adapt to an environment. Culture is reified as a group is isolated or closes their doors to outside influences. Culture is mixed as a group situates itself in the traffic of

---

105. Rynkiewich, *Soul, Self, and Society*, 38–39.

106. Failure to acknowledge history and cultural evolution will lead to ethnocentrism or what Harris refers to as "ethnomania." In his rebuttal on the Stolen-Culture Myth, "All cultures consist of a mélange of elements derived from other cultures as a result of direct or indirect contact and diffusion, and this holds as much for Egyptian as for Greek culture. Indeed the more developed and complex a society is, the more its culture (and subcultures) will reflect the influence of near and distant diffusionary contacts and the greater in turn will be that society's cultural influence. That is the lesson that needs to be taught in the name of multiculturalism, not the ethnomaniacal idea that Greeks stole philosophy and mathematics from black Africans." Harris, *Theories of Culture in Postmodern Times*, 119.

communication and trade. Culture is influenced as it chooses to be open to foreign elements. In this global and technological world, mixing of cultures is inevitable. However, the mixing seems to have a certain limit. Suffice it to say that humans determine the extent of the outside influences they allow. The Tsinoys likewise are filtering other cultural elements to add, modify, or delete from their hybrid of cultures.

All of the Tsinoys interviewed studied in Chinese schools in the country. All of them can read, write, and speak English and Filipino. However, not all are fluent in Minnanhua or even Putonghua. The younger generation preferred to combine two or more languages. Most respondents recognized that they are hybrids culturally as evident in their use of language/s, and even in their preferred cuisines, practices, and mindset.[107] A handful still see themselves as "pure" Chinese or practicing only Chinese culture.

A Minority among the Minority

The following present the case of Chinese Filipinos with Chinese citizenships and the case of Overseas Chinese Filipino Workers. Their stories demonstrate how as a minority group they can further be marginalized.

The Case of the Chinese Citizens

See believes that 90 percent of the present Chinese in the Philippines have already acquired Filipino citizenship because of the 1975 Naturalization Act of Marcos.[108] Hence, those who retain their Chinese citizenship become a minority among the minority. One must not assume that they are all citizens of China although the OIs and NIs are predominantly from China. When China became communist in 1949, the Philippines aligned itself with the United States in recognizing Taiwan as the official Chinese government until 1975. Henceforth, the Tsinoy with Chinese citizenship

---

107. They have acquired Filipino values like **pakikisama** (camaraderie) and **utang na loob** (indebtedness) as they also spread their values of thrift and hard work. Their Confucian ethical value of respect for elders is amplified with the Filipino **mano po** practice. **Mano po** is the practice of placing the hand of the elderly on one's forehead as way of showing respect. The use of **po** and **opo** for yes instead of **oo** in replying or conversing to elderly is also a sign of respect. Their mindset is also influenced by the long standing Filipino culture of **mañana** habit (Spanish for tomorrow, procrastination habit) or the **lusot** (get away with it), **lagay** (bribe it), and **lakad** (**padrino** system which is the godfather system or finding someone in power for help or patronage).

108. Teresita Ang See, individual interview by author, 29 July 2012.

can be considered a "citizen" of China or Taiwan, depending on their political inclinations.

The classification "citizen" is actually "imaginary," especially for the local-born second-, third-, and fourth-generation Chinese. They are not legally or actually citizens of either China or Taiwan. Most of them have not been to either country. The category of "citizenship" is a classification by the immigration bureau. Both China and Taiwan nevertheless welcome overseas Chinese to become their subjects.

The immigration laws in the Philippines continuously changed during the American Period.[109] Chu summarizes this development. In 1902, a child born to a Chinese father and a Filipina mother was considered a Chinese until the age of majority by virtue of *jus sanguinis*. In 1909, the Chinese imperial government also imposed *jus sanguinis*, thus making all Chinese born outside China subjects to China. In 1917, the Philippine Supreme Court applied *jus soli* making it legal for those born in Philippines to choose Filipino citizenship. However, in 1935, the law reverted back to *jus sanguinis* and this is in effect until the present.[110]

Filipino citizenship has been withheld from the Chinese for the longest time. In 1971, Chinben See and Pagkaisa aggressively lobbied for the *jus soli* principle of citizenship at the Constitutional Convention that year. They believed that citizenship would help speed up the integration process.[111] The *jus soli* or citizenship by birth argument asserts that the Chinese to have the right to Filipino citizenship by virtue of birth in the country. Philippine law grants Filipino citizenship only by *jus sanguinis* or paternal descent. A child with a Filipino father automatically acquires Filipino citizenship; but a child with a Filipina mother and non-Filipino father needs to wait until the age of eighteen to decide which citizenship to follow. A child with a non-Filipino father and mother is also considered an alien but can apply for naturalization to acquire Filipino citizenship, but not on the grounds of *jus soli*.[112]

109. See appendix I.

110. Chu, *Chinese and Chinese Mestizos of Manila*, 396–97.

111. In 1970, Chinben See together with Bernard Go, Fr. Charles McCarthy, Teddy Catindig, Harry Chua, Agnes Cuatico, Rosalinda Cua, and Napoleon Co, instituted Pagkakaisa sa Pag-unlad. Pagkaisa aims to see national integration of the Chinese in the Philippines. Unfortunately, Pagkaisa dissolved during Martial Law. Kaisa became the successor of Pagkaisa. After Chinben's death, Kaisa was founded and organized in 1987 in memory and fulfillment of Chinben's dream. See, "Bridge-Builders," 503–4.

112. Acosta, "Resolving Citizenship Issue."

It is unfortunate that local-born Chinese (including the second-, third-, and fourth-generation Chinese) are still required to apply for naturalization to become citizens of the Philippines. The root of this problem can be traced back to the colonial era when Chinese migrants were ostracized. Tsinoys are born in the country, study in Filipino colleges, and many pay their taxes dutifully; but citizenship is still deprived from them, making them citizens of no country. They are like nomads with no permanent country. They are what Bhabha describes as "unhomed."

Is naturalization difficult? Information on the website of the Bureau of Immigration shows that application for naturalization to obtain Filipino citizenship amounts to ₱140,000 or around $3,000.[113] This amount only includes the application form and processing fees. It does not include the other expenses, such as medical and legal expenses. If the applicant is employed, there is also the possibility of salary deductions for being absent during the process of application. In many cases, the demand for bribes and the required "express fee" jacks up the expenses. One Tsinoy claimed that he spent half a million pesos for the whole process, another shared that it cost three hundred thousand pesos.

With no guarantee of being accepted as a citizen of the country and with the big amount of money needed, not to disregard time, effort, tears, headaches, stomachaches, and leg aches (from too much standing and queuing), the Tsinoy would have second thoughts about acquiring citizenship. Therefore, when a Tsinoy remains a Chinese citizen, it does not necessarily mean they do not desire to acquire Filipino citizenship or that their loyalty is to China and not the Philippines. The long and costly process of applying for citizenship discourages them. Not all Tsinoys are rich, not all have the capacity to pay that amount of money for citizenship.

Many Tsinoys with Chinese citizenship long for the day when they will be recognized as citizens. It will be a joy when they finally can recite the pledge of allegiance **Panatang Makabayan** or sing the national anthem **Lupang Hinirang** without a doubt that they are Filipinos in reality and in their hearts.

---

113. The initial processing fee payable to the government is forty thousand pesos. Another fifty thousand pesos upon the approval of the petition and again fifty thousand pesos upon the taking of the oath of allegiance to the Republic of the Philippines. Bureau of Immigration, "Administrative Naturalization Law of 2000."

THE CASE OF OVERSEAS CHINESE FILIPINO WORKERS

Much has been said about the contributions of the OFWs (Overseas Filipino Workers) to the economy of the country with their remittances to their families back home. For this portion, I want to acknowledge that among the millions of OFWs hailed as "Bagong Bayani" or new heroes by the Philippine government, there were Chinese Filipinos. They are the OCFWs or Overseas Chinese Filipino Workers. There are even Chinese citizens employing Taiwan or China passports to work abroad. Their ambivalent identity and nationality gives them tremendous uncertainty and insecurity. What will happen to them if the host country where they are working suddenly decides to deport them? Where will they go? China? Taiwan? The Philippines? These Tsinoys experience the same scenario as their predecessors, "overstaying Chinese," did back in 1950s.

I interviewed five Chinese Filipinos in the category of overseas worker. Out of the five overseas workers, only one was a Chinese citizen. The rest were Filipino citizens.

James was born and raised in the Philippines, but spent most of his life within the Chinese community. In college, he experienced discrimination because he is a Tsinoy. One time, his classmates refused to help pay their share in a group project and asked him to shoulder everything, because, as they say, he is Chinese and therefore rich. James' parents are actually OCFWs working in Taiwan. They used to have a store in Manila, but because competition was tough, they had to close their business. His parents, who were formerly *towkay* or bosses, became factory workers.

James eventually joined his parents in Taiwan and applied for Taiwan citizenship. He recalled that in high school, some Chinese teachers called him *hoan-á gong* because his Putonghua was not good. In college, some Filipino classmates teased him because he speaks Filipino with a Chinese accent. When he started working in Taiwan, the Taiwanese discriminated against him because they find his Minnanhua has a Filipino accent and his Putonghua is poor.

Robert, another informant, has been working in Taiwan for twelve years now. He has not yet applied for Taiwan citizenship. In his opinion, since Taiwan no longer requires military service in exchange for citizenship for male Chinese Overseas aged thirty-five and above, he will just wait until he reaches that age. He observed that the Taiwanese were mostly friendly. He experienced less discrimination because his Putonghua is good, although he finds his Minnanhua was below Taiwanese standards.

Like James, Robert loves the Philippines. Although he prefers to live in the Philippines, the living standard in the Philippines causes him to have second thoughts.

The problem of low salary is one of the main reasons many Chinese Filipinos and Filipinos chose to work abroad. In the case of Arlene, a second-generation CM, she wanted to live independently with the hope of becoming more mature and responsible. So even without her parents' approval, she went to Singapore for two years. She enjoyed her work and if not for her parents, she would not want to return to the Philippines. Arlene is multilingual; being fluent in English, Filipino, Minnanhua, and Putonghua gave her some advantage at work. But her most important asset, she confessed, is her Chinese facial features. She easily adapted the Singaporean accent, and she was often mistaken for a Singaporean. Hence, she experienced less discrimination.[114]

Margaret believes she also became more mature and independent by working and living alone in Australia. She learned to appreciate different cultures and respect different people in this multicultural country. Although she is a college graduate from the Philippines, she worked as a server for a time in a restaurant in Australia. This made her realize the importance of respecting people of different ethnicities and different social statuses. With her mestizo background, she has no problems mingling with both Filipinos and Chinese abroad. However, she wishes that she had taken her Putonghua classes more seriously because the Chinese in Australia are Putonghua speakers. She did not experience much discrimination.

After working for two years as an architect in Saudi Arabia, Wendel wanted to live and start a family there. He noticed that the peace and order situation is better than the Philippines. There is no fear that personal belongings left unattended would be stolen. People generally abide by their laws. They work diligently. Wendel observed that, in the Philippines people often feared the Muslims, but he felt very safe in Saudi Arabia surrounded by the Muslims. On the contrary, he felt unsafe living in the Philippines even though it is a Catholic country because of frequent robberies and thefts. The only reason he returned was because of the discrimination he experienced from his Sudanese boss who preferred Indonesians over Filipinos.

114. According to Arian, discrimination was not allowed in Singapore. It was unlawful. Arian also worked in Singapore for several years. He was an informant for the CM category.

Out of the five respondents, Wendel and Arlene both worked for two years and then returned to the Philippines for good. Wendel presently helps in his uncle's business while Arlene works in a big company. James, Robert, and Margaret continue to work abroad. They believe they would have a better life staying there than coming back. James finally felt at home in Taiwan after receiving Taiwan citizenship in 2013. Robert and Margaret remained Filipino citizens but they have no issues living abroad.

All found themselves very much affected by their experience working abroad. Their exposure to another country enabled them to see the need for the Philippines to improve and change. This exposure also created in them a bigger heart to understand people marginalized by either ethnicity, social status, or religion. Their unhomely situations and unhomed identities had helped them become more mature and better citizens. At the same time, this unhomely nature also led them to seek a place to call their home.

Conclusion

Benedict Anderson coined the term "imagined communities" to refer to the emergence of nations. He defines a nation as an imagined political community that is inherently limited and sovereign. It is "imagined" because the people within the nation can never know every person in the country. And yet they all unite and believe they all belong to one country governed by the same rulers and laws. However, the nation is limited as its borders set the parameters of its territory. It is sovereign as it gives freedom not bondage under religious structure or dynastic rule.[115]

The Tsinoys with Chinese citizenship have "imagined citizenship." The nature of their Chinese citizenship or Taiwanese citizenship is "imaginary" because they are not in reality citizens either of China or Taiwan. They do not have a national identification number to prove they belong to China or Taiwan. Their only connection or proof of citizenship is their passports. They even have to acquire visas to enter Taiwan or China. They are people of "no permanent country" to call their own. They are children of the Chinese immigrants who were not able to acquire Filipino citizenships. Their parents or grandparents may have been victims of the Cold War. These OIs may have been "overstaying Chinese," or as Luther calls them, "trapped Chinese." The difficult and long process of naturalization usually becomes the barrier for them to apply for Filipino citizenship,

---

115. Anderson, *Imagined Communities*, 6–7.

not to mention the huge amount of money required. Such situations led to unhomely positions. The Tsinoys are suspended in space where they at times feel unwanted by the Philippines and even China or Taiwan.

Their immigrant status in the Philippines set many limitations. The Philippines provide them permanent residency but not the right to acquire land and properties. They pay taxes but cannot vote. They can venture into business but not as sole proprietor. They must be in a partnership or corporation with Filipinos. They can enter schools and universities but not at the expense of the state. They can get a college degree but not a licensure. They have China or Taiwan passports but will still need visas of China or Taiwan to enter those countries. Their status as a minority among the minority further adds to their displacement and unhomely feelings. Despite all these, these Tsinoys already consider the Philippines as their beloved country and home. As one Tsinoy remarked, "*tseng chha sī miâ nì* (the only difference is the name or citizenship)."

As for the OCFWs, they experienced culture shock the first time they worked abroad. They went through a series of adjustments as they adapted to the new culture and language. They went through unhomely situations and unhomely feelings. Upon returning home, they experienced reverse culture shock. With a new perspective, they think that the Philippines needs to change, to improve their economy. They were shocked by the piles of garbage; crowded cities; tormenting traffic; widespread poverty; lack of peace and order; and unending government corruption. Such scenarios add to their dismay and dislocation as many years of working abroad made the other country more like their home than the Philippines. Once again, they experience unhomely feelings and displacement. If given a choice, four out of five would wish to live outside the country. The Philippines will merely be a country for vacation and memories.

PART 3: SINICIZATION OR FILIPINIZATION OF SPOUSES IN INTER-ETHNIC MARRIAGES AND THEIR OFFSPRING THE CHINESE MESTIZOS

Chu believes that the Chinese tend to employ negotiations in different situations, manipulating and switching identities in most instances during the Spanish and American Period. For instance, the Chinese were taxed the heaviest in the Spanish Period; because of this, many allowed their children to become Spanish citizens. During the American Period and following the spread of nationalism in China, the Chinese had to consider some internal (e.g., location, situation) and external (e.g., political, historical) factors before deciding on their citizenship. Chu observes, however, that the Chinese during this period may have Filipino citizenship, but remain culturally Chinese. The Chinese may intermarry with Filipinas but they will make sure that their children are Sinicized rather than Filipinized.[116]

Chu connects the rise of Chinese nationalism in the late 1920s with the Nationalist Party's (GMD) establishment of China as a republic. This development also influenced the Chinese in Manila, so that in the 1930s, they became more nationalistic and close-knit. Chu believes that it was during this time period that the word *chhut-sì-á* 出世子 was used to refer to the Chinese Mestizos. The Minnan word *chhut-sì-á* means someone born outside (China) with the connotation of impurity. He believes that this word is only used in the Philippines. Most of the Chinese born outside China during this time were offspring of inter-ethnic marriages between Chinese and Filipinas. The Chinese made a conscious effort to turn their *chhut-sì-á* offsprings to *lanlâng* or *lan e lâng* (our own people).[117]

The last part of this chapter will present the possibility of Sinicization, Filipinization, hybridization, and Resinification in inter-ethnic marriages and their children the Chinese Mestizos.

Reversed Identities in Marriage: Filipino to Chinese, Chinese to Filipino

Paul A. Rodell argues that the Filipinos are often hospitable, but with regard to marriage, the Filipinos also tend to be endogamous. First, Filipino parents prefer their children to marry someone within their locality. Close proximity ensures close family ties. Second, finding a mate of higher economic status is welcomed since such linkages help the family's community standing. Rodell argues that the wealthy families have a tendency to find partners for their children within their social class. Third, the Filipinos rarely consider marrying someone from a different region or linguistic group. Filipinos are willing to cross such boundaries only when there are social or economic advantages. Rodell observes that

---

116. Chu, *Chinese and Chinese Mestizos of Manila*, 392–98.

117. Ibid., 395.

poor Filipinas are generally the ones attracted to marry ethnic Chinese.[118] Lastly, religion is an important criteria for finding a mate.[119]

Rodell notes that the Iglesia Ni Cristo and Roman Catholics do not intermarry because of doctrinal considerations. The Muslims also forbid marrying non-Muslims without conversion. He concludes that even with modernity and urbanization, finding a mate has its constraints. Even with the loosening of some traditional strictures, there remain some clear demarcations, and crossing such boundaries only invites opposition.[120]

These factors are useful in understanding endogamous practices of the Chinese Filipinos. Locality, economic status, ethnicity, language, and religion are the criteria they consider in choosing a spouse. Economic considerations are a major factor in crossing such boundaries, says Rodell. These criteria are created to prevent, discourage, or assist in the crossing of boundaries. Another criterion may be added to Rodell's list, namely, urbanization and migration. Metro Manila has been an attractive place for many rural-to-urban job seekers. Thus, Manila has been a cultural melting pot since the Spanish Period.[121]

Chinese immigrants belong to a large ethnic minority in Manila.[122] They are not immune from this mixing of cultures and languages, as well as inter-ethnic marriages. They are also influenced by Filipino culture.

118. The results from the limited sample show that the ten hybrid couples were either of the same economic status or the other was from a higher level. Most of the Filipino spouses come from middle class families, two are from upper middle class, and one from lower middle class. Most of the Chinese spouses come from upper middle class families, two are from middle class, and one from lower middle class. The findings seemed to agree with Rodell's observation that only poor Filipinos/as were attracted to marry ethnic Chinese. But then, that raised the issue of who is poor or what is poor. Such categorization is very subjective. It can be based on figures such as income or ownership. Yet the fact remained that economic status did play a major role as pointed out by Rodell.

119. Rodell, *Culture and Customs*, 128.

120. Ibid.

121. Caoili notes that two-thirds of the migrants to Metropolitan Manila are from urbanized regions of Central Luzon, Southern Luzon, Western Visayas and Central Visayas. He calls Metropolitan Manila a "primate city" meaning it is disproportionately grown in population throughout the centuries as compared to other parts of the country. Caoili, *Origins of Metropolitan Manila*, 42–43, 68, 70–77. The "Manila-centric" mentality is proof of the country's failure to develop other parts of the country thereby leading to unequal distribution of people, resources, and income.

122. See, "Case of the Chinese in the Philippines," 155–56. If 52 percent of all Chinese in the Philippines live in Metro Manila, then there are more than half a million of them in this region alone.

Further, the expectations of Filipino society and the demands of Filipino politics are factors that contributed to the shaping of Chinese Filipino's beliefs and behavior.

What kind of hybridity is produced in inter-ethnic marriages between Chinese and Filipinos today? Are the families Sinicized or Filipinized in terms of language and cultural practices in the home? I classify the Chinese and Filipino spouses as "Reversed Identities." This is to point out the reality that one of the partners generally adopt and adapt to the other culture in order to maintain harmony in the family, while the other partner has fewer adjustments to make. The hybrid family is not a 50/50 proposition, but rather it tends to employ a dominant culture which dictates the language used at home and how the couple raises the children. Since the mother has the biggest influence on the children, her ethnicity is usually the crucial factor whether the family will be more Sinicized or Filipinized.

I interviewed ten people from ten inter-ethnic marriages; five Filipino spouses and five Chinese spouses, five were males and five were females. Eight found their partners in the work place, except for two who met through referral of friend or relative. Among the ten Chinese spouses, they are all Tsinoys. There were four CMs, two second-generation Cantonese, and four second-generation Hokkien.

Hybrid Partnerships: Going Against Tradition

> "Most Chinese are open for boys to marry Filipinas but not for their girls to marry Filipinos. My two brothers marry Filipinas. There is no opposition or not that strong opposition." —Nara[123]

Nara (a Cantonese) confessed that there was great opposition on her side of the family when she and Chester (a Filipino) started their relationship. When they decided to marry, her siblings neither opposed nor encouraged her decision. Nara and Chester had a civil wedding in 1986 but none of her family members attended the event. The first year they were married, they were not invited to attend the family's Christmas and New Year

123. Nara was born in 1955. She is a second-generation native born but remains a Chinese citizen. Both her parents were Chinese citizens. She had a master's degree in history from the University of Santo Tomas while her husband Chester was a graduate of Ateneo de Manila's Master of Business Administration program. They have two children. Nara, Chinese Spouse individual interview by author, 19 July 2012.

celebration. Despite all these, Nara had no regrets. She admitted she was prepared for whatever consequences.

Although her family did not forbid her to visit them, she knew she was not welcomed. With much patience and perseverance, she faithfully brought her children to visit her parents every Saturday.

> In spite that they do not talk to you, I'll bring the children to my parents' house every Saturday. Until such time that they just ignore you (*di ka pansinin*). Just be persistent. When I give birth to my second child who is a boy, he is so cute. And you know that Chinese prefer boys over girls. [Crying and smiling] My mother secretly tells me that my son is her favorite grandson. I think that breaks the ice. But I did not abandon the idea (reconciliation). I did not isolate myself. *Di ka pansinin, sige lang* (Even if they will ignore you, it is okay). *Di ka na naman tinataboy na* you cannot go back (You are not driven away that you cannot go back home). Until the ice thaw, I just keep going back. In God's time *lang talaga* (truly). Persistence, perseverance, in spite of all persecutions.[124]

Out of the five Chinese spouses interviewed, only Nara faced this level of opposition. Lovely, the other Chinese female in this category, felt free to marry a Filipino. Her mother was a Chinese Mestiza while her father was a pure Chinese. She married Miguel, a native of Southern Luzon and whom she met at work in 1998.

Wendel, Adam, and Andrew were the three Chinese males interviewed for this category. Their families have no problem with them marrying Filipinas. Wendel is a CM.[125] He married Rachel, a Filipina.

Adam admitted he was afraid to marry a Chinese because he did not like the idea of marrying someone from a higher economic standing to avoid the pressures of providing the same luxury as she used to enjoy before getting married.

> To tell you honestly, I am a Chinese but if I will, you know, court a Chinese, I think I cannot meet their standard. I am from a poor family. Even the thought of courting, I dare not think about it. It is okay if I will be able to raise her economic level than to pull

---

124. Nara, Chinese Spouse individual interview by author, 19 July 2012.

125. Wendel's grandfather was very much against his parents' marriage. His father was a Chinese immigrant while his mother was a Filipina. But his grandfather mellowed when his father suddenly died of heart attack and his mother died a month after. His grandfather never forced him to find a Chinese wife.

her down to a lower level. I do not like to be looked down. That is what I do not like. That's why I did not court a Chinese, not even a *hoan-á* that is rich. I do not like the idea that she used to enjoy a luxurious life then I will bring her down. I will be more proud if I will be able to lift her up to a higher level.[126]

When Adam (b. 1959) began courting Jenny (b. 1973), her family initially doubted his sincerity because of their age gap, and his being a Chinese. To prove he was serious with Jenny, he immediately proposed marriage, and they were wed in 1994.

Andrew (a Cantonese) was a tourist guide when he met Sally (a Filipina) in a Nihongo class. Sally was working in a hotel back in 1994 when Andrew, who is ten years older, began courting her. They experienced no opposition from both his and her families. Her work was Andrew's greatest hurdle but his persistence paid off.[127]

The Filipino spouses, in contrast, experienced greater opposition. Edna (a Filipina) experienced opposition from her family, but not from her Chinese spouse's family. Glenda and Bernice (Filipinas) experienced opposition from both sides of the families. As for Faustino and Ace (Filipinos), their Chinese spouses' families were opposed to the relationship.

Faustino (b. 1957) married Ashley (b. 1960), a second-generation Chinese. She worked as a secretary in a company where he was the driver. Initially, she was interested with his **kumpareng** Chinese (Chinese friend), but Faustino was able to woo her with his patience. His social status is an additional obstacle on top of his ethnic origin in winning the approval of Ashley's parents.

> Category C **ako, isang hamak na drayber kaya di agree**. (I belong to class C category, just a poor driver that is why they disagree with our relationship.) My wife fought for our relationship . . . She did not have regrets but sad with the situation.

> Every time there is an occasion; I will bring my wife and daughter to their house. I will just wait outside the gate until they are done. Christmas, birthdays, or other occasions. Sometimes there is food set aside for me. On December, Christmas 1991, I brought them to their house and waited outside as usual. [Tears forming in his eyes] Then Ashley came out calling me, "Papa

126. Adam, Chinese Spouse individual interview by author, 4 July 2012.

127. After college, Sally spent three years in Germany and six months in Switzerland studying.

and mama are looking for you, they said you must go inside." So I entered in. I am so happy that after persevering for two years, her family finally accepts me. Her family tells me "*Wala ka naman masamang tinapay* (Filipino idiom meaning no bad blood in you)." They see how I work hard and take care of Ashley and our daughter. That is the happiest December in my life. From then on, I accompany my father-in-law every time he will go to Ongpin to shop or eat at his favorite restaurant Ling Nam then buy baked goods at Eng Ho. Every Sunday, we go there, even to his barber. He always pays even if I volunteer to pay. He gets angry when I insist to pay. He will tell me, "*Itabi mo na lang yan para sa mga apo ko* (Just set them aside for my grandchildren)."[128]

Ace waited for ten years before he married his wife Ellen, a CM. Ellen's Chinese father was initially opposed to their relationship, but after ten years of courtship, her parents gave them their blessings.

There are some conflicts in the beginning. Ellen's father is a Chinese. He is not in favor of our relationship. With patience, *dalaw-dalaw* (visit their home). *Hatid-sundo sa* school (I accompany her to school and accompany her home).[129] After ten years of steady, they decided we should marry. Ellen's mother is a Filipina.[130]

Glenda, Bernice, and Edna encountered difficulties as well because of inter-ethnic marriages. In 1979, Glenda (b. 1959) met Teddy (b. 1941), who is a second-generation Chinese. Glenda did not mind their age gap. Her relatives had to check his background to make sure he did not have a wife in China before her father gave his approval.

Glenda recalled how he brought *pasalubong* (a gift) when he picked her up from work, and her boss yelling, "Glenda, *nandiyan na si kabise* (Glenda, *kabise* is here.)"[131] Teddy's elder brother was against the relationship because he was arranged to marry a Chinese woman earlier, but he backed out in his desire to find "true love."

128. Faustino, Filipino Spouse individual interview by author, 25 July 2012.

129. Traditional Filipino courtship is usually composed of *dalaw* or visiting the girl in her house. This is one way to show respect for the girl's parents and to prove one's good intention. *Hatid-sundo* is also a way of courtship. As a gentleman, he will always ensure the safety of the woman he is courting or going steady with. Therefore, it is necessary that he will find ways to accompany her home after school or after work.

130. Ace, Filipino Spouse individual interview by author, 25 July 2013.

131. *Kabise* is boss.

Bernice (a Filipina) met Eddie (a Chinese) through their common friend. When she started dating Eddie, her friend Joey warned her "***Sige, tigas ng ulo mo ah, iiyak ka lang.*** Chinese *mama papa niya* (Go ahead, you are so hard headed. You will end up just crying. His father and mother are Chinese)." Her mother also told her to stop entertaining Eddie early on when he started calling her at home. She advised, "Chinese *yan, ibang ugali niyan, iba kultura nila*. (They are Chinese. They behave differently and practice a different culture.)" Bernice also sensed opposition from Eddie's family. Although Eddie's two older brothers both married Filipinas and another brother married a CM, this did not change his mother's treatment of Bernice. When they got married, she recounted how her mother-in-law ignored her whenever she brought her children to visit their grandmother. It took a while before this treatment changed.

Edna was her town's beauty queen and was just sixteen when Art, a second-generation CM, pursued her. Their courtship was swift but their relationship was not smooth. Art's family liked her very much. One of his uncles even taught her how to speak Minnanhua. Her family sadly disapproved of the relationship. Her family warned her,

> They tell me, "*Ay* Chinese *yan. Pag napangasawa mo yan naku di ka makakalabas ng bahay. Di ka na makakahawak ng pera. Di ka na makakapasyal sa parte mo.* (He is a Chinese. If you marry him, you will never go out of the house. You will never handle money. You will not be allowed to visit us.)" I am so angry that they will suddenly change their minds. Art's family already *namanhikan* (asks for the girl's hand for marriage) and we already agreed to marry. My *kuya* (big brother) said he will do anything even to cry with tears of blood just for me to retreat. They saw me as *pasaway* (stubborn) and that they cannot change my mind anymore. My father slapped me in his anger for I insisted to marry Art. I tell them that I will follow him and that I have made up my mind. Eventually, the wedding pushed through. My father accompanied me to Manila to buy my wedding dress ... Everything my family feared is the opposite of what really happens ... [Chuckling] I handle our finances. I have my own business. I can go out every Sunday.[132]

These stories presented the problems of inter-ethnic marriages. The oppositions were real and painful as these couples went against the

---

132. Edna, Filipino Spouse individual interview by author, 15 June 2012, Quezon City.

traditional value of endogamy. The thought of being ostracized by your family because of your choice of life partner was agonizing. Nara cried throughout the interview especially when she recalled how her mother gave her the cold treatment when she married Chester. Faustino could not help but cry when he shared how he was not welcomed by his wife's family. Bernice cried as she talked about her mother-in-law's indifference and coldness toward her. Edna was teary eyed when she recalled being slapped by her father. Ace waited ten years to prove his sincerity to his wife's family. Teddy's brother threatened not to attend his wedding. "Was it worth it?" asked Nara to herself. She replied, "Fifty-fifty, I guess."

From these stories, ethnicity seems to be the greatest barrier in inter-ethnic marriages. Right at the core of the problem of inter-ethnic marriages is the issue of distrust and estrangement. Distrust could be in the area of fidelity, ability to provide for the family, and continuing family ties. In the area of fidelity, the Chinese or Filipino parents definitely want their sons or daughters to find a spouse who would remain faithful and loyal. Marriage is sacred among Roman Catholics in the Philippines. Further, there is no divorce in the Philippines.

Both ethnicities considered the role of the man as the main provider while the wife was the nurturer. Traditionally, women in both cultures stay at home and care for the family.[133] With modernity and postmodernity, women were no longer confined in the houses. The fear of being tied inside the home became a reason for some Chinese women to look for Filipinos as spouses rather than a very traditional Chinese. Unfortunately, many Filipinos also had a traditional understanding of roles of men and women. In the case of Nara, she realized that Chester is very conservative "*parang* Chinese" (Chinese-like) when it comes to family. He left all the children to her care. Lovely is able to continue to work just as she wanted but she became the major provider for the family because of her husband's gambling problem and his extra-marital affairs. Both these Chinese women later in their interviews admitted that their prejudices to marry Chinese men backfired. Nara realized that cultures and personalities were major factors that needed to be considered in marriage. Lovely presently would prefer a Chinese over a Filipino based on her personal experience.

---

133. Rodell, *Cultures and Customs*, 123.

Both ethnicities upheld family ties. The fear that their son/daughter would eventually become Sinicized or Filipinized brought threat to their own culture and traditions as well as connections with family and kin.

SINICIZATION OR FILIPINIZATION OF FAMILY

> "The children learn very little (Minnanhua) because we rarely use the language at home. My husband's Filipino is way better than mine. Only in times when we do not wish our Filipino helpers to understand our conversation then we *kóng lanlâng ōe la, kóng lanlâng ōe la* (speak Minnanhua, speak Minnanhua). [Laughter] The children do not speak the language even among themselves. *Bô le kóng ná, bô le kóng.* (They do not speak the language, they do not speak it.) [Laughter] My children at least understand the language. They all studied in Chinese school. **Baka kung** *hoanáng-hoaná* (Maybe if I am very Filipina), they may never learn the language." —Edna[134]

Edna admitted she was very much influenced by Chinese culture. She had to adapt and adopt some elements of Chinese culture and learn their language because she lives in Binondo and does business with Chinese. To some degree, she was Sinicized, but she still see herself as *hoan-á* not *lanlâng*. She believes that not learning the language places her in a disadvantageous position, whether in social gatherings, and more so in business. This motivated Edna to learn Minnanhua, and to be precise both in intonation and grammar. She observed that many Chinese today no longer preserved the purity of their language, **halo-halo na** (mixed already).

Glenda shared that, in their home, they favored Filipino culture and language over Chinese culture and language. She was liberated from the pressure of learning Minnanhua and living with in-laws because Teddy's parents had passed away already when they met. The fact was she discovered her husband was very Filipinized. They sent their children to Chinese school to learn Minnanhua and Putonghua for their advantage in finding work in the future. Nevertheless, they did not force the children to speak the language at home. "**Kung matuto then maganda.** (It will be great if they learn the languages.)" Interestingly, her husband had always desired to see all his children, especially the eldest son, marry Chinese

---

134. Edna, Filipino Spouse individual interview by author, 15 June 2012.

spouses. She considered it absurd to force endogamy to their children when he himself married a Filipina.[135]

Bernice might not live with her in-laws, but she is constantly in contact with them during holidays and birthdays. With this, she has to learn how to deal with them and relate to them. As they live with her parents and eldest sister, her husband is the one who needs to adjust and relate to her family. He became very close to her father. Her eldest sister helped take care of their children while the two of them work in the same company. They sent their eldest to an exclusive Catholic boy's school and chose Chinese class for his elective. The youngest attended a newly opened Chinese school in their area.

Ace and his CM wife Ellen sent their three children to a Chinese school. His in-laws helped them financially especially when the children came along. Living in the Binondo area and working in a Chinese company, Ace is well oriented with the Chinese culture. His Minnanhua is not very fluent but he could understand a little. His wife spoke Minnanhua to the children. Nevertheless, the usage of Filipino was still predominant at home. He observed his children and most Chinese children living in Manila preferred to speak in Filipino rather than Minnanhua.

Faustino and his Chinese wife Ashley sent one of their daughters to a Chinese school when they were still living in Caloocan City. By the time they moved to Retiro in Quezon City, they sent the children to a private Filipino school near their house. They spoke Filipino at home. His mother helped take care of the children when they were small and whenever they had difficulty finding a nanny.[136] He could not deny the fact that he was also influenced by Chinese culture with marriage and his work (in a Chinese company). His children also acquired two cultures but Filipino culture was dominant. His children actually blamed their mother for her failure to teach them Minnanhua which could be to their advantage as they sought employment.

135. Out of the four children, the eldest daughter married a Filipino while the eldest son married a CM. The other two were not yet married. Glenda gave her children the freedom to choose since they were the ones who will **makikisama** (live with them). She imparted to her children Filipino virtues like being courteous and respectful, being humble and not looking down on others. She appreciated Chinese kinship and family ties. She finds the Chinese responsibly taking care of their families. When Teddy passed away, his elder brother supported them financially.

136. In the interview, Faustino also used the word *hoan-á-po* to refer to Filipina house helpers. It seems like he did not find the word wrong or he did not know the real meaning behind the word.

Out of the five Filipino spouses interviewed, only Edna mastered Minnanhua. Ace and Faustino can understand a little but cannot speak very fluently. Both are working in Chinese companies in Manila Chinatown. Bernice and Glenda do not speak Minnanhua since they do not live with their Chinese in-laws.[137] In these five families, only Edna and Ace used Filipino and Minnanhua interchangeably in their respective homes. The rest used Filipino only. All families sent their children to Chinese schools or had some kind of Chinese language education.[138] But in the homes, Filipinization rather than Sinicization occurred especially in their way of raising the children. All Filipino spouses still see themselves as Filipinos but agree they were influenced by Chinese culture to a certain degree. Hence, hybridity for them was more on compartmentalization, having the ability to employ different cultures in different situations with different people.

With regard to the five Chinese spouses interviewed, two were CMs while three were "pure" Chinese. Interestingly, four of these families primarily used English and Filipino in their homes. Only one used Filipino only.[139] Two families sent their children to Chinese schools where they learned Minnanhua and Putonghua. The other three sent their children to Filipino schools due to proximity. Given a choice, if there was a nearby

---

137. Edna lived for at least two years with her Chinese mother-in-law. Faustino's wife had to live with his mother for a while as well. For this reason, Ashley probably opted not to speak Minnanhua to the children in respect for her Filipina mother-in-law living with them.

138. Edna, Glenda, Bernice, and Ace send their children to Chinese schools or had Chinese language education. Faustino send one of his daughters to a Chinese school but later send the two daughters to a private Filipino school. This in part affected his daughters learning of the Chinese language and connection with the Chinese community.

139. Nara's children had learned a little Cantonese through the years. She confessed she usually spoke the language when very angry. Her children learned Minnanhua and Putonghua in school. But they usually used English and a little Filipino in their conversation. Andrew's children also used mostly English and a little Filipino at home. They learned Minnanhua and Putonghua in school. Wendel tried to teach his children Minnanhua but only the youngest seemed interested. Both children studied in a private Filipino school that did not offer Chinese language class. Adam forbade the speaking of Bisaya at home but was fine with Filipino. He wanted his children to at least understood Minnanhua even if they could not speak fluently. He was saddened by the fact that his vicinity did not have a nearby Chinese school. Lovely no longer enforced speaking Minnanhua at home. Her son could not speak or understand the language. She sent him to a private Filipino school near their vicinity. It used to offer Chinese language class but eventually stopped when enrollment was low.

Chinese school in their place, they would send their children to Chinese schools.

In the area of culture practiced in the home, Adam, Lovely, and Wendel admitted that their respective families were more Filipinized than Sinicized. Although they imparted the good values or practices of Chinese culture, Filipino culture remained dominant. In the cases of Adam and Wendel, their Filipina wives were more influential in raising the children. Naturally, the Filipino culture became dominant. In the case of Andrew, his Filipina wife had more influence with the children but their Chinatown environment contributed as well, thus balancing two cultures. Sally, herself a linguist, was very encouraging and supportive to her children learning many languages. Andrew and Sally sent their daughter to China for summer study tours. Nara also saw herself as the main propagator of culture in the home. She evaluated their home as more Westernized Chinese culture, an assimilated Chinese style and not conservative traditionalist. For the Chinese spouses' category, it was evident that they tended to be more Filipinized than Sinicized. They had mixed the two or more cultures into their homes but Filipino culture remained dominant. Since their Filipino/a spouses could not speak Minnanhua or Cantonese, they were willing to do the adjustment and switched to the Filipino or English language.

Adam saw himself as a hybrid in the sense that he had mixed the two cultures and could not be one without the other. Lovely saw herself as hybrid but more Filipinized already. Wendel, Nara, and Andrew saw themselves as hybrid but not totally losing their Chineseness. Hybridity for them was the ability to switch from one culture to the other. It was more on compartmentalization, mixed and yet unmixed since one could still identify one culture from the other.

Table 3. Hybrid Partnership Culture Scale

Informant	Spouse	Chinese Language Education for Children	*Language/s the Children Can Speak or Understand	Language/s Used at Home	Sinicized, Filipinized, or Both
Ace (Filipino)	Ellen (CM)	Yes	English, Filipino, Putonghua, and Minnanhua	Minnanhua and Filipino	Both
Bernice (Filipino)	Eddie (Chinese)	Yes	English, Filipino, and Putonghua	Filipino	Filipinized
Edna (Filipino)	Art (CM)	Yes	English, Filipino, Putonghua, and Minnanhua	Minnanhua and Filipino	Both
Faustino (Filipino)	Ashley (Chinese)	Yes (partial)	English and Filipino	Filipino	Filipinized
Glenda (Filipino)	Teddy (Chinese)	Yes	English, Filipino, Putonghua, and Minnanhua	Filipino	Filipinized
Adam (Chinese)	Jenny (Filipino)	No	English and Filipino	Filipino	Filipinized
Andrew (Chinese)	Sally (Filipino)	Yes	English, Filipino, Putonghua, and Minnanhua	English, Filipino, and Minnanhua	Both
Lovely (CM)	Miguel (Filipino)	No	English and Filipino	English and Filipino	Filipinized
Nara (Chinese)	Chester (Filipino)	Yes	Cantonese, English, Filipino, Putonghua, and Minnanhua	Cantonese, English, Filipino, and Minnanhua	Both
Wendel (CM)	Rachel (Filipino)	No	English and Filipino	English and Filipino	Filipinized

*The degree of fluency for each language varies for each child and family.

CONCLUSION

Alfonso, Layo, and Bulatao did a study on inter-ethnic marriages in 1980 entitled *Culture and Fertility: The Case of the Philippines.* They cite the social distance study of Macaraig back in 1931 to 1932 and discover the sample preferential difference. Out of thirteen nationals, the Americans and the Spanish Mestizos are most preferred by Filipinos, whereas the Chinese and the Japanese are least preferred. Alfonso, Layo, and Bulatao acknowledge the fact that the Chinese are still deemed undesirables even though they have been in the country for centuries. The Filipinos remain distant toward the Chinese. There are limits to their social acceptance of the Chinese which depended largely on economic benefits such as business partnerships or being *compadres* in baptismal or wedding sponsors. As marital partners, the Chinese ranked the lowest. Nevertheless, many Filipinos have 10 percent Chinese blood running in their veins. Further, a survey made from 1960 to 1969 shows that there were 805 inter-ethnic marriages between Chinese males and Filipinas and 583 inter-ethnic marriages between Chinese women and Filipinos. Alfonso, Layo, and Bulatao conclude that there are more inter-ethnic marriages between Chinese and Filipinos/as than the 890 marriages between Chinese and Chinese.[140]

Considering that immigration of Chinese nationals stopped in 1940 and reopened only in 1975 when Marcos established diplomatic ties with China, most of the single Chinese Filipinos would have to find spouses among themselves. The limited number of Chinese Filipinos posed the limitation of choices in finding spouses. There was the problem of imbalance of males and females since most immigrants were males.

Second, it also caused delays in marriage thus creating a bachelor society among many Chinese men. Teddy and Adam were eighteen years older than their spouses while Andrew was ten years older than Sally.

Third, the environment was favorable for the minority Chinese Filipinos/as to find suitable partners among the dominant Filipinos/as. Eight out of ten informants for this category found their spouses in the workplace. Most Chinese Filipinos would be exposed to the dominant world of the Filipinos after finishing Chinese high school or when working. Many would no longer be confined within Chinatown or kept in predominantly Chinese environment like Chinese schools. The environment factor then became crucial for the eligible Chinese Filipino bachelors and bachelorettes in finding their choice of partners in marriage. It was then nearly inevitable for inter-ethnic marriage to happen between these two ethnic groups living in the same country.

140. Alfonso et al., *Culture and Fertility*, 21–22.

With hybrid partnerships, the homes of these informants were mostly Filipinized rather than Sinicized as evident in their usage of Filipino language and culture. For many of the OIs, there was a correlation between language and culture. The dropping of the Minnanhua language was a strong indication of the loss of Chinese culture and identity. Hence, many older generations disagree with inter-ethnic marriages for fear of the loss of Chinese culture. And for this reason, the OIs appreciated the Resinification brought about by the NIs.

The findings in this limited sampling confirmed that there is a correlation between language and culture. Out of the ten inter-ethnic marriages, only four families employ some degree of Minnanhua usage aside from Filipino and English with the children. The rest used Filipino and/ or English only. Out of the four families, the mothers played a major role in the learning of the language. Nara and Ace's CM wife Ellen spoke Minnanhua with the children. Edna spoke Minnanhua even though she was a Filipina. Sally was a Filipina but encouraged her children to learn Minnanhua and Putonghua.[141] The location and environment are also significant in the learning and usage of the language. All four families sent their children to Chinese schools. Three out of four of these families lived in Binondo when they started their families. Therefore, four out of ten have incorporated Sinicization aside from Filipinization in their families.

The spouses in inter-ethnic marriages had to realign themselves, their identities and their cultural inclination, in the kind of culture they would create or had created. They negotiate what language or languages to use and what traditions to follow.[142]

141. Nara and Chester, as well as Andrew and Sally, encouraged their children to excel and learn multiple languages for their advantages in their future careers. These two couples had higher educational attainment than the rest of the informants that led me to a further observation. These parents have higher goals and higher expectations for their children. They inevitably sought opportunities for their children to experience what they had experienced for their personal growth.

142. In these hybrid partnerships, many of them did not discuss with their spouses what culture and language to employ in their homes. They simply adapted and adjusted as they went along in their marriages. The Chinese spouses who lived with Filipino in-laws had to refrain from speaking Minnanhua as a sign of respect to the elders. Such were the situations of Bernice's Chinese husband and Faustino's Chinese wife. Adam, Wendel, and Lovely decided to just use Filipino and English at home since their spouses could not speak Minnanhua. The three of them were fluent in Minnanhua but they used the language in their work not in the home. Their homes eventually became more Filipinized than Sinicized. However, when asked how they saw themselves, all three still affirmed that they had not totally lost their Chineseness.

I therefore concluded that Sinicization or Filipinization of oneself or a family was an intentional construct that can lead to transferring, negotiating, compromising, or discarding of cultural element/s. Cultures are constructed over the course of time with whatever materials or elements are contingent or available. Cultures are contested on a daily basis, thereby leading to propagation, negotiation, or elimination. With propagation, cultures are transferred from one person to another or one generation to another. With negotiation, there are practices, beliefs, or characteristics changed, compromised, mixed, reinvented, or discarded. Once again, culture is proven to be constructed rather than a given inherent in the blood or genes. Ethnic groups differ from one another as they exemplified distinct characteristics, beliefs, practices, and languages. Therefore, problems will definitely occur in inter-ethnic marriages in addition to the problems and issues of normal marriages. Endogamy and exogamy are personal choices. They have their advantages and disadvantages. However, the real culprit in opposing inter-ethnic marriages are the stereotypes and prejudices we have accrued throughout the years.

Chinese Mestizos: Prejudices and Perceptions

For centuries, the idea of being mixed, biracial, multiracial, creoles, mullatoes, mestizos, or hybrids has been abhorred by societies. Young traces the history of the notion of hybridity from a Western perspective in his book *Colonial Desire*. He notes that "hybrid" simply means half-bred. He reports that, in 1823, Webster defined it as a mixture of two species pertaining to animals and plants. Later, the term came to be used to refer to interracial offspring. The racist's disdain for hybrid offspring does not spring from genetics, however, for the hybrids often are more hardy and adaptive than "pure" parents. Thus, the term "hybrid vigor" is applied to increased adaptability. The derision when applied to humans derives from the white superiority complex. The argument on whites and blacks coming from different human species give rise to different theories. Young claims that these theories on race are actually hidden theories of desire, specifically the tension between sexual desire for black or brown female bodies and repugnance of the idea of a mixed race sexual union.[143]

During colonialism, hybridity was viewed negatively. Conversely, it was during this period that products of mixed union increased. The

---

143. Young's premise in his book is that the colonizers are obsessed with the colonized people and their possessions. Young, *Colonial Desire*, xi–xii. See also appendix J.

intermingling of different ethnic groups due to trade, conquests, and migration since ancient times have been avenues for inter-ethnic relationships. Those living on the borders cannot escape the possibility of contact and union that gives birth to hybrid people.[144]

DIMINISHING PREJUDICES ON HYBRIDS

> "It is never an issue that I am a *mestizo* in (Chinese) school. In fact, most of the students in our school are *mestizos*. I have *mestizo* friends and pure (Chinese) friends. There are more prejudices toward the New Immigrants." —Chris[145]

There seemed to be diminishing prejudice toward the CMs today as evident in the data gathered. In the past, the pure Chinese called the CMs *chhut-sì-á* 出世子, meaning someone born locally, but perceived them as impure and corrupted. With the influx of NI, these Chinese from the mainland perceive the local Chinese whether pure Chinese or mixed breed as *chhut-sì-á* mainly because they were born and resided in this country. Some NI perceived them as *hoan- á*, because they saw them as having acquired the positivist outlook in life of the Filipino people. Joaquin Sy, a CM himself, writes,

> The typical Chinese concept of identity stresses blood relations and since Chinese mestizos are common descendants of the Chinese and Filipinos, the Chinese mestizos should feel a high degree of closeness and affinity to both races and should act as natural bonds or links in Chinese-Filipino relations. But this is not always the case. In Philippine history, the relationship of the Chinese mestizos to both the Chinese and Filipinos was not always pleasant and harmonious. In fact, there were times when such relations were characterized by varying degrees of discrimination, friction and antagonism.[146]

Sy agrees with Wickberg that the CMs during the Spanish period would have been pro-Spain, pro-Philippines, and anti-Chinese to varying degrees. And yet, the CMs are the revolutionaries and contribute to the making of the Philippine nation. Sy argues that the historical and social realities have contributed much to the Sinicization or Filipinization of the

144. See appendix J for more discussion on Chinese Mestizos during the Spanish Period.

145. Chris, CM individual interview by author, 22 July 2012.

146. Sy, "Changing Role," 121.

CMs. Therefore, it is not the bloodline that really determines ethnicity and identity but it is the situational and environmental factors that play the biggest influences.

Further, the Chinese fathers are usually absent. This leaves the Filipina mother and Roman Catholicism as the major influences in the Filipinization of the CMs in the past. Nonetheless, the establishment of Chinese schools in the late nineteenth and early twentieth century led to the Sinicization of some of the CMs. Sy adds that during this period, the more Chinese education a CM receives, the more Sinicized he/she becomes, the more he/she looks down on the Filipinos.[147]

The seventeen CMs interviewed for this category were further classified as first generation, second generation, third generation, and fourth generation. The purpose for such elaborate classification was to detect which culture would tend to remain dominant one generation after the other. What were the possible factors that contributed to the process of Sinicization, Filipinization, or hybridization which was the continuous mixing of two cultures? How did the hybrid nature affect their identities?

The following were some of the stories shared by the CM informants regarding prejudices on their hybrid nature. The fact that most CMs knew both the Minnanhua and Filipino languages was an advantage to them. Yet, there were times when the CMs experienced deep sadness as they overheard Chinese criticizing Filipinos in Minnanhua or Filipinos criticizing Chinese in Filipino.

Jennet (CM 1) confessed that she was hurting whenever she heard Chinese calling Filipinos *hoan-á* or commenting "***Kasi** hoan-á **eh** (Because they are barbarians).*" Similarly, she disliked Filipinos calling Chinese ***intsik beho*** or ***tsekwa***.

> ***Nasasaktan din ako*** (I am also hurting). ***Kasi may*** blood ***akong*** Chinese and Filipino (Because I have in me Chinese and Filipino blood). I cannot be loyal to just one. I have two kinds of blood flowing in me. We must treat all people equal, no matter what race . . . We need to be respectful because they are human beings.

> I experience being prejudiced in a Chinese class in high school. You know whenever I got home from school I will share to my sisters about my teacher. Then I find out this teacher had taught my other sisters. I cannot understand why this teacher was like

147. Ibid., 122–24.

that. She is a Christian and I study in a Christian school. When you enter the classroom, if you are a pure Chinese, you will be seated in front. If you are half Chinese, the teacher will make you sit at the back. In cases when two students are quarreling, she always sides with the pure Chinese even when this student is clearly wrong. Not fair **na** *sin-se* (Not a fair teacher). She always favors the pure Chinese. There is racial discrimination. When I met this teacher that was the time I first became aware of racial discrimination.[148]

Growing up, her mother taught all her children that they should use *Huilípin-lâng* (Filipinos) and not *hoan-á*. Her parents also taught them to be respectful and accepting of all kinds of people or races. Her father was never ashamed of the fact that he started as a **kargador** (porter) when he first came to the Philippines in 1940. He said that "**malinis na trabaho 'yan kesa magnakaw** (it is a decent job and better than to steal)." Once she shouted at their house helper, her father scolded her not to treat the house helper that way. He reminded her they were already marginalized because of the nature of their job, her treatment added to their pain.

Arian (CM 1) experienced being prejudiced by Filipinos because of his Chinese features, particularly his slanted eyes. When he was young, he and his cousin once fought some Filipinos. They accidentally hit a Filipino boy as they played with their new skateboards. Looking back, he laments,

> The boy returns with some big boys and before we know it, we are fighting on the street. **Nakakalungkot lang isipin.** (This is really sad.) The next morning, my mother found feces on our house's door knob. In the end, I am still scolded by my mother even though I am just defending myself . . . Since my features are so Chinese, that I think becomes the reason for the fight and not because of the boy got hurt . . . Filipinos will always think this is their country. As long as you look Chinese, you are not part of here. Even if you are Filipino citizen, as long as you do not look Filipino, you are not a Filipino.[149]

Chris' (CM 1) father is a Filipino and his mother is a second-generation Chinese. He experienced prejudices in the Chinese community because of his Filipino features and Filipino last name. Through the years,

---

148. Jennet, CM individual interview by author, 13 June 2012.
149. Arian, CM individual interview by author, 9 June 2012.

he learned how to answer when a Chinese asked him, "Are you Chinese?" He simply answered, "Yes." He admits,

> What I like about Chinese is that if they know you are Chinese, they will accept you. Similarly, what I do not like is that if they learn you are *hoan-á*, **yun na** negative **na** (they already have negative responses). Normally, (when people ask if I am a Chinese), it depends on who asks. If I assessed they are prejudice, I will say yes I am a Chinese. Sometimes, I say I am half but I know Minnanhua. I mostly understand the language but cannot speak fluently. **Kasi pag nalaman nila di ka makaintindi marami pa sila sinasabi.** (If they learn you cannot understand Minnanhua, they will make lots of remarks.)[150]

All seven first-generation CMs attended Chinese schools. Only two grew up in Manila Chinatown. Three were fluent in Minnanhua, and the rest can understand but cannot speak fluently.

The five second-generation CMs have no problems being mestizos. They studied in Chinese schools and four of them even grew up in Manila Chinatown. Three of them are fluent in Minnanhua, and the two can understand but have difficulty speaking. Two out of five experienced prejudices because of their physical appearances.

Casey (CM 2) has more Chinese features and she has a Chinese last name. Whenever people asked her, "Chinese **ka ba**? (Are you Chinese?)" She usually answered them that she is Chinese but just 75 percent.

> When I first enter college and people ask me, are you Chinese? I will say I am Chinese but I also have Filipino blood. It is an advantage to have Filipino blood. In college, most of the people around you are Filipinos. If you are a Chinese, they judge you and discriminate you. They will say that you Chinese dislike us Filipinos and so on. But if you have Filipino blood, you are less likely to be judged . . . My Filipino classmates like to tease my Filipino and say, "**Ba't ganun ka magsalita?** (Why do you talk like that?)" When I hear them using words like **intsik** or **intsik beho**, I will tell them in a polite way that that is not nice.[151]

In spite of being discriminated against, Casey had many Filipino friends in college. She was able to mingle with them and establish good relationships with them.

150. Chris, CM individual interview by author, 22 July 2012.
151. Casey, CM individual interview by author, 10 June 2012.

Steven (CM 2) has a very dark complexion. Having a Chinese surname, people often asked if he is a Chinese. He observed,

> In college, sometimes the Chinese are still singled-out and discriminated. I am not discriminated **kasi di naman ako mukhang** Chinese (because I do not look like a Chinese). [Laughter] Sometimes, my (college) professors will ask if I am a Chinese because of my Chinese last name. But I am never discriminated by Filipinos. I am discriminated at times because of my physical features in the Chinese community and even in the Chinese church. I kinda feel I am an outcast because of my looks in the Chinese community and even in the Chinese church. But since I am attending this church for a long time already, they know me and I do not feel that way anymore. In the beginning, it is really hard (to be accepted).[152]

Lani's (CM 2) father is a second-generation Chinese and her mother is a first-generation CM. Her maternal grandmother is a Spanish Mestiza who married a pure Chinese. When she entered college, she experienced culture shock. Although her Minnanhua was not very good, she grew up in the Chinese community and attended Chinese high school. So she identified herself as Chinese rather than Filipino. She had difficulty relating with her Filipino classmates. She discovered that they were very different in how they do things, especially on handling money. She begged her father to help her transfer to a Chinese college because she felt out of place.

Nadine (CM 2) is fluent in Minnanhua. She studied in a Chinese high school and graduated in a Chinese college. She presently works in a Chinese school and spends most of her time within the Chinese community. Like Nadine, Benson (CM 2) is limited within the Chinese community. His fluency in Minnanhua made him very Chinese; but his fluency in Filipino and physical features made him very Filipino.

The five third-generation CM informants have no issues with discrimination or prejudice. Could it be that this is indication of diminishing prejudices on hybrids? Is it possible that in this global age, people are more accepting and less discriminating? Or is it, because four of the five informants are still studying in Chinese high schools, they are less exposed to the predominant Filipino community? Joshua and Rick are both studying in Chinese schools and very fluent in Minnanhua. Both of their

152. Steven, CM individual interview by author, 15 July 2012.

fathers are second-generation CMs who married Chinese women; both their *a-má* (paternal grandmothers) are CMs who married Chinese men.

Harry (CM 3) and Hal (CM 3) have a half Indonesian and half Filipino father. Their paternal grandfather is half Dutch and half Indonesian. Their paternal grandmother is a Filipina. Their mother is a second-generation CM. Their *gōa-má* (maternal grandmother) is a first-generation CM while *gōa-kong* (maternal grandfather) was a Chinese. They used to attend a Chinese school but recently transferred to a Filipino private high school because it provides better training in science and math education. The twins like the new school better than the Chinese school because they do not have to attend Chinese classes. They could understand Minnanhua but could only speak a little. They did not have difficulty mingling with their Filipino classmates. They considered themselves Filipinos.

Carding (CM 3) is the only third-generation CM informant who had totally cut off ties with his Chinese relatives. He grew up within the Filipino community. He never brought out the issue that he was a *mestizo*. Although he worked in a Chinese company, he never revealed to his employer or fellow employees about his Chinese ancestry. He saw himself just Filipino. Sy points that,

> Before the (Second World War) war, the Chinese mestizos were looked down upon in the Chinese community, but in the larger Philippine society, they were generally accepted as Filipinos and no longer existed and acted as a distinct social class or group. On the other hand, some Sinicized mestizos chose to be considered as Chinese and acted as such in the Chinese community, without necessarily advertising their being mestizos. This seemed to show that at that time, the Chinese mestizos had made their choice. Either they chose to be Chinese and stay with the Chinese community, or decided to be Filipinos and totally integrated into the mainstream of Philippine society.[153]

Language in the Hybrid Home

"Chinese (language) is confined in the (Chinese) school, **pag-uwi** no more (when you get home we no longer speak in Chinese)... Even in school, (we) speak Tagalog (Filipino)." —Billy[154]

---

153. Sy, "Changing Role," 124. I believe Sy means assimilated though he uses the term integrated.

154. Billy, CM individual interview by author, 4 July 2012.

Language is an important factor in determining whether a CM is Sinicized or Filipinized. The ability to speak and/or understand Minnanhua is crucial for one to engage in a conversation, socialize, or develop deep relationships with the people in the Chinese community. Conversely, the ability to speak and/or understand Filipino is important to socialize or build relationships in a Filipino community. Language is a significant marker of ethnicity. It enables one to participate and be accepted in a community. Yet language is progressive. It continues to change and evolve. It borrows words or produces new words. Rarely used words can eventually become extinct.

Peter Burke names the Philippines as his example of linguistic borrowing and linguistic hybridity. He contends that mixed languages today have gained respectability.[155] The phenomena of multiple languages present in a conversation among the Chinese Filipinos is proof of cultural hybridity at work. The EngChiLog (English, Chinese and Tagalog), TagLish (Tagalog and English), ChiLish (Chinese and English), or ChiLog (Chinese and Tagalog) combinations in communication are examples of hybrid languages. The interviews are evidences of how they mix two or three languages at the same time during conversations.

Out of the seventeen CMs informants, only eight speak Minnanhua at home. The rest used Filipino. These eight CMs are able to speak fluent Minnanhua mainly because the Chinese or CM parent used the language to talk with them. The first-generation CMs usually encountered a dilemma with the language since one of the parents is a Filipino. The tendency is to use Filipino at home since the Filipina mother is usually the one taking care of the children while the Chinese fathers worked. None of the six Filipina mothers of the first-generation CMs speaks Minnanhua, although four of them can understand the language. Only Chris' Filipino father learned to speak a little Minnanhua. No wonder that only three out of seven first-generation CMs can speak fluent Minnanhua.

The second-, third-, and fourth-generation CMs can further their Sinicization or Filipinization depending on the ethnicity of the spouse they choose. Such is the case for the five CMs who are fluent in Minnanhua. Their CM parents opted to marry Chinese spouses that aid in the propagation of the Chinese language and culture in the home. The Chinese schools may help in the Sinicization process by providing Chinese classes or the setting that provides opportunities for socializing with

155. Burke, *Cultural Hybridity*, 46.

other Chinese students. But this is still not a guarantee that the children will become fluent in Minnanhua or Putonghua. Seventeen informants attended Chinese schools, yet only eight were fluent in Minnanhua. Nevertheless, it was the conscious decision and desire of the individual to choose to learn and employ whatever language and culture. Such was the case of Darla (CM 1) who chose to learn Minnanhua said,

> Actually, papa is not strict when we keep on speaking in Filipino. We ourselves (siblings) want to speak Chinese. I married a pure Chinese and that has all the more helped me speak Minnanhua. Also, my work here (Chinese company) makes me speak Chinese. My father is okay with us talking to him in Tagalog. He emphasizes more on us being good citizens, maintain a good name (integrity), and be content with what you have . . . Mama knows the word *kàw* 狗 which means dog. One time, she thought we are cursing her and calling her a dog. I told her that we are just counting and saying *kāw* 九 or nine.[156]

Joshua (CM 3) and Rick (CM 3) have their parents to thank for making sure they learn and speak Minnanhua. They are fluent in Minnanhua, English, and Filipino. Joshua and Rick shared that they speak Minnanhua at home and English in school. Joshua added that he speaks Filipino with their house helper. Rick knew a little Bisaya[157] and enjoyed learning different languages.

Arian regretted he was not able to speak Minnanhua fluently.

> One thing we blame our father is that he never enforced us to speak in Minnanhua . . . He (Father) argues that it is the responsibility of the Chinese school to teach us how to speak in Hokkien. Further, if we speak in Hokkien, this may create conflict with my mother.[158]

Lani also blamed her father for failing to teach her and speak to her in Minnanhua. At home, her CM mother preferred Filipino as well. In her father's viewpoint, it is enough that he sent them to a Chinese school where they should have learned the language.

In this context, there are at least two avenues wherein a person can learn Minnanhua: (1) through the parents who speak the language with

156. Darla, CM individual interview by author, 4 July 2012.

157. *Bisaya* is the dialect spoken in the Visayan and Mindanao areas of the Philippines. Rick's mother is a Chinese Filipino from Mindanao.

158. Arian, CM individual interview by author, 9 June 2012.

children at home, and (2) by studying in a Chinese school. Further, a third avenue depends on the will factor. The Chinese schools cannot force the students to speak Minnanhua since not all are also able to. Most Chinese schools actually teach Putonghua not Minnanhua. The students use Minnanhua only when fellow students will converse with them in that language. However, most CMs and even Tsinoy informants claim that they use English and/or Filipino when talking with their classmates in school. Steven shared that when he was still a student in a Chinese high school, nobody spoke Minnanhua anymore. Also, some parents prefer that their children learn Putonghua instead of Minnanhua. The younger generation Chinese whether Tsinoys or CMs, employed trilingual EngChiLog (English, Chinese, and Tagalog). Still others preferred just Filipino, like Chris. He narrated,

> Mother speaks to us in Hokkien (Minnanhua). We just listen but still reply in Tagalog (Filipino). My father can understand Hokkien and speak a little Hokkien. We, the children, **bihirang-bihira mag-Hokkien** (rarely speak in Hokkien) . . . Tagalog is my heart language.[159]

Jennet's Chinese father was actively involved in his children learning Minnanhua. Her Filipina mother made a conscious effort to help her children learn the Chinese language and culture by hiring a Chinese tutor.

> Papa speaks to us in Chinese and mama in Tagalog. No issues. Papa said he speaks to us in Hokkien so we will learn the language. He never gets mad in teaching us. He is very gentle and patient. He uses stories to teach us Hokkien. His methods make us respectful to him, not negative . . . As much as my father wants to teach us Chinese, he is always busy with work. My mother hires a Chinese tutor to help us in our Chinese subjects.[160]

Most of the informants admitted that their Chinese fathers were usually absent because of work, leaving them with Filipina mothers. So they are not exposed much to the Chinese language. Billy admitted he had difficulty learning the language while growing up.

> Growing up, my father wants us to speak *lanlâng ōe la* (Minnanhua). But since our environment is usually Filipino, **nahirapan**

159. Chris, CM individual interview by author, 22 July 2012.
160. Jennet, CM individual interview by author, 13 June 2012.

din kami (we have difficulty speaking Minnanhua). Once we go out of the house, our playmates are Filipinos. Naturally, we speak more Filipino than *lanlâng ōe*.[161]

His father sent all six children to Chinese school hoping they could learn Minnanhua. However, even his Chinese or CM classmates speak mostly Filipino. His youngest sister is the only one who became fluent in Minnanhua. Looking back, Billy believed that his sister's Chinese friends in high school influenced her in speaking Minnanhua. Friends and environment are two other factors in enforcing or losing a language. Fely (CM 1) found herself losing her ability to speak Minnanhua because she rarely used it. She observed her children are also losing their Minnanhua because they live in an environment that is predominantly Filipinos, "*khe kong hoan-á ōe, khe kong hoan-á ōe la*. (They keep on speaking Filipino, they keep on speaking Filipino.)"

Growing up, papa speaks in Chinese. His Tagalog is terrible. Mama speaks to us in Tagalog. My Minnanhua is not *malalim* (deep). Especially now that I live in a Filipino community, my Minnanhua is disappearing. It comes back when I speak with Chinese . . . Mother understands Hokkien but never speaks it even though they were married for many years.[162]

All of the CM informants are very fluent in Filipino but only eight are fluent in Minnanhua. Among those who were not fluent in Minnanhua, five could still converse fairly well with the language since they understood the language though they preferred to speak in Filipino. Three can understand very little Minnanhua and only one does not know the language. Most OIs and older Tsinoys tend to consider a CM as Chinese or Sinicized based on their ability to speak and/or understand the language. Therefore, the language had more weight and emphasis in relation to culture more than the skin color or physical features. But learning a language was not easy. It takes determination and will.

---

161. Billy, CM individual interview by author, 4 July 2012.
162. Fely, CM individual interview by author, 15 July 2012.

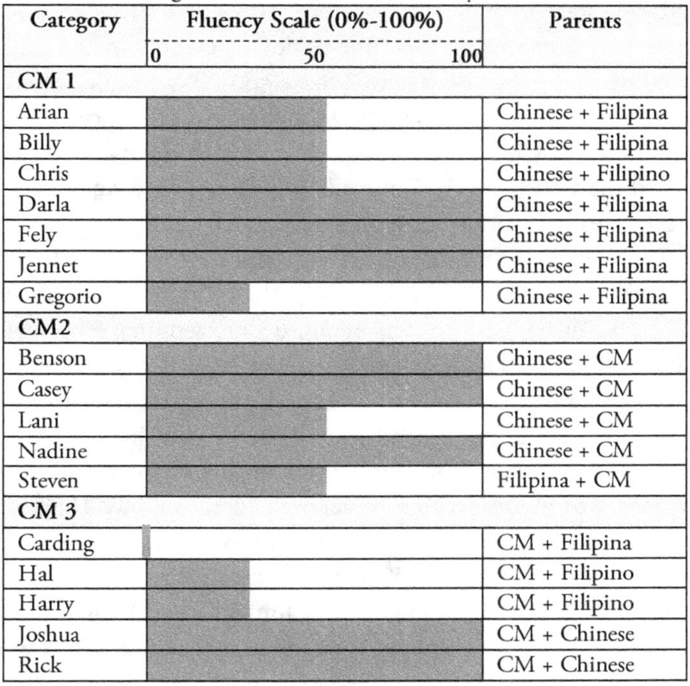

Category	Fluency Scale (0%-100%)			Parents
	0	50	100	
CM 1				
Arian				Chinese + Filipina
Billy				Chinese + Filipina
Chris				Chinese + Filipino
Darla				Chinese + Filipina
Fely				Chinese + Filipina
Jennet				Chinese + Filipina
Gregorio				Chinese + Filipina
CM2				
Benson				Chinese + CM
Casey				Chinese + CM
Lani				Chinese + CM
Nadine				Chinese + CM
Steven				Filipina + CM
CM 3				
Carding				CM + Filipina
Hal				CM + Filipino
Harry				CM + Filipino
Joshua				CM + Chinese
Rick				CM + Chinese

Figure 3. Minnanhua Fluency Scale

CONCLUSION

Chu believes that in analyzing CM identity, "it is important to examine the intersections of class, gender, religious, generational, and ethnic identities."[163] He studied mostly the lives of prominent and rich Chinese merchants and their offspring through inter-ethnic marriages with *indias* and Chinese Mestizas. He discovers that the rich Chinese or Chinese Mestizo merchants of Manila during the late nineteenth century practiced what he calls social endogamy or marrying within your class. This was to ensure that the wealth will be confined within one's family or increase one's social status. He adds the need to study the familial structures whether the father had more than one wife. Bigamy and polygamy were practiced by rich Chinese merchants.[164] Chu claims that

163. Chu, *Chinese and Chinese Mestizos*, 275.

164. The wife in China was usually left to take care of the husband's aging parents and ensure posterity. The wife in Manila could be a Chinese but at this time period,

Sinicization rather than Hispanization remained stronger among the Chinese and CMs during this time period as evident in the continuous inter-ethnic marriages between Chinese and CMs from one generation to another. Again, the CM mothers might have influenced the sons to intermarry with CMs rather than *indias* as they themselves were more Sinicized than Hispanized. Chu calls this the "slowed down" process of Chinese "mestizo-ization" or indigenization.[165]

Chu's idea of social endogamy is useful for this research because it strengthens the results from the data gathered that the CMs who married Chinese or CM spouses will be more Sinicized than Filipinized. This research did not study the class issues but did discover that six out of ten second- and third-generation CMs interviewed have one Chinese parent. These six families send their children to Chinese schools and employ Minnanhua at home though in varying degrees. All six of these informants see themselves more Chinese than Filipino. The other four CM informants have one Filipino parent or in the case of Harry and Hal, a Filipino-Indonesian parent. They see themselves as more Filipino since their knowledge in Minnanhua is very limited even though three out of four studied in Chinese schools. Carding totally cannot speak or understand Minnanhua and cut off ties with the Chinese side of the family. Interestingly, Steven is now more Sinicized with his involvement in the Chinese church and working in a Chinese company. He is learning Minnanhua through his church and workplace.

Halley's (CM 5) genealogy reveals that her ancestors did continually marry Chinese spouses that enhanced further the Sinicization process. This is Resinification through endogamy. Hence, Halley is very Chinese looking and very fluent in Minnanhua. Halley's maternal great great grandmother was a Spanish Mestiza who married a pure Chinese. This made her great grandmother a Chinese Mestiza (CM) who also married a pure Chinese. Her grandmother then was a third-generation CM who again married a pure Chinese. This made her mother a fourth-generation CM who, in her turn, married a pure Chinese. Halley's case confirms

---

it was usually a CM. The CM wife usually provided an important role for the Chinese merchant with her knowledge and network in both Chinese and Hispanic cultures. Chu believes that these CM wives were very much influenced by their Chinese fathers or possible CM mothers, hence, they were mostly abled in doing business. In his research, 49 out of 69 CM wives were proprietresses. Ibid., 266–68.

165. Ibid., 269–70. Chu includes a statistical data that shows the Chinese men's preference for CMs than *indias*.

Chu's theory of "slowed down" Chinese "mestizo-ization" or I will simply call it "slowed down" Filipinization or hybridization for this context.

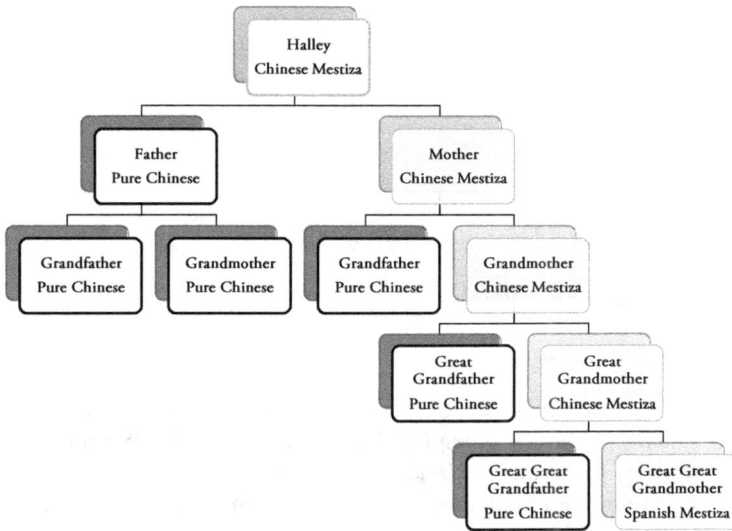

Figure 4. Resinification through Endogamy

I concluded that there are five factors that influence the development of ethnic identity or the Sinicization or Filipinization process: (1) Parent/s; (2) School; (3) Friends; (4) Environment or Location: (5) Will factor. Sinicization, Filipinization, Resinification, and hybridization are then social cultural constructs that people (most of the time) intentionally and consciously build in their lives that reveal their understanding of their identities and cultural leanings. However, people may also unintentionally or unconsciously apply cultural elements as they go about their lives or as they face situations and make decisions along the way which cultures to adapt or adopt. The CM will be more Sinicized if one identified more with one's Chinese heritage or Chineseness and more Filipinized when identified with one's Filipinoness.

5

Hybridity or Homogeneity:
Analyzing the Tsinoy Ethnic Identity

"When people ask us if we are *Tiong Kok Lâng* (Chinese), we usually say we are *Tiong Kok Lâng*. But the *Huakiao* (Sojourners) are different. The *Huakiao* are *Tiong Kok Lâng* who came to live in the Philippines. At present, the Philippines is a poor country and has no money. Our status as *Huakiao* also downgraded. Today, when we go abroad as overseas Chinese from the Philippines, people looked down on us. The standard changes, earlier times it was not like that. For example, between Chinese people from different geographic locations. During those times when the Philippines was still rich, the government was very rich, when we as Philippine overseas Chinese went abroad, we were very much welcomed in Taiwan. But now, the Philippine overseas Chinese go to Taiwan to work and earn money. This time it is different, they now look down on you. They see you as nothing. Your status changed. Times are changing. The same Chinese in different time periods have different outcomes." —Milo[1]

RYNKIEWICH POSITS THE IMPORTANCE of looking into the sociocultural constructs to understand the different factors that lead to the development of one's identity or an ethnic identity, because for him, culture is not static. As times changes, culture also changes, and with it, the people. He reminds the readers to be critical of sensational news about "Stone Age" people who are said to have never changed.

1. Milo, Tsinoy individual interview by author, 23, June 2012.

Everybody changes all the time, though the rate of change differs from people to people. All people have a local history, including a variety of traditions that come from the ancestors and are deployed to shape the future. In addition, there is interaction over space. These people, whoever they are, are not completely isolated, even if they live on an island. They have had and continue to have encounters with other people marked by cooperation and conflict, and linked in a web of exchange, and thus in a network that includes the diffusion of innovations. So, although the culture, society, ecology and history of a people constitute a local system, that system is also part of a larger system of social relations.[2]

Various elements conditioned by one's historical setting affect the development and construction of the behavior, status, and identity of an individual, and ultimately, the group/society. Elements such as the culture, society, and ecology are crucial in acquiring a "more complete model for explaining people's way of life or even a multicultural community."[3] Consequently, these elements also lead to different responses of other people toward a particular group and different outcomes in different periods of history.

Anthropology and other social sciences have long been asking questions focusing on the individual as influenced by the Enlightenment Period. However, the assumptions concerning the individual are givens and have not been examined or questioned adequately. Rynkiewich writes that only recently has anthropology begun to examine the cultural assumptions about what a person is or how a person is constructed in a society. Since people change as their culture changes, their identities and statuses also change within their society. These in turn affect the perceptions of the other people around them. The postmodern culture is contingent, constructed, and contested.[4]

2. Rynkiewich, *Soul, Self, and Society*, 65.

3. Questions such as, "Given the existence of an individual, for example, a baby just born, how does that person grow to become a member of society? What are the developmental steps? What are the pitfalls? What happens when things go right and the person is socialized? What happens when things go wrong and the person becomes a deviant? How can the individual negotiate society's attempt to proscribe behavior and make the individual conform to society's norms?" Rynkiewich, *Soul, Self, and Society*, 66.

4. Ibid., 38–39, 64–65, 77.

Milo shared the reality that the present Chinese Filipinos are often regarded as inferior by many Taiwanese since they no longer go there as tourists, students, or compatriots but rather as factory workers and employees seeking a better salary and future. As times change, statuses and identities also change along with culture, society, ecology and politics. Rynkiewich poses the challenge of continuing studies and research on what is a person; understanding how a person constructs his or her own identity and how one develops one's social relations and many other roles in life. He believes that anthropology has not yet fully probed this topic and missiology has completely ignored it.[5]

Below is an attempt to discover the identity of the present Chinese Filipinos.[6] The gospel message can be more effectively shared and presented if we understand who they are. Such understanding also aids in the contextualization of the Scripture for the present generation. As Schreiter writes,

> Culture has become an increasingly important category for understanding the world and the construction of theologies. The first generation of contextual theologies used integrated concepts of culture to help assert local identity, and integrated concepts continue to be very useful in this regard. At the same time, the mixing of cultures today requires additional approaches. The fact of this mixing, and the new hybridities it is forming, probably explain why cultural analysis seems to be gaining ground over social analysis in much of the literature today. In a multipolar world, one cannot assume that the social structures are all the same, or that they are perceived in the same fashion.[7]

Studying culture in juxtaposition with the present changing world is undoubtedly important. However, this study focuses primarily on

5. Ibid., 67.

6. See also chapter 1 on Research Problem and Research Questions.

7. Robert Schreiter points that the integrated concepts of culture has dominated both sociology and anthropology since these disciplines started. He defines integrated concepts of culture as "patterned systems in which the various elements are coordinated in such a fashion as to create a unified whole." Schreiter observes that this concept of culture characterized the traditional society that is self-enclosed, self-sufficient, and governed by a rule-bound tradition. This corresponds to those societies that lived "fairly contented lives in their culture" that they do not bother to venture outside their boundaries. Nevertheless, such thinking and understanding is no longer applicable to our present globalized deterritorialized world. Schreiter, *New Catholicity*, 47–49, 60–61.

cultural hybridity and how this affects the identity of the Chinese Filipinos as an ethnic minority. By understanding their identity and culture, this study aims to help the Chinese churches in their evangelism and discipleship ministries of the Chinese Filipinos.

In this chapter, I will discuss the following issues. First, I will explore the questions concerning the self-perception of Chinese Filipinos. Do they see themselves as homogenous purist or cultural hybrids? Second, I will discuss the possibility of Sinification, Filipinization, and Resinification. Third, I will investigate whether the Chinese Filipinos are integrated or assimilated. Fourth, I will examine the nature of cultural hybridity of the Chinese Filipinos today. The purpose of all this is to see whether the hybridity of the Chinese Filipinos is compartmentalized (or what Robbins calls "mixed yet unmixed") or whether it is fused that produces a third culture. This portion will also review whether their cultural hybridity exhibits the characteristics of Bhabha's unhomely and third space theories and/or Barth's situational theory. Finally, based on the above analysis, an assessment will be made whether the Chinese Filipinos themselves are primordialist or constructivist.

ARE THE CHINESE FILIPINOS HOMOGENOUS PURISTS OR CULTURAL HYBRIDS?

> "We are mixed already. We are affected by our everyday life. *Yung* everyday *niya na naranasan, nakagawian, ginagawa, masasanay ka na … Maski pa sabihin na mahirap mag-*adjust, *masasanay ka rin kasi.*" (The everyday experiences, habits, chores, you will get used to them. Even though you will have difficulty adjusting, you will get used to them eventually.)
> —Benjie[8]

Benjie believes that the Chinese Filipinos are cultural hybrids because they are constantly affected by the different situations and the changes happening around them as they live in this country. He also believes that all humans have the ability to adapt to different situations. I began this research with the question whether the Chinese Filipinos see themselves as culturally pure or culturally hybrid. Based on the informants' responses, I conclude that many already see themselves as cultural hybrids. However, there are still some who see themselves as purists.

---

8. Benjie, Tsinoy individual interview by author, 21, July 2012.

In this study, I use the term "homogenous purist" to refer to the Chinese Filipinos who still perceive themselves as Chinese in culture and hope to preserve the purity of their bloodline. In contrast are the cultural hybrids or those whose cultural practice and/or bloodline are no longer pure but "tainted."

As mentioned in appendix K, Tracing Chinese Ethnocentrism, Edward Schafer refers to Lu Chun as a zealous ethnic puritan who banned inter-ethnic marriage in China and promoted segregation in AD 836.[9] Also discussed is the ethnocentric tendencies of the Chinese as evident in the writings of Chao Ju-Kua when he referred to non-Chinese as barbarians.[10] The homogenous purist tends to see oneself as having or practicing Chinese culture similar to those Chinese in China, Taiwan, or Hong Kong. They believe they still retain the purity of their ethnicity and bloodline through endogamy. They also classify Chineseness or Chinese culture according to the physical features; residence, association, and participation with other Chinese; Chinese education; usage of Chinese languages like Minnanhua, Cantonese, and/or Putonghua; and/or practices of endogamy, filial piety, ancestral worship, Confucian values, Buddhism, and Daoism. They see themselves as traditionalists and conservatives. They may or may not have ethnocentric tendencies.

The majority of the Old and New Immigrants (Adults) I interviewed show characteristic of a homogenous purists because of the following reasons. First, they see themselves essentially Chinese only. This is evident in their usage primarily of Minnanhua in conversation and Putonghua for writing and reading although a number are fluent in English. They are actively engaged or connected with the Chinese community. They still adhere to endogamy, filial piety, and other Chinese cultural practices and beliefs. They are all immigrants or former immigrants posing their affinity to China as homeland, particularly for the NI. Many of the OIs and even NIs, whether with Filipino or Chinese citizenship, already consider the Philippines as their present home and country. Nonetheless, they still insist they are Chinese in terms of culture. Second, as immigrants, especially the NIs who recently arrived, their Chineseness has not been tainted or influenced by the dominant culture.

The NIs surprisingly find the Chinese Filipinos as essentially Chinese, especially the older generation or OIs. They appreciate how the

9. Schafer, *Golden Peaches*, 20–22.

10. Chao, *Chu-Fan-Chï*, 159–62. See also Scott, *Prehispanic Source Materials*, 71n 18, 73.

Chinese Filipinos preserve the Chinese culture in the areas of festivities, language, marriage, and family. However, the NIs see the young Tsinoys as more Filipinized or Westernized in terms of language and thinking. As Peter says, they are like bananas, yellow on the outside but white inside. The OIs also see the Tsinoys as hybrids, some in terms of culture, and others because of their bloodline with inter-ethnic marriages. Interestingly, a number of second-generation older Tsinoys still see themselves as Chinese only. There are NIs who see the Tsinoys as *hoan-á*. The younger NIs, however, see themselves as hybrids (bi-cultural or multi-cultural) because they cannot evade the Western influences anymore.

The cultural hybrids, in contrast, are those Chinese Filipinos who have recognized the inevitable exchanges of cultural elements and/or inter-ethnic marriages in this global and migratory age. Many see themselves as essentially Chinese with Chinese culture as the dominant culture but also practicing other culture/s. Those who see themselves essentially Chinese believe they are pure in terms of bloodline but not culture. Those who see themselves as hybrid in bloodline all the more see themselves as hybrid in culture. Some CMs call themselves "half-half" or "50-50". This label indicates, not only their bloodline, but also their cultural practices at homes. They are biracial or bicultural. The spouses in inter-ethnic marriages find themselves either Sinicized, hybridized, or Filipinized.

The Tsinoys, CMs, and even some OIs can no longer evade the reality of hybridization. They all find the present Chinese culture to have been influenced by the Filipino culture after living for a period of time in the Philippines. They also see Western influences, in particular the American culture, in education, choice of entertainment, and in their preferences and consumption of goods. The colonial mentality remains strong among the present Filipinos and Chinese Filipinos.[11] This is largely because the medium of instruction in the country is English and many of the books used are from the United States. It is unavoidable for many Filipinos and Chinese Filipinos to be exposed to American literature and culture. Not to mention the American pop culture, both in music and Hollywood movies, which are widely accepted and patronized by both Filipinos and Chinese Filipinos. Arjun Appadurai notes that the Filipinos

---

11. E. J. R. David defines colonial mentality as a perceived ethnic or cultural inferiority with centuries of colonialism under Spain and the United States that result in "automatic and uncritical rejection of anything Filipino and an automatic and uncritical preference of anything American." David, *Filipino-American Postcolonial Psychology*, 85.

can render perfect American music. This shows their affinity and patronage to American entertainment.[12]

Among the cultural hybrids, some cannot say that they are "pure" Chinese in bloodline because they cannot know for sure their ancestral tree or lineage. Their inability to speak pure Minnanhua, Cantonese, or Putonghua sometimes cause shame and sadness. They regret not taking seriously their Chinese education. Some OIs even forecast the eventual extinction of Minnanhua and the inevitable increase of the use of Putonghua among the Tsinoys. They struggle with the idea of calling a person *lanlâng* (Chinese) when he/she cannot speak *lanlâng ōe* (literally, "Chinese language," in this context referring to the Minnanhua).

The cultural hybrids may be fluent in one or more Chinese languages but, usually, they borrow many terms from both Filipino and English. Their transitional words in conversations are often in Filipino, words such as **kasi** (because), **basta** (as long as/provided), **sayang** (unfortunately), **tsaka** (also), and **pero** (but). There are times using Minnanhua will best express their thoughts, and at other times, Filipino or English is best. The trilingual usage is common among the Tsinoys. EngChiLog and EnRAWGen are realities they cannot escape. They feel powerless in maintaining an untainted Chinese culture. The second-, third-, fourth-, or fifth-generation Chinese may have difficulty defining the Chinese culture; partly because they are lost as to which country should be their point of reference: China, Taiwan, Hong Kong, or other Chinese in Southeast Asia.

Aside from external influences, both local and international, the politics and sociological circumstances throughout Philippine history have forced them to adapt and even adopt different identities or cultures to survive and thrive in this country. When the 1975 Mass Naturalization Law was enacted, many Chinese changed their citizenship to Filipino, giving their loyalty to the Philippines. When the kidnapping of Chinese Filipinos was at its peak in the 1990s, many protested resulting in the creation of the Movement for Restoration of Peace and Order and the Citizens Action Against Crime. The Tsinoys rallied against kidnappings and criminality. Teresita Ang See became well known as an anti-kidnapping advocate.[13]

12. Appadurai, *Modernity At Large*, 29.

13. It was in the wake of Charlene Sy in 1993 that Teresita Ang See became an anti-kidnapping advocate. Charlene was a fifteen-year-old high school student kidnapped on her way to school. Unfortunately, she was killed as the police exchanged fire with her abductors. Prior to this, the kidnap-murder case of two teenagers Kenneth Go and

For the homogenous purists, homogeneity and hybridity clash. Nevertheless, the OIs admitted that the social changes and forces of the present world are too strong, against which even a strong desire to maintain cultural purity is not enough to compete. The cultural hybrids do not see homogeneity and hybridity as mutually exclusive. They serve as proofs of this possibility, ones whose ethnic identity is Chinese but whose loyalty is to the Philippines. They are Chinese by ethnicity and Filipinos by nationality. Their cultural practices remains primarily Chinese, but have mixed with some Filipino and other cultures. This raises the question: can one consider this as homogeneity and hybridity at the same time? Or is this a form of hybridity, but having one dominant cultural influence?

The Chinese Filipinos today are predominantly cultural hybrids with the Chinese culture and/or language remaining dominant. The degree to which this is true varies, as some of the younger generation tend to employ English only or Filipino only in conversation, although many remain fluent in Minnanhua. The degree of dominance can be illustrated as a bar with two poles. The end of one pole is Chinese and the end of the other pole is Filipino. The center represents equal mixing or hybridization. The degree of Chineseness or Sinicization and the degree of Filipinoness or Filipinization often depends on the influences surrounding the person.

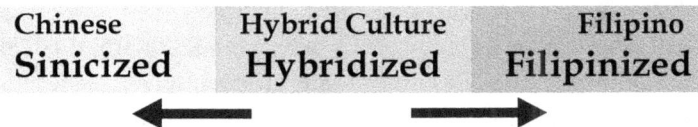

Figure 5. Culture Scale on the Degree of Dominance

Myron Uy Ramos caused a lot of rage and fear to the Chinese community. They were abducted in Binondo, the very heart of the Chinese community. Moreover, they were terribly tortured even after the huge ransom was paid to the kidnappers. The reason for the torture and murder was to send out a clear message by the kidnappers to the Philippine National Police (PNP) official who had tried to cut into the ransom payment that they needed to back off. See, "Long Wait." It is no wonder that the Chinese Filipinos would rather keep silent and not report to the police for fear of the lives of their loved ones. Kidnapping cases seem to have lessened at present or probably they are not reported.

Murat Bayar's article "Reconsidering Primordialism" proposes the theory of ethnic distance as a variable in understanding the level of integration of immigrants. He explains ethnic distance as "the degree to which two ethnic identities have been solidified as opposed to each other and hypothesizes that the higher the ethnic distance between immigrants and the host society the lower the level of integration, holding other things constant."[14] I will take this up again in more detail in the last part of the chapter.

SINIFICATION, FILIPINIZATION, OR RESINIFICATION

> "Dominant culture (at home)? Chinese *pa rin* (Chinese still). 60 to 75 percent Chinese. My mom is the one who adjusted. She became close to my *a-má* (grandma). *A-má* is very Chinese. My mom is the one who adjusted." —Arian[15]

Arian is the youngest among three siblings. His family speaks Filipino at home since his mother is a Filipina. But they were all sent to Chinese school. He reminisced about being comfortable enough growing up in the Chinese community that when he moved into the Filipino community as he entered college he experienced culture shock. He gauged his family's Chineseness on the middle of the bar. However he believes that, in terms of values and character molding, he and his siblings are more Chinese than Filipino. He admitted that his Minnanhua is not good. If he were fluent, he thinks he would be more Sinicized.

As I have explained in the part 3 of chapter 4, the process of Sinicization, Filipinization, or Resinification is an intentional construction of one's culture and identity. This intentional construction not only applies to the spouses of inter-ethnic marriages or Chinese Mestizos, but to all Chinese Filipinos. Sinicization, Filipinization, or Resinification will not just happen for the Chinese Filipinos being an ethnic minority. The process requires, to a certain degree, conscious effort on their part to decide which cultural elements must be transferred, negotiated, compromised, or discarded. Although a conscious decision is not possible at all times, usually their decisions will determine on which pole of the bar they will lean to.

Schreiter discusses in his book *The New Catholicity* that as globalization homogenizes the world, paradoxically, there is also the heightening

14. Bayar, "Reconsidering Primordialism," 1651–52.

15. Arian, CM individual interview by author, 9 June 2012.

of the particular. He then lays out three cultural logics that contradict globalization and homogenizing of culture:[16] Antiglobalism, Ethnification, and Primitivism. His idea of ethnification is similar to the phenomenon of Sinicization, Filipinization, and Resinification. Schreiter defines ethnification as

> the process of rediscovering a forgotten identity based on one's cultural ties. It is about the assertion of local identity, especially amid the experience of social change and cultural instability . . . Establishing ethnic identity, then, is rarely an easy task. Mixing or hybridization is normally the actual case; purity in identity is hard to come by.[17]

Schreiter recognizes that ethnification gives rise to contextual theologies as this process focuses directly on one particular minority. For this reason, I see the importance of understanding the present cultural inclination of the Chinese Filipinos as well as how they perceive their identity. The ethnification among the Chinese Filipinos is the assertion of the Chinese culture as the dominant culture in the midst of the many other cultures competing for their patronage. Here I have traced the development of the Chinese culture or particularly the "Chinese Filipino culture" through different channels and avenues like integration, endogamy, language, and education.

INTEGRATION OR ASSIMILATION

> "The Yuyitung Brothers were the pioneer advocates of the integration process of the Chinese Filipinos before Chinben See and the Kaisa. They were the Chinese Commercial News chief and publisher." —Jimmy[18]

Senator Joker Arroyo wrote an article as tribute to the Yuyitung brothers who fought for the integration of the Chinese Filipinos.[19] They sought

16. The homogenization in globalization must not be confused with the homogenous purists as discussed already. In globalization, homogeneity is the idea of having one world culture similar to McDonaldization or Cocalization. However, the homogenous purists for this study refers to a particular ethnic minority who seeks to maintain their culture as they live in a country with a different dominant culture.

17. Schreiter, *New Catholicity*, 21–27.

18. Jimmy, OI individual interview by author, 4 July 2012.

19. Arroyo actually writes "assimilation." But based on the interviews of OIs about the Yuyitung brothers, I believe they were adhering to integration.

Filipino citizenship yet were denied. They encouraged the Philippine government to recognize China as the legitimate Chinese government contrary to the Cold War propaganda. Rizal and Quintin Yuyitung were two brave men who fought against giants of their time. They were journalists living in the Philippines where the United States had a foothold and Communism was considered an enemy. They were regarded as advocates against the ideals of the pro-GMD Chinese community at that time. They fought against bureaucracy and red tape in government as they sought citizenship for the Chinese in the country, and against Marcos and his fear of Communism as well as for freedom of the press. They were imprisoned and deported to Taiwan for trial, then sentenced to jail in 1970. Arroyo, who once was Rizal Yuyitung's attorney, called these two ideal Filipinos. In his words,

> But it is thanks to the Yuyitung brothers, as the tandem came to be famously known, that Filipino-Chinese have come to be regarded unstintingly by all Filipinos as true brothers beneath their differing complexions and accents. For these two ethnic Chinese brothers had demonstrated their indisputable fraternity with Filipinos less by a superficial commonality of blood as by their profound willingness to sacrifice everything for the freedom of all Filipinos.[20]

Because of the Yuyitung brothers, Marcos developed the idea of administrative naturalization versus the long and often corrupt legal naturalization.[21] The sacrifices of these brothers bore fruit to the advantage of the present 90 percent of Chinese holding Filipino citizenship. The acquisition of Filipino citizenship enable the Chinese Filipinos to move out of the crowded Manila Chinatown and hence, help in the development of the different suburbs in Metro Manila as they build houses, schools, churches, businesses, hospitals, and many other institutions.[22] The Chinese Filipino community has a lot to thank the Yuyitung Brothers for, as well as all those who have helped in the integration process.

As the Kaisa emphasizes, the Chinese Filipinos seek integration into mainstream Filipino society but still want to maintain their Chinese culture. Yet the interviews gathered show that there were Chinese Filipinos

---

20. Arroyo, "Rizal Yuyitung."

21. Ibid.

22. Guéguen, "Moving from Binondo," 124–25.

who through inter-ethnic marriages assimilated into the Filipino community and were Filipinized.

Bayar points out that integration varies in definition for different countries. But basically it refers to "the degree to which immigrants and the host society have common values, social cohesion and social incorporation." Again, with the ethnic distance theory, this helps explain the integration process and varied integration levels of the Chinese Filipinos.[23] Considering these, it seems best to conclude that the present Chinese Filipinos are integrated into the Filipino mainstream society though there are varied levels of integration that correspond with their levels or degrees of Sinicization and/or Filipinization. A considerable percentage are slowly assimilating into the Filipino community with inter-ethnic marriages and cutting off ties with the Chinese community. Those who eventually cut off ties usually have non-Chinese education, non-Chinese contact and associations, and non-Chinese cultural inclination.

This study finds the Chinese Filipinos integrated into the Filipino society because of the following. First, they are presently more known as Tsinoys or Chinese Filipinos or Filipino-Chinese than the negative labels they used to be called by the Filipinos. The diminishing name calling and increasing public acceptance of Chinese Filipino celebrities and politicians such as Kim Chiu, Enchong Dee, Richard Yap, Alfredo Lim, Sherwin Gatchalian, and many others are proof of the acceptance of their presence and the recognition of their contributions to the country. In 2012, President Benigno "Noynoy" Aquino declared the Chinese New Year as a national holiday when in the past, only the Chinese community has celebrated this event. Presently, the whole Philippines commemorates this day.[24]

Second, 90 percent of the Chinese are Filipino citizens already.[25] Their acquisition of Filipino citizenship has enabled them to belong to a country. They are able to own estates and businesses allowing for their progress. Such are the cases of high-profile Chinese Filipino businessmen like Henry Sy, Lucio Tan, John Gokongwei, and George Ty, who are part of a very small percentage of the Chinese communities, albeit often used for stereotyping. Nevertheless, many others have established themselves

23. Bayar, "Reconsidering Primordialism," 1651–52.

24. Official Gazette, "Proclamation no. 295, s. 2011."

25. Teresita Ang See, individual interview by author, 29 July 2012.

as Filipinos in their businesses, professions, families, and communities; and in many ways, contributed to the progress of the nation.

Third, they are still prioritizing Chinese education by sending their children to Chinese schools. Although they seek to be part of the country, they also seek to return to their cultural roots or cultural heritage. As an ethnic minority, their ambiguous identity and unhomely situations will oftentimes lead them back to their cultural roots. There is also the possibility that getting Chinese education is to learn another major language which is Putonghua. Therefore, the Chinese education should not be confused with political adherence or loyalty to China or Taiwan but rather to celebrate one's cultural heritage or to advance one's business or professional opportunities. This must be made clear to avoid branding the Chinese Filipinos as seeing China or Taiwan as their homeland. As explained in chapter 4, almost all informants already see the Philippines as their home country, even those who are immigrants or who have Chinese citizenship. They love the country and they feel they are already part of it.

Fourth, they are still employing Minnanhua and Putonghua in communication, although fluency is at present a problem. Many OIs and older adult second-generation Tsinoys find this as a crisis. Thus, the influx of NIs becomes a welcome development. The NIs contribute to the Resinification and revitalization of the Chinese language and culture. The Tsinoys specifically employ three languages in their everyday conversation. Many can still speak and/or understand the Minnanhua but not Putonghua since many regrettably did not take seriously their Chinese classes. The OIs and NIs may use primarily Minnanhua while the Tsinoys and Chinese Mestizos may use three or two languages or just Filipino. The NI Youth prefer to use Putonghua rather than Minnanhua. This use of language depends largely on the leanings of the families whether more Sinicized or more Filipinized.

Fifth, they are still, in general, practicing endogamy out of preference. This fosters cohesiveness, unity, and propagation of the Chinese Filipino culture though not necessarily "the Chinese culture." Endogamy is one major factor in the continuance or transferring of kinship ties, culture, and language. Parents play the important role of propagating and teaching the language, culture, and proper behavior. This is contrary to some Chinese Filipino parents who believe that the Chinese schools are solely responsible for the Sinicization of their children. Endogamy or exogamy are preferences, not absolutes. Endogamy does not necessarily imply ethnocentrism, and exogamy does not necessarily suggest multi-culturalism. Prejudices and discrimination are universal to all people of all ethnic background and nationalities. These can be avoided as one intentionally addresses and confronts the tendency to label and stereotype the other.

WHAT KIND OF CULTURAL HYBRIDITY?

Sally's *a-má* (grandmother) has been living in the Philippines all her life mingling with both Chinese and Filipinos. She used to own a store in Tondo. At present, she is retired and living with her daughter in an apartment in Manila Chinatown. *A-má* is still very pleasant, alert, and enthusiastic. Whenever she talked with me, she used straight Minnan-hua. However, when speaking to her Filipino neighbors, she used straight not broken Filipino. Her apartment building consisted mostly of Chinese Mestizo and Filipino tenants. Moreover, I noticed she is very amicable with all the neighbors.

Upon seeing the son of her Filipina neighbor, she greeted him, "*Oh birthday mo di ba, ano handa mo? Ano pakain mo?* (Hey, isn't it your birthday? What have you prepared? What food will you serve?)" Then, she saw her former neighbor visiting another neighbor. She called out to him and said, "*Oh ano pasalubong mo sa akin?* (Hey, what have you brought for me?)"

A-má has truly understood the Filipino culture. It has been a Filipino custom to tease or even put pressure on someone who just had a birthday to treat friends with food and drinks. If someone leaves home for vacation or work and returns, he/she is usually asked for a *pasalubong* or souvenir from wherever one came from. No wonder *a-má* can easily live amidst them. Now the question is whether *a-má* has been influenced by these Filipino values or she simply used this knowledge when dealing with them? Is cultural hybridity a part of her that cannot be singled out? Is hybridity compartmentalized and used as needed?

I have already stated that most Chinese Filipinos are more cultural hybrids than homogenous purists. Many of those interviewed are struggling to really understand whether their hybridity is simply compartmentalized or fused and cannot be taken apart. As they evaluate their experiences and everyday life, they discover that they are negotiating two or more cultures and at the same time they have these two or more cultures in them. Due to their constant exposure and constant practice of other cultures than just the Chinese culture, they have already imbued these into their minds and into their lives. They know how to operate between two or more cultures and yet they continue to see the Chinese culture as the dominant one. Therefore, the fact that they can still recognize which culture belongs to which ethnicity, they are compartmentalizing.

Lewellen correctly notes that compartmentalization is the ability to use selectively the appropriate culture for a situation. This can also be understood as having "multiple selfs." Such are the cases of the Chinese Filipinos who juggle between cultures to maintain harmony and unity in the community and country. Hiebert describes compartmentalization as adapting the culture we are in but separating these different cultures in our minds. Hiebert's point of reference are the missionaries who speak the local dialect and know local customs but remain an American or British or whatever nationality as soon as they are back in the private comfort of their homes.[26] With many kinds of Chinese Filipinos, I remain open to the possibilities of either Lewellen or Hiebert's understanding of compartmentalization. They are certainly hybrids, very much like Robbins's "mixed yet unmixed."

This "mixed yet unmixed" nature demonstrates four important features of the Chinese Filipinos. First, this hybrid nature characterized the resistance of the Chinese Filipinos to be fully Filipinized. Their affinity to their Chinese roots remains strong. They are inclined to maintain the Chinese culture as the dominant culture. Sinicization is still strongly adhered though hybridization seems stronger as reality seeped in. The idea of compartmentalization is at work when resistance to conform or fully embody another culture is present.

Second, this nature is similar to Barth's situational approach wherein culture is hybridized in the sense of negotiations, manipulations, adaptations, and adoption. The crossing of borders every now and then resulted to knowledge and proper response to other ethnic groups. The Chinese Filipinos apply Barth's situational approach in their everyday lives as they negotiate their way into the mainstream society or comingle with Filipinos. Their acquired knowledge of Filipino language and culture through education, exposure to Filipinos, media, and the internet enabled them to apply appropriate responses in different situations to avoid conflict and problems. They have adapted in their residence in the country. They even adopted the Filipino language as one of their languages. The fact is they

26. Lewellen, *Anthropology of Globalization*, 99; Hiebert, *Anthropological Insights*, 106–7.

are fluent in Filipino though with a different accent. They are comfortable with the language and it is used together with Minnanhua and English to fully express what is in their hearts. I can echo Chu's observation that the Chinese employ negotiations, manipulations, accommodations, and adaptations for survival and/or for profit.[27] This "mixed yet unmixed" nature is to their advantage as they can easily switch from one identity to another or one culture to another.

Third, they have created their very own culture based on the cultures to which they are exposed. I see this as an "enhanced hybrid culture." It is a unique Chinese Filipino culture and can only be found among them and not anywhere else in the world. It cannot be either just Chinese or Filipino culture but aptly called the Chinese Filipino culture. Lawrence J. C. Ma points out the significance of space, place, and mobility in understanding identity in the book *The Chinese Diaspora*. He utilizes the Chinese in Canada and the United States as examples of varied Chinese diasporic communities vis-à-vis a homogenous group as perceived by mainstream citizens.[28] Only a Chinese Filipino can fully understand the Chinese Filipino language and culture. Two obvious examples of this enhanced form of culture are the trilingual usage called EngChiLog and the reality of EnRAWGen (English Reading and Writing Generation).

The Chinese Filipinos usually employ three languages in conversation to best express themselves. In chapter 4, I argued that the failure to master the languages leads to borrowing of terms to fully express one's thought. However, it can also be that the Chinese Filipinos so fully understand the Filipino and American cultures that they see fit to use terms in either of these languages in conversations. For example, there are Chinese Filipino jokes that other ethnicities cannot understand. When translated, it loses its humor. If Americans have "Knock-Knock" jokes, then Filipinos have "Use-in-a-Sentence" jokes. A popular Minnanhua joke in the eighties was "Use Chiquito and Paquito in a sentence."[29] "Chiquito *nā bô lāi, li tiò Ēng* Paquito. (If this knife is not sharp then use another one.)"

27. Chu, *Chinese and Chinese Mestizos of Manila*, 8–12.

28. Ma and Cartier, *Chinese Diaspora*, 26. In the book *Scattered and Gathered*, Sadiri Joy Tira contends that "Diaspora is not a new phenomenon," since human migration is ancient as well as mission and evangelism. Tira, preface to *Scattered and Gathered*, xv.

29. Chiquito was a famous Filipino comedian. Paquito Diaz was a famous Filipino actor who always played the role of the villain.

Another is instead of using the Minnanhua expression *"góa gin-ná"* (oh my son), the Chinese Filipinos tend to use the Filipino expression *"**hay naku**"* (or **hay, anak ko**) which has the same meaning.[30] The younger Tsinoys today evidently tend to use the American expression "oh my God" popularized through media. There are even transitional words in Filipino adapted and somehow owned by the Chinese Filipinos through the years. Even the OIs use these transitional words. Words like **kasi** (because), **tsaka** (also), **baka** (maybe), **paano** or **pa'no** (how), **sige** (okay), and **bahala** (whatever). Then again, there are things that can only be best expressed in Minnanhua. Some informants are like Edna who uses the Minnanhua when she does not want to let her house helper understand their conversation. This is clearly instrumental or situational in approach.

The Chinese Filipinos today are EnRWAGen who read and write in English but prefer to speak in trilingual. They love to watch Hollywood movies, read American novels, or listen to American music but remain a Tsinoy at heart. The Chinese Filipino is a hybrid of two or more cultures that are "mixed yet unmixed" that produces an enhanced culture that may or may not necessarily be to their advantage. Some informants observed that they are familiar with many languages and cultures but they are not fluent or expert in any one of them.

Fourth, this "mixed yet unmixed" nature is ambivalent and ambiguous similar to what Bhabha calls unhomed or unhomely, a third space or third culture. The OIs and NIs are unhomed with their sojourning nature. The Tsinoys are unhomed with their dual identities as both Chinese and Filipino. The Chinese citizen Tsinoys have "imaginary" citizenship as they truly have no permanent country to call their own. Their unhomely situations are likely to remind them of their difference from the dominant Filipinos but also push them to seek a place of belonging. Hence, this unhomely nature also makes them desire citizenship and identify with Filipinos as one people in one nation. The Chinese and Filipino spouses in inter-ethnic marriages are unhomed as they were ushered either into a dominant Chinese or Filipino community and culture. The Chinese Mestizos have this unhomely feelings when neither the Chinese or Filipino community accepts them because of physical appearance or language fluency. The Overseas Chinese Filipino Workers all the more feel unhomed in other countries as they adjust to new environments and try to identify themselves in terms of ethnicity and nationality.

---

30. The expression *"góa gin-ná"* is sometimes pronounced as *"wa ka-na."*

ARE THE CHINESE FILIPINOS PRIMORDIALIST OR CONSTRUCTIVIST?

> "When migration stops then purists stop and hybrids stop and all will be Filipinized." —Hendrick[31]

Based on the interviews, I conclude that the Chinese Filipinos are mostly constructivists. Their presence in the country and comingling with the Filipinos exposed them to different socio-political, historical, and cultural situations or influences. They are evolving and developing alongside the global and technological changes happening in this twenty-first century. The phenomenon of construction and reconstruction of identities is evident in their ability to negotiate, adapt, and adopt in different political, social, and cultural changes.

However, even with centuries of comingling with the majority Filipinos since Pre-Hispanic Period, they have not yet fully assimilated. They persist as an ethnic minority. Appadurai notes that primordial ethnics are more alive than ever.[32] This leads to my reconsideration of primordialism for the Chinese Filipinos. Hendrick sees migration as the major factor for the continuance of Chinese culture in the country. He believes that once the influx of new immigrants stops, the Sinicization stops. The hybridization continues for a while but eventually also stops as borders are closed. It is then possible that after many generations, all Chinese Filipinos will eventually be Filipinized.

Our present age is global and migratory in nature, hence, mixing of cultures is inevitable. This continuing mixing seems to imply a never-ending construction and reconstruction of identities, as well as a never-ending proliferation of new combinations of identities. Conversely, as most informants revealed, they continue to adhere predominantly to Chinese culture as they also practice other cultures. The ethnic identity persists in this postcolonial era. How can primordialism and constructivism be reconciled then?

Jonathan Friedman presents his views on authenticity and identities in "The Politics of De-Authentification: Escaping from Identity, a Response to 'Beyond Authenticity' by Mark Rogers." He reminds us that all positions, whether essentialism or constructionism,[33] may be politically

---

31. Hendrick, Tsinoy individual interview by author, 28 June 2012.

32. Appadurai, *Modernity at Large*, 143.

33. Constructionism and constructivism are non-essentialists or opposite of primordialism or essentialism.

motivated as much as socially or anthropologically motivated.[34] Friedman stresses that identity or identification implies boundary making. These identified boundaries are perceived, recognized, and distinguished from their surroundings. In other words, Friedman argues that as long as one can be distinguished from another, this implies specific properties that can define or identify a particular person or group as such. This is coherence or sameness or sharedness. This sharedness is not simply a given that one has but rather a given that one does. The doing is what makes the identity. This is not to disregard contesting the meanings and using of identities.[35]

Friedman contends that essentialism cannot simply be dismissed because it is often related to colonialism and racism. It is still a valid theory to explain persisting or reemerging ethnicities. Since identities are constructed with boundaries as markers, essentializing is unavoidable. Constructivism is not the only theory that can explain culture, identity, and ethnicity. In fact, it may not be the most applicable theory for all cultures. Friedman explains that as one carefully studies a culture, one will discover a "core of experiences" shared by people that resonate with their identities. This sharedness is the common denominator that the people perceived as a unifying factor. He concludes that there is much "cultural continuity in the renaissance of indigenous identities, the process is and has been global-local from the start."[36]

It is true enough that the Chinese Filipinos remain essentially Chinese in culture and identity as they share a core of experiences. But their Chinese culture is no longer the same as the culture in China, Taiwan, or Hong Kong. They have constructed an enhanced Chinese Filipino culture, mixed yet unmixed, uniquely their own. The constant migration of Chinese nationals into the country has contributed to the tension of Sinicization or Filipinization of the Chinese Filipinos. But then again, even in Sinicization or Resinification of the Chinese Filipinos, the cultural practice is not tantamount to loyalty to China or Taiwan. We must not confuse nationalities with ethnicities.

Anderson popularizes the notion of "imagined communities." We must acknowledge that the Philippines is composed of different ethnicities and the Chinese are just one of the many ethnic minorities. Different

---

34. Ibid., 129. Appadurai calls this virus primordial bug. Appadurai, *Modernity At Large*, 143.

35. Ibid., 129–30.

36. Ibid., 130–35.

ethnicities can live in harmony with one another as they share one country and treat each other with respect and value. They can celebrate their respective cultural inclinations and continuous usage of their languages or dialects and still pledge loyalty to the host country.

Bayar distinguishes ethnicities from nationalities as one of his seven arguments why primordialism needs to be reconsidered. He writes,

> American, Canadian and Australian are not ethnic categories and do not have ethnic connotations (Joppke 1998). Hence, being Irish-American does not contradict primordialism because it is not the reconstruction of ethnic identity. Instead, Irish is an ethnic identity and American is a national identity, with which an individual can simultaneously identify himself or herself.[37]

Bayar argues that primordialism and constructivism are often described as opposing views. He agrees that ethnic identities are not genetic but nurtured by environment. Nevertheless, a person is usually nurtured by one's parents. Upon conception or birth, one cannot choose his/her ethnicity or parents. Therefore, the "genetic" element is not without basis. This will be appropriately called blood ties or kinship. These are the "givens" or assumed characteristics that Geertz laid out. Bayar also cites the findings of Cavalli-Sforza's genetic analysis of 2,000 populations and 100,000 individuals. The result shows that certain markers of ethnicity such as language, assumed kinship, and physical features are correlated with genetic proximity. However, he emphasizes the need to study ethnicity in all dimensions aside from biological or genetics.[38]

Bayar returns to the works of Shils and Geertz to argue for the idea of "varying degrees of affinity" or levels of attachments to "givens" or what he calls multiple dimensions such as blood, kinship, language, customs, and religion. He believes that the key in reconsidering primordialism is to reconsider his theory of "ethnic distance" to explain the varying degrees of influence or acceptance of a particular culture. He admits that in primordialism, ethnicity is fixed and maintains one single identity, as opposed to constructivism, in which it is socially constructed and maintains multiple identities. But Bayar clarifies that the single identity has multiple dimensions or many "givens" and the degree of affinity for each

---

37. Bayar, "Reconsidering Primordialism," 1647.
38. Ibid., 1642–45.

dimension varies, which in turn describe the kind of ethnicity the person or group has.[39]

Bayar's idea of ethnic distance to describe the varied degree of affinity to different givens makes sense. This is similar to my findings that the Chinese Filipinos maintain a dominant culture that makes them essentially still Chinese. Like Bayar, I cannot simply dismiss primordialism because of the resurgence and persistence of ethnic groups. The fact that the world has not attained one global culture means that primordialism is still a topic that must not be negated.

Nonetheless, I cannot apply primordialism in the case of the Chinese Filipinos. Their admission that they are hybrids culturally already aligns them with the constructivist view. Their "enhanced culture" or "mixed and not yet mixed" nature connotes continuing construction. The very idea of undergoing a process or a shifting of identities implies something constructed, whether it involves negotiations or flexibility. Sinicization, Filipinization, or Resinification can thus be seen as constructivist processes. However, I find the constructivist view lacking in the sense that it cannot satisfactorily explain the persistence of certain "givens" in an ethnic group, or like in the case of the Chinese Filipinos as having a dominant culture among the mixing of cultures. Lewellen may argue that this is cultural or political.[40] But how will constructivism explains the period wherein the constructed culture is being propagated, transferred, applied, and practiced for a period of time? Will not that time frame place the ethnic group as primordial? Can constructivism explain the reification of ethnicities in multiculturalism and the continuing persistence of a constructed culture for a period before it is reconstructed again?

Kanchan Chandra satisfactorily answers my questions with her four arguments on what constructivism is not. First, constructivism is not negating biology but rather interpreting its raw facts in relation to how this affect one's identity. Second, it is not constructing something out of thin air but acknowledging that the essence of identity is "imagined" construction from history and that we are products of a "prior process of construction." Third, it is fluid but not necessarily always in the process of continuous fluidity or change. Fourth, ethnic identity in constructivism

---

39. Bayar, "Reconsidering Primordialism," 1641, 1652.
40. Lewellen, *Anthropology of Globalization*, 106, 108.

does not always mean there is instrumental calculation or material or psychic benefits.[41]

I conclude that the Chinese Filipinos are constructivists. First, the discussion on Sinicization, Filipinization, and Resinification shows that the practice of a particular dominant culture is eventually an intentional construct. Second, they are culturally hybrid but maintain their Chineseness as the dominant culture, thus, they show the characteristic of mixed yet not really mixed. They "feel" primordialist about their identity but in fact they act in a constructivist way to maintain identity. Third, throughout history, there were Chinese Filipinos who decided to assimilate into the Filipino community and became Filipinos by ethnicity and nationality. The Chinese Filipino ethnic identity is therefore fixed yet not really fixed. With their sojourning characteristic, they may even migrate to another country and identify with the new country. They may change their ethnic identity in time. Fourth, they employ multiple identities to negotiate in different situations. It is the adaptability of the human beings that enables them to be one and also the other.

41. Chandra, *Constructivist Theories*, 149–55.

6

Mission among Chinese in the Philippines

ON NOVEMBER 10, 2013, the St. Stephen's Parish celebrated its 110th anniversary. It is the oldest existing Chinese Protestant church in the Philippines established by the Episcopalian Bishop Charles Brent. The Philippine Chinese Protestantism or Philippine Chinese evangelical churches can look back to a 110-year history.

Bishop Brent's theological and ecclesiological conviction recognized the validity of the Roman Catholic Church. When he came to the Philippines at the start of the American colonization, he prevented the Protestant Episcopal Church from joining the Evangelical Union of the Philippine Islands. This union was an interdenominational body of seven missionary and Bible societies established to promote cooperation and comity among Protestants as they "bring true evangelical Christianity to the Roman Catholic masses."[1] Brent considers the Roman Catholics as "churched"[2] and thus limits the Episcopalian ministry to three groups of people who are not even nominally Christian: the Chinese community in Manila, the Moros on the southern islands of the Philippines, and groups of people in mountainous areas and other remote regions of the islands who follow the traditional primal religions of the Philippines.[3]

In the accounts of Shao,

---

1. Jones, *Christian Missions*, 95.

2. "[When] Brent witnessed firsthand the incompetence and immorality of the Roman Catholic clergy in the Philippines, he was strongly tempted to begin Episcopal work among the Catholic population." Ibid., 78–79.

3. Ibid., 95.

The St Stephen's Church was the first church of the new diocese, and was organized primarily for American civilian and military personnel. However, Bishop Brent noticed that in the congregation then were Chinese worshippers who came from Xiamen, Fujian. Knowing the dire need for mission work among the Chinese, Bishop Brent recruited Hobart E. Studley to work in the Philippines. He was an American fluent in Amoy, and at that time a missionary of the Reformed Church of America residing in Xiamen.

The first Chinese worship service, on 8 November 1903, was held in a rented quarter along San Fernando Street. There were ten attendees. The worshippers came from various denominational backgrounds.[4]

From ten attendees in 1903, there are presently about 24,000 Chinese Filipino evangelical Christians (CFEC) of different denominations in the whole archipelago.[5] This raises several questions. First, what kind of belief system do the Chinese Filipinos have? In line with this, is there a need to evangelize and disciple the present 1.2 million Chinese Filipinos if 85 percent consider themselves to be Christians already?[6] Second, what are the challenges of the Chinese Filipino evangelical churches given the cultural hybridity of the present generation Chinese Filipinos? Third, what is the role of the CFEC in both local and global missions?

CHAP CHAY LOMI BELIEF SYSTEM: CULTURE AND EVANGELISM

> Author: Uncle,[7] what is your religion? Are you a Roman Catholic, Protestant, Buddhist, or Daoist?

4. Shao, "Channel of Blessings," 414. Amoy 廈門 is the English transliteration of the Minnanhua term *Ēmn̂g* or Xiamen in Putonghua. It is used to refer the coastal city in the southeastern part of China as well as the language spoken which is also known as Hokkien or Minnanhua.

5. There are about 2 percent CFEC in the Philippines. Wan, "Mission among the Chinese Diaspora," 40. If the present Chinese Filipino population is 1.2 million, there are 24,000 CFEC. The real number may be lower since there are Chinese Filipinos switching to Filipino mega churches like CCF (Christ Commission Fellowship), GCF (Greenhills Christian Fellowship), and VCF (Victory Christian Fellowship).

6. See discussion on religious affiliation of Chinese Filipinos in ch. 1 on Review of Related Literature section by Teresita Ang See.

7. The Chinese Filipinos usually call elderly men "uncle" as a way of showing respect toward them, not necessarily implying blood relations.

Benson: *Ták-hāng ma sìn* (I believe in everything). If they invite me, I go with them. **Lahat pinupuntahan** (I join all kinds of religions).

Author: So which Protestant church do you attend?

Benson: *Chhin chhái* (Any).

Author: How did you join such services?

Benson: Some people invited me, like my friends. There's nothing wrong joining all kinds of religions. All is good. All religions teach us to do good deeds. If they teach us to do bad things, then, we will not join them anymore.[8]

[Then the phone rang, Benson answered the phone. It was a friend inviting him to attend another Chinese Protestant church service.]

Benson (CM 2) disliked offending his friends so he cordially accepts invitations from Christian friends to attend church activities. His goal is primarily to maintain harmonious relationships with friends, not necessarily faith in Christ. He remains open, however, to join any religion that teaches good things.

See observes that the Chinese Filipinos tend to be syncretistic in their religious life with their pragmatic mindset. The daily uncertainties of profit or loss in their businesses become fertile ground for strengthening religious beliefs and superstitions.[9] She notices that they accept all kinds of religions because they believe all religions teach people to do good deeds. Further, anything that works or brings luck must be true and observed. See is amused that the Chinese Filipinos easily mix different faiths without problems. One example is that they will consult the Chinese calendar for *ho jít tsi* 好日子 (lucky dates) for engagements, weddings, and baptisms, while accepting Roman Catholic or Protestant rites for these.[10]

Like Benson, Nellie saw religions, whether Buddhism or Christianity, as channels for one to learn how to be a good person. Switching from

8. Benson, CM individual interview by author, 19 June 2012.

9. Conwell observes that the late nineteenth-century Coolies became superstitious due to hardships and tyranny of government. Conwell, *Why and How*, 41–43. See more discussion in appendix G.

10. See, *Chinese in the Philippines*, 3:181–86; See, "Case of the Chinese in the Philippines," 155–56.

one religion to another to maintain harmony is a practical way to face challenges in life. She shared,

> Let me share to you, you listen. When I was small, I live on Benavidez Street just beside Hope Christian High School. *hm tióh hō hoai chhù-pi liáh-khì khì le pài* (So our neighbors forced us to go to church). Me, my younger sister, and my younger brother, the three of us, we went to church every Sunday. But then my foster mother made me marry a Buddhist. My mother-in-law was a Buddhist, but not a devout one. So I didn't go to church anymore to avoid trouble. I saw that they were very kind to me. My mother-in-law asked me to go with her to *Seng Gōan Sì* (a Buddhist temple). I was afraid to have problems with my in-laws so I obeyed her. I observed the Buddhists are very good people so why not join them . . . My friends would tell me stories of Christian daughter-in-law quarreling with Buddhist mother-in-law. I don't like that. Later, we moved out from my in-laws and live on Asuncion Street. Our children attended a Christian school and we let them attend church on Sundays. My in-laws did not oppose this. Today, I consider myself having no religion . . . When I visit America, I join my eldest son in attending Protestant churches.[11]

Nellie confessed she has no religion though she willingly joins other religious rituals or services. Three NI adult informants share the same mindset. Although they are willing to join various religious activities, they see Buddhism as a Chinese religion and Christianity a Western religion.

> I . . . [Paused for a few seconds] . . . believe in everything and I believe in nothing. [Laughter] Back in China, most people are Buddhists. When my mother went to temple I followed her. If she went to church I also followed her. [Laughter] My uncle is a Roman Catholic. As I came to the Philippines, I also join my uncle and attend Roman Catholic church. [Laughter] —Li[12]

---

11. Nellie, Tsinoys individual interview by author, 28 June 2012.

12. During the interview on this topic, Li kept stopping himself from saying *tsiàh kàu* (eat religion) and instead say *sin pút kàu* (believe in Buddhism) or *sin Thien tsú kàu* (believe in Roman Catholicism). The idea of *tsiàh kàu* traced back in China when religion is likened to a rice bowl or being a Christian is actually a rice Christian. A rice Christian or rice-bowl Christian is someone who turned to Christianity for its material not spiritual benefits. Li, NI individual interview by author, 24 July 2012. See also Yang, "Chinese Conversion," 239–45.

> All religion just teach you to do good . . . I personally have no religion. (Back in China) We do not believe in Mao Zhedong like he was a god. It's not like that. If you are a Buddhist, if we really face trouble, can Buddha help us? We solve our problems by ourselves . . . Buddhism in China existed thousands of years already, the roots are very deep. When Western religions went in, Roman Catholicism and Protestantism, one portion will accept but not majority. Since our ancestors are Buddhists, how can you expect them to change? —Ping[13]

> I have no religion but my wife and daughter are Roman Catholics. I go with them to church on Sundays. I also go with my (Chinese Filipino) friends to temples. I follow people around but I personally have no belief or conviction. —Peter[14]

Uayan sees that the pragmatic Chinese Filipino will seek to maintain harmonious relationship with the dominant religious group (Roman Catholics or Protestants) and the minority group (Buddhists or Daoists). This results in their syncretistic tendency. Uayan notes that this pragmatic approach makes God distant and unapproachable. Thus, mediators like lesser gods or magic are needed to address everyday life's issues and problems. She observes,

> For pragmatic, syncretistic Chinese Filipinos, the most important religious matters include: the meaning of life and death, the nature of the good life, security, knowing the future in order to live well and avoid misfortune, and finally, dealing with morality and evil.[15]

Bernice shared how her Chinese husband during college submitted a letter declaring that he was a Buddhist even though he was a Roman Catholic to avoid attending theology classes (a required course in Catholic universities). Pragmatism in this case rules over the religious sphere as one manipulates and negotiates one's religion to achieve one's desired goal. The pragmatic mindset dominates in the thinking and practice of the everyday life of some Chinese Filipinos, and permeates their religious practices as well.

13. Ping, NI individual interview by author, 25 July 2012.
14. Peter, NI individual interview by author, 24 July 2012.
15. Uayan, "Chap Chay Lomi," 72.

The following is an overview of religious affiliations of the 59 key informants interviewed individually. They were classified into six categories.

Table 4. Religious Affiliation of the 59 Key Informants From the Six Categories

	Protestant	Roman Catholic	Buddhist	Mixed Religion	No Religion	Did not mention
Old Immigrants (4)	2		1			1
New Immigrants (7)	3			1	3	
Tsinoys (17)	12	1	1	2	1	
Chinese Mestizos (17)	9	5		3		
Spouses (10)	4	5				1
Unhomed (4)	3	1				
TOTAL: (59)*	33	12	2	6	4	2

*30 out of the 33 Protestants attend church regularly. 10 out of the 12 Roman Catholics go to church regularly. Six informants openly shared their mixed beliefs of Buddhism, Daoism, Roman Catholicism, and others. Four have no religion while two failed to share what were their religion.

Aside from the pragmatic mindset, Uayan believes that the Chinese Filipino worldview is a mixture of different elements borrowed from here and there. Different religions like Catholicism, Protestantism, Buddhism, and Daoism are combined with animistic beliefs and practices of Chinese folk religion. Consequently, she calls the Chinese Filipino worldview as *chap chay lomi*.[16]

The married couple Paolo and Lani confessed that they believe in Buddhism, Roman Catholicism, Protestantism, and even in fortune telling and other superstitions. Paolo humorously called their belief system as "Chopsuey."[17] He shared that he became Roman Catholic while studying in a Catholic university in college. He continued with his Buddhist faith for his mother's sake, who, incidentally, is both a Buddhist and a Roman Catholic. She faithfully pilgrimages to Manaoag as well as *Lam Hai*.[18] Paolo bought an expensive statue of Buddha in Indonesia hop-

16. Uayan, "Chap Chay Lo Mi," 65.

17. Chopsuey is a Chinese dish of mixed vegetables. It is also used in reference to mixing of this and that.

18. Our Lady of Manaoag is a popular destination in Pangasinan, Philippines, of Marian devotees. It is a religious shrine that claims to have miraculous results. *Lam*

ing that after he has it blessed by monks, he can display it in his store and will bring him good business. He saw geomancy as simply common sense and not just superstitions. He and his wife tried joining Chinese Filipino evangelical churches with the encouragement of their wedding godparents. Religion looks more like a channel for good fortune and not a set of creeds or beliefs.

Nadine is a Roman Catholic, but she believes that all religions teach people to do good. She acknowledged that she has a **halo-halo** or mixed beliefs.

> Actually, ah what we practice is like (this). Mama, she goes to (Roman) Catholic church. Papa, is more of temple, **kasi** (because he is) Chinese. But then we also go to those YGC (Youth Gospel Center) **di ba** (right)? And then CGC (Christian Gospel Center), so Protestant, **di ba** (right)? So **halo-halo** (mixed), back then (in high school) until now ... (Having mixed religions) It's more of combination of both worlds, Chinese and then the Filipino **di ba** (right)? Then you have your **barkada** (friends) or other influences (school, friends, family). **Kasi kina** (Because for) papa and mama, it is okay for you to join other religions as long as you are happy or it's your choice. As long as you do good. Since for them, religion is for you to know what is good and bad. As long as you don't convert them. [Laughter][19]

Nadine considered the Christian faith as Filipino or Western religion while Buddhism is the Chinese religion. This is evident in her opinion when she said that her father is a Buddhist because he is a (pure) Chinese. Her mother, being a first-generation CM, is a Roman Catholic. Nadine concluded that Roman Catholicism is the Filipino religion. Nadine also described her mixed beliefs as combination of two worlds, Filipino and Chinese, as she herself is a second-generation CM with Filipino and Chinese blood running in her veins.

Steven observed that his Filipina grandmother has a mixed belief system.

> **Lola** (Filipina grandmother) is a Christian. When we were still little, she was the one who brought us to (Protestant) church ... We have an altar at home but we do not offer food. **Ang** weird **nga eh** (It's really weird). My grandmother is the one who burns incense. I already told her to stop doing it. Even though she is

---

Hai is a popular place for Buddhist devotees.

19. Nadine, CM individual interview by author, 21 June 2012.

the (evangelical) Christian in the family but she continued the (Chinese) tradition she got from my **Lolo** (Chinese grandfather)—that is, putting up an altar to burn incense for my great grandfather (her husband's father). She is just continuing the tradition. She never forces me to do *paì paì* (ancestral veneration) but she makes my *sió-bĒ* (younger sister) do it. **May halo pa rin yung paniwala ni Lola** (Grandma still has mixed beliefs).[20]

Chu suggests that a reevaluation of the Catholicity of the Chinese Filipinos is necessary. He reasons that it is easier to simply see all the Chinese Catholics as "insincere" in their faith as observed by missionaries. Their mixing of different religions may be regarded as pragmatic and for personal gain rather than authentic faith. But there are devout Chinese Catholics. He challenges the need to understand the Chinese religious worldview to better understand how "sincere" they are in their faith or faiths.[21]

Their "mixing" of Christian and Chinese gods to worship could be ascribed to what other scholars call "religious syncretism." But would not using "syncretism" as a way to describe their behavior, from the Catholic monotheistic perspective, beg the question: does this not prove that Chinese converts could never be "good" Catholics? How can we reinterpret the behavior of the Chinese converts without resorting to an either-or proposition, and toward a more nuanced and non-Eurocentric way? I propose to do this by relating some of these practices that had often been criticized by Catholic missionaries and Western observers to some of the cosmological worldviews of the Chinese.[22]

Chu discusses how the Chinese concept of ghosts and gods affect their behavior and how they do religion. Chu surveys the Spanish Period Chinese and CMs's concept of ghosts and gods were often fuzzy. Ghosts for the Chinese did not apply only to spirit beings but also to foreigners whom they called barbarians or "white devils."[23] Chu believes that the Chinese turning to Roman Catholicism was very much affected by their cosmological understanding that there were many gods in this world. In order that they will prosper and find good fortune, they need to appease

---

20. Steven, CM individual interview by author, 15 July 2012.
21. Chu, *Chinese and Chinese Mestizos*, 190–93.
22. Ibid., 192–93.
23. Ibid., 194.

the new ghosts or new gods by worshipping them, burning incense, giving them gifts, and establishing relationships.[24]

In line with Chu's discussion, Chiu-Eng Tan recognizes the limitations of Western understanding on Chinese polytheism. She writes,

> Some Western missionaries in their zealous evangelization of China, condemned Chinese polytheism as idolatry but failed to understand folk beliefs and practices as seen by the people themselves. They also desacralized the Chinese beliefs of the spirit world and imposed their own Western dualistic worldview on Chinese religions.[25]

Tan's research in 1996 showed that the CFEC also practiced what she calls "folk Christianity." She discovers that some CFEC remained superstitious and ignorant of the teachings in the Bible. They continued in their adherence to both Christian faith and folk Chinese religions as well as fortune and luck. She raises the question, how can one reconcile this mixing of beliefs with a monotheistic religion?[26]

Tan argues that the Chinese people had a concept of a supreme being as early as the Shang Dynasty (1600 BC–1046 BC). This was evident in their calling of a god called Shàngdì 上帝. Under Shàngdì, there were other deities such as God of Wind, God of Cloud, God of Sun, and God of Moon. There were also earthly deities like god of earth and grains, god of rivers and mountains.[27]

During the Zhou Dynasty (1065 BC–256 BC), Tiān (T'ien) 天 was used in reference to heaven and for the supreme deity. Tiān by this time was viewed as a personal Being who took care the affairs of men. However, the people continued the use of divination to seek guidance and fortunes. Daoism is homegrown in China from the fourth century BC while Buddhism came from India and Tibet around AD first century. These religions turn humans into saints and gods. Even ancestral worship, which traced back to ancient China, believed in the deification of the ancestors. This helped us comprehend the cosmological worldview of the Chinese Filipinos. They are not simply superstitious or polytheistic.

---

24. Ibid.

25. Tan, "Cosmos, Humans, and Gods," 25.

26. Ibid., 5–6.

27. Ibid., 39.

Their belief system traced back to their ancestors and passed on from one generation to another.[28]

Tan presents the idea of reciprocity between humans and gods as: a favor done is a favor due. Thus, when food or incenses are offered to the gods, the gods in turn will protect or bless the humans. She also differentiates their concept of gods and ghosts. Ghosts are deceased humans who failed to enter into the afterlife and are left roaming on earth.[29] This idea of reciprocity further encouraged the adding of gods to their existing list or collection of gods, as well as the propagation of the tradition of ancestral veneration and filial piety.

Chu is right in his observation that the Chinese turning to Christianity was actually adding new gods instead of a replacement of their former gods, since their cosmological understanding is that there are many gods or spirits. His assessment is that the Chinese apply extension rather than replacement in conversion.[30] The Christian God then is the Supreme Being yet there are also many other lesser gods. Chu's observation and evaluation on the Chinese Filipino way of doing faith or religion help explains why Buddhism blended well with Daoism and eventually the Christian faith as they live in the Philippines.

Chu points out that the Chinese Filipino "mixing" tendency of different faiths, such is the idea of extension rather than replacement, does not necessarily mean false faith or insincere faith or even syncretism. Chu is trying to prove that there are Chinese Filipinos with authentic faith in Christianity, but this faith coexists with other faiths. If this is the case, can such kind of faith or faiths can be viewed other than syncretism?[31] Given

28. Ibid., 39–42.

29. Ibid., 42–43.

30. Chu, *Chinese and Chinese Mestizos of Manila*, 197.

31. Hiebert defines syncretism as combination of Christianity and other religious beliefs that produces a "Christo-paganism." He observes that syncretism results in a gospel that loses its message and integrity. He disagrees with the old method of *tabula rasa* wherein the folk religions and practices are completely ignored or dismissed. Yet at the same time, he discusses the dangers of syncretism without proper or critical contextualization. Without proper contextualization, there will be a failure of addressing the underlying wrong assumptions from the old beliefs and practices as the people accept the new religion or belief. Hiebert et al., *Understanding Folk Religion*, 19, 21, 194–95. Schreiter argues for a more positive understanding of syncretism or "at least a balance between the positive and the negative understanding." He agrees that syncretism must be contested because our goal is to uphold the "faithful transmittal of the Word of God entrusted to us." He concludes that syncretism and synthesis are essentially the same as they seek to form the religious identity of person/people. However,

that the Chinese Filipinos are sincere in their faith in different religions, there is a need to help them eventually decide to let go other gods and only worship the God of the Bible.

Figure 6. Chinese Filipinos praying and burning incense

Tan's research presents the need to help these Chinese Filipinos to obey faithfully the biblical teachings to be authentic Christians. This study also affirms the Chinese Filipino tendency to mix different religions. The interviews show how they perceive religions as an avenue to know how to be good; to find prosperity and thwart bad luck as in the case of Paolo and Lani; to develop or maintain harmony in the social sphere; and to continue the traditions passed from ancestors. There is then a need to evangelize, re-evangelize, and/or disciple the Chinese Filipino Roman Catholics and Protestants to become authentic believers and faithful followers of Jesus Christ.

whether syncretism or synthesis, the goal is always to construct local theologies in agreement with biblical teachings. Schreiter, *New Catholicity*, 63, 83, 144–58.

Tan suggests we need to help them understand that there is only one true God; idolatry is wrong and that there should be no other gods; trust in God's goodness and provision; and study the Scriptures like the Bereans. Tan also points out the importance of reminding them about the reality of spiritual warfare and relying on the Holy Spirit as our only mediator.[32] Churches need to intentionally address these issues of mixed beliefs and find ways to help their members and non-believers discover the truth and remain faithful in obeying Scriptures.

Both verbal and nonverbal testimonies are important. Nonetheless, the nonverbal testimony is usually more real to the Chinese Filipinos. Since they see religion as teaching people to do good deeds, they usually judge Christians whether or not they do what they preach. Authenticity through our life testimony is very important and sometimes impacts them more than our words. Our care and concern for them are as important as our preaching of God's truth to them.

CHALLENGES FACED BY CHINESE FILIPINO EVANGELICAL CHURCHES

The Chinese Filipinos have evolved through the years in their cultural identity as well as spiritual adherence. The profile in chapter 4 shows that there are actually different kinds of Chinese. Appropriate methods of ministry must be applied to each kind/group of Chinese Filipinos. There is no one method of evangelism or discipleship or worship or mission that is applicable to all Chinese Filipinos or Chinese Filipino evangelical churches. As there are different kinds of people, there are different kinds of churches. In application for the present Chinese Filipino evangelical churches, they may reconsider or reexamine how they do church to remain effective, relevant, and in conversant with their target ethnic group. This portion brings out two challenges based on the research made by Catherine Guéguen on Chinese Filipinos in Metro Manila: the issue of language and the issue of space. These challenges will raise more questions than give answers.

Guéguen, a geographer who maps out the movements of the Chinese Filipinos in Metro Manila through the years, notices that there is a lack of clear information from the Philippine government regarding the figures of Chinese Filipino population. She discovers that in 1970, about 100,000 of Chinese origin lived in Manila. By 1990, the number

32. Tan, "Cosmos, Humans, and Gods," 352–55.

of Chinese-speakers was 3,482 households. In the year 2000, there were 40,000 Chinese-speaking persons in Metro Manila. Manila has the largest number with 17,799 Chinese-speakers. Quezon City has 9,533 while Caloocan City and San Juan City have less than three thousand respectively.[33] She deduces that many Chinese Filipinos may no longer speak Chinese or they did not declare the Chinese language as their mother tongue. She also adds that most Chinese-speaking are probably elderly adults who did not adopt Filipino citizenships; such was the case in Caloocan City which has 2,619 Chinese Filipinos and 2,849 Chinese citizens.[34] Since most Chinese Filipinos prefer to be trilingual, they may consider themselves not fluent enough in Minnanhua to declare it as their mother tongue. Nonetheless, the issue of language and identity cannot be dismissed.

This research shows that the second-, third-, fourth-, and fifth-generation Tsinoys interviewed prefer to be trilingual (Minnanhua, English, and Filipino) in conversation but use English in reading and writing. Though there are still a considerable number who are fluent in Minnanhua, most of them cannot resist the majority who are bilingual or trilingual. As the OIs admitted, the present forces in society are too strong to compete with, hence, many of the Tsinoys are losing Minnanhua.

See assesses that 90 percent of the present Chinese population in the Philippines are below 50 years old. These local-born Chinese do not read Chinese newspapers or join Chinese organizations.[35] This means that the other 10 percent are the elderly Chinese, aged 51 and above. This group of Chinese reads Chinese newspapers and joins Chinese organizations. The *World News* 世界日報 is currently the top Chinese newspaper in the country. It has a readership of 20,000 all throughout the country. The 20,000 is roughly 2 percent of the more than one million Chinese Filipinos. All these evidences confirm that the majority of Chinese Filipinos are definitely EnRAWGen and may or may no longer be fluent in Minnanhua. It also means that the Chinese Filipinos at present are composed of very young people. In line with this, how should the Chinese Filipino evangelical churches respond to this present situation?

The demographics show clearly that the majority of the Chinese Filipinos today are young, EnRAWGen, trilingual, and very much hybrid

33. Chinese-speaking means Minnanhua speakers.

34. Guéguen, "Moving from Binondo," 119, 122.

35. See, *Chinese in the Philippines*, 3:21.

in cultural mindset and practice. The churches need to reconsider their present strategies on how they can be more effective in reaching the majority group without neglecting the minority elderly or homogenous purist group.

To cite a situation, the Chinese Filipino evangelical churches had bilingual services since the 1980s. The preacher uses Minnanhua and an interpreter will translate to English. Many big churches have all English services since the 1990s in recognition of the rising number of EnRAW-Gens. However, the small churches maintain the traditional bilingual services. In view of the current cultural hybrid Tsinoys, should the church consider an EngChiLog service? Or eventually just have English services or Filipino services? This leads us to the second issue. What about the elderlies or NI who only speak Minnanhua or Putonghua? How should the church go about these changes and remain relevant and effective in reaching all kinds of Chinese Filipinos?

At present, the United Evangelical Church of the Philippines (UECP) divides its services based on the different kinds of Chinese Filipinos living in Manila. Their first service starts as early as seven in the morning and targets the elderly Chinese Filipinos. It is an all Minnanhua service. The worship songs, sermon, and even the presider speaks in Minnanhua. This cuts down much of the time in translating compared to a bilingual service. The second service is the largest group. This is the all English service. The last worship service is the bilingual service that targets those elderlies and Tsinoys who prefer to wake up later on Sunday mornings and catch up on the last service. This church also has an outreach ministry to the NIs. UECP hired four full-time NI pastors just to minister to these NIs. The other churches I visited have an all English service first then one or two bilingual services.

The issue on language is also connected to other related issues like ethnicity and culture. This brings into conversation the application of Donald McGavran's Homogenous Unit theory or Andrew Walls' Indigenous Principle and Pilgrim Principle among the Chinese Filipino evangelical churches. I propose that establishing ethnic churches is a choice in doing church or mission. In the midst of globalization, the persistence of ethnicities or social classes and other forms of associations and groupings confirms the appropriateness of the Homogenous Unit theory and the Indigenizing Principle. These are a few of the many tools and principles in doing church. It is not the core of mission or church growth. It may not be applicable to all people or churches.

Walls presents the existing tension among Christians as being at home and yet not really at home with his Indigenizing Principle and Pilgrim Principle. These principles bring out the "unhomely" nature of Christians. The Indigenizing Principle is the acknowledgment that it is impossible to separate an individual from his/her relationships with his/her society and culture. This leads to the desire to indigenize—to live as Christians and remain a member of one's own group or society. This principle also reflects one's strong desire to find one's identity and a place to belong or a home. In contrast, the Pilgrim Principle reminds us that we are pilgrims and sojourners. This world is our temporal abode. This principle shows the universalizing factor of Christianity. We are Christians and members of a particular church but we are all part of a bigger church, the universal church. The kingdom concept binds us as one.[36] The danger lies in the church's failure to intentionally address issues on racism and prejudice which leads to fostering and nurturing sentiments like ethnocentrism and discrimination.[37]

Another challenge that the Chinese Filipino evangelical churches have to face is where to find these Chinese Filipinos. We have to know where to find them in order to meet them and minister to them. In 2008, See writes that 52 percent are living in Metro Manila.[38] This shows their tendency to concentrate in the urban than rural areas. Moreover, 52 percent means half of the whole Chinese Filipino population of the Philippines can be found in Metro Manila. This information can help Chinese evangelical churches reexamine their strategies on how they reach the Chinese Filipinos for Christ. What steps can help them make greater impact among the Chinese Filipinos in their respective churches and communities?

Guéguen's research shows that for a long time the Chinese Filipinos settled in Binondo, also known as the Chinese district. By the 1960s and 1970s, they started to move to the outskirts of the city where residential subdivisions or townhouses also known as "villages" were growing in popularity. In the 1970s, there were 100,000 people of Chinese origins living in Manila, 5 percent were living in the suburban areas. She believes that those who lived in the suburbs were those who have acquired

36. Walls, *Missionary Movement*, 7–9.

37. Douglas C. McConnell proposes an "intentional confrontation of prejudice" as part of homogenous churches' formation to avoid racism. McConnell, "Confronting Racism and Prejudice," 387.

38. See, "Case of the Chinese in the Philippines," 155–56.

citizenships and therefore were able to own properties. She adds that these Chinese no longer have to use fake names to own properties but can freely use their names to buy lands. The Chinese Filipinos consider buying lands as investments. Guéguen sees this new freedom as opportunities for the Chinese Filipinos to build "villages" and "subdivisions" with their own identity as well as for their own security and convenience.[39]

Guéguen observes that there are class criteria among the Chinese Filipinos. During the postwar era, the rich Chinese choose to live close by with the rich Filipinos in Forbes Park, Makati City. The middle class Chinese live in Quezon City while the lower middle class and poor live in Manila.[40] This is where the *chhi goā* (suburbs) and *chhi lâi* (city) became popularly used by Chinese Filipinos themselves in the 1970s to distinguish those who live in Manila proper and those who live in the suburbs. As discussed in chapter 4, those who live in *chhi goā* are perceived by those in *chhi lâi* as more Westernized or Filipinized. However, we must be careful in making clear-cut distinctions. As there are poor Chinese Filipinos in *chhi goā*, there are also rich Chinese Filipinos in *chhi lâi*. As there are traditionalist in *chhi goā*, there are also very Westernized or Filipinized in *chhi lâi*.[41]

Guéguen notes that the development of these urban "villages" is actually small-sized urban units called "micro-urbanism" settlements. These groups of settlements or units form together a small town. She cites three reasons for the creation of such "villages": cultural, sharing the same social profile, and security.[42] Guéguen also made another important observation. She sees the creation of the new urban areas inevitably created jealousy that led to the many kidnappings of the Chinese Filipinos in the 1990s and 2000s. Moreover, the walls, fences, and even security guards posted outside subdivision gates were proven not impenetrable. She writes,

> The areas occupied by the Chinese are known to everybody, whether they are used for the purpose of work or residence. It is easy to trace their movements and find out when they use their vehicles everyday. These urban enclaves are far from being impenetrable; it is possible for someone to jump over the fence or a wall to look for a few spots that can be used to set up a trap.

39. Guéguen, "Moving from Binondo," 122–25.

40. Ibid., 124–26.

41. See also ibid., 135.

42. Ibid., 126.

> Behind the kidnappings is a highly organized criminal network which targeted the Chinese community. Information could also be obtained from collaborators in the local police or the army.[43]

The Chinese Filipinos are an ethnic minority that in some ways persists in their traditionalism and cultural adherence by unifying themselves in clustered neighborhoods. Guéguen wonders what kind of integration these "micro-urbanism" settlements bring in the different urban areas of Metro Manila. She concludes that these are enclaves surrounded by walls and fences and security guards.[44] I see their settlements as "mixed yet unmixed" settlements. On a bigger scale, they are found living among Filipinos but they are actually living among Chinese.

In another article, Guéguen suggests that the identification of Binondo as Chinatown does not necessarily mean the majority of residents are Chinese but rather they are important economic players of the community. She believes that this framework is also applicable to the many Chinese scattered in different parts of the country. Their presence in one block, building, subdivision, or barangay does not constitute dominant residency of the whole city, town, or even neighborhood. She recommends the need to go to them, to find them, to know where they are really situated and not simply relying on labels or old notions.[45]

Guéguen discovers that

> statistical data for the numbers of Chinese and Filipinos living in the same space show that the Chinese make up only six percent, at the most, of the total population of a local administrative unit (barangay). According to the figures, they are never the majority group, except in some streets or residential buildings where there is Filipino domestic staff.[46]

Guéguen's findings remind us once again the dangers of clumping and relying on stereotypes. Her discovery that Binondo district is no longer made up predominantly of Chinese Filipinos and that they compose about 6 percent of every barangay in Manila leads us to rethink where to really find them. It can be that many Chinese Filipinos have businesses in downtown Manila but reside in other cities of Metro Manila.

43. Ibid., 127.
44. Ibid., 121–22, 127, 134–35.
45. Guéguen, "Boundaries, Spaces and Populations."
46. Guéguen, "Moving from Binondo," 127.

Finding them may be tough but there are clues such as high walls, fences, subdivisions, buildings, and specific blocks on a street. The Chinese Filipino evangelical churches must make use of the available information such as Guéguen's or See's to acquire a better knowledge and understanding of the present Chinese Filipinos. The Chinese Filipino evangelical churches must be willing to go through the valleys and rivers, thickets and bushes, to seek and save the lost for Jesus.

CHINESE FILIPINO EVANGELICAL CHRISTIANS' ROLE IN LOCAL AND GLOBAL MISSIONS

On November 8, 2013, one of the strongest typhoons ever recorded in history struck the Philippines. Thousands dead and thousands left without homes, hungry, cold, and traumatized by the experience. The Filipinos are overwhelmed with the foreign aid pouring into the country for the typhoon victims. The total foreign aid pledged is ₱25.5 billion or $566 million.[47] Many Filipinos contributed to their ability to help their *kababayan* (countrymen). The Chinese Filipinos also do their share in helping the victims.

The places that were hit the hardest are Leyte and eastern Samar, particularly Tacloban City. There are two Chinese schools in Tacloban City, namely, Leyte Progressive High School and Sacred Heart College. After the typhoon, the schools were not able to open. The city lost electricity and communication lines were interrupted. Looting and chaos prevailed immediately after the storm, which forced many residents to flee and find refuge in Metro Manila or nearby provinces. Many Chinese schools in Metro Manila sent help (in monetary and in kind) to the victims. They also offered free tuition, free uniforms, and school supplies for the students of these two Chinese schools and other Chinese schools affected by the typhoon. They assisted these children and youth in their relocation to Metro Manila and to continue their schooling. Some Chinese schools went extra miles, like providing temporary housing and counseling for these students.[48] This is only one of the many examples of how the

47. Official Gazette, "Typhoon Yolanda"; Foreign Aid Transparency Hub, "Total Foreign Aid Pledge."

48. Two examples of online announcements made by two big Chinese schools are the following. "We have seen on TV and read in the newspapers about the sad plight that the 7.2 magnitude earthquake and super typhoon Yolanda have brought to your areas. It is our sincere desire to help you by extending an invitation for you to continue your interrupted education at our school, Grace Christian College. You will be

Chinese Filipinos are generous in responding to crisis. There are many other Chinese Filipino organizations and institutions that reached out and helped. The Chinese Filipino evangelical churches also responded with help. The Christian Bible Church of the Philippines (CBCP) alone was able to raise ₱1.8 million or approximately $40,000 cash to donate to different institutions that directly help the Yolanda victims.

This research has 59 key informants interviewed individually, 33 of whom were Protestants. Most of them are members of Chinese evangelical churches in the Philippines. They are Chinese Filipino Evangelical Christians (CFEC). As CFEC, this portion will lay down two reasons why they can be pivotal in both local and global missions. First, the CFEC are predominantly cultural hybrids. Their hybrid nature contributes to their advantage in terms of language, culture, and education. Their hybrid nature enables them to negotiate and cross boundaries, which makes mission among one's own group as well as other groups possible.

The CFEC are multilingual. Most of them are fluent in Filipino and English. Many can either understand or speak Minnanhua. Some can converse in Putonghua. Their knowledge in different languages and cultures opens doors of opportunities to do evangelism and discipleship among fellow Chinese Filipinos, Filipinos, or cross culturally.

The United Evangelical Church of Malabon envisions the need to provide a place for the elderly Chinese Filipinos whether Christians or non-Christians for association and activities. They are mostly Minnanhua speakers. Since many of these elderlies' family members are busy at work or in school, they are usually left at home, lonely and without

---

welcomed as our scholars, free of tuition and miscellaneous expenses, as well as books. We can also help you look for boarding places around our campus." Grace Christian College, "Campus Bulletin." "In cognizance of their plight, our school, as a gesture of humanitarian spirit and outpouring of love and compassion, posted in the official website and the Facebook our acceptance of students enrolled in Chinese-Filipino schools in affected areas of Tacloban, Samar, Bohol, and Palawan with completely free school fees. They can immediately continue their studies in our school at the soonest possible time so that they can move on with their lives quickly. We also announced the availability of free school and P.E. uniforms and dormitories for these students, now that their homes are completely washed away by the storm surges, looted, or pulverized by the destructive earthquake. The reaction has been positive and uplifting. On November 18, twenty four (24) students from Leyte Progressive School, Sacred Heart School, and two colleges in Tacloban City, plus a school in Ormoc City enrolled. Some have places to stay in Manila while several will stay in the school dormitory. As of last count, there are now 39 students from kindergarten to college levels. We expect to have some more coming in as soon as they can find a way to reach Manila." Te, "CKSC Cares for Typhoon Yolanda Victims."

companionship. The church opens their multipurpose hall every Tuesday and Thursday for these seniors. They facilitate different activities like exercises, crafts, games, and seminars for them. They also provide transportation with a minimal fee. Church members volunteer their time to make friends with these elderlies and hope to encourage them and bring them to a knowledge of who Jesus Christ is.[49] CFEC who are fluent in Minnanhua can reach out to such elderlies.

Those who are fluent in Putonghua can venture to minister to the NI or the one billion Chinese in the mainland. There are Chinese evangelical churches that have outreach programs specifically to the NIs. A number of faculty members in Biblical Seminary of the Philippines teach Putonghua module classes in China, countries in the Middle East, and Spain aside from teaching in the Putonghua track of the seminary. Their knowledge in the Putonghua language is used not just locally but globally.

The hybrid CFEC can serve as missionaries here and abroad with their ability to speak in English. An example of this is the Gerizim Evangelical Church (GEC). GEC is not a big church but it has several members who are cross-cultural missionaries here and abroad. They do not simply support missionaries but support their own home-grown missionaries. These CFEC are missionaries to China, Haiti, Madagascar, and the United States.

Second, the CFEC are an army of many possibilities of ministries and mission work. The CFEC must rethink how they can be good stewards of the resources the Lord has entrusted to them. They need to reexamine how faithful they are with their talents, skills, and other resources. Many Chinese Filipino evangelical churches have outreach programs, usually to the poor Filipino in their community. Their knowledge in Filipino gives them the opportunity to preach the gospel to the Filipinos. They employ their talents and skills in helping the Filipinos as well as share their time, energy, and finances.

To illustrate, CBCP started a Slum Ministry in 1993 that reaches out to the Talayan Riverside community. This community lives just behind the church and is composed mainly of informal settlers or squatters living in poor and depressed community. CBCP organizes and distributes yearly Christmas goods for every family in that community. This is made possible through the generosity of the church members.

---

49. Tanganco, "Bringing God's Love to the Elderly."

The church also has a weekly Saturday Kids' Bible Club open to all the children in the slum community. The Saturday School is held in the church. CBCP willingly open their classrooms and facilities for these children. Many church members volunteer their time and energy to teach the children Bible stories and lead them to godly lives. There is also a weekly free medical consultation for them. They can avail free medical consultations and quality medicines at very low cost. Veteran doctors, a dentist, and nurses volunteer to help give free medical check-ups. CBCP have also partnered with Filipino churches to reach out to the slum community since 1997.[50]

This is just one church using all the possible means to make a difference in their community and their country. As I have discovered in this research project, the CFEC are in a position where they could use their hybrid culture and their resources, whether skills, talents, or money, as opportunities to serve God in local and global missions.

50. CBCP, "Our Ministries."

7

Conclusion and Recommendation

THE IDENTITIES OF THE Chinese in the Philippines have evolved and have been redefined through the past several centuries. They were traders who journeyed to find greener grass. They were Coolies as the demands for such labor guaranteed entrance to the Philippines. They were *kabise* or bosses of retail and wholesale stores. They were Tsino or Chinese during the Spanish Period and even in the American Period. When the Philippines became independent and a sense of nationalism swept the country, the Chinese acknowledged their gratitude to the Philippines for giving them a place for refuge by calling themselves Filipino-Chinese.

The second- and third-generation Filipino-Chinese have realized the Philippines is their only country, their homeland. They called themselves Tsinoys and Chinese-Filipinos, contending that Filipino is the noun while Chinese is the adjective. Presently, the hyphen is dropped and they are simply called Chinese Filipinos. They are Chinese in ethnicity and Filipino in nationality. They are Chinese whose loyalty resides in the country and not China or Taiwan. They are Chinese and Filipinos, a cultural hybrid. This section will review the questions raised at the beginning of this study. The research concludes with the following discoveries made.

First, the Chinese Filipinos cannot be classified merely as Tsino (Chinese) or Tsinoy (Tsino and Pinoy) since there are many kinds of Chinese Filipinos, many interrelated and overlapping identities, as presented in chapter 4. They are the Old Immigrants, New Immigrants, Tsinoys, Unhomed Chinese Filipinos, Chinese Spouses in Inter-ethnic Marriages, and the Chinese Mestizos. They share core experiences and practices and yet they also differ in various ways.

191

Second, most informants, including those with Chinese citizenships, accept the term Tsinoy to refer to the Chinese in the Philippines. A number dislike the term and prefer to be called Filipino-Chinese or just Chinese.

Third, most of the informants see themselves as cultural hybrids rather than homogenous purists. Interestingly, most of the OI and NI Adults see themselves as Chinese only and can then be categorized as homogenous purists. The second-, third-, fourth-, and fifth-generation Tsinoys and even the NI Youth see themselves as cultural hybrids.

The Old or New Immigrants are Sojourners turned Settlers or still sojourning. They are Settlers as they decide to plant their roots in this country when circumstances are favorable to them. They are Sojourners as they continue to decide whether to stay or move elsewhere. These Sojourners are transnationals and cosmopolitan capitalists. They are Huáqiáo (overseas Chinese) or Chinese in diaspora. They have strong affinity to their country of origin. They have preserved their Chinese culture and heritage.

The Tsinoys are Huárén (Chinese people in diaspora) or Huá-yi (of Chinese descent). They were born and grew up in the country. They are taxpayers and mostly Filipino citizens. They are cultural hybrids since they cannot deny that they are influenced by Filipino and Western cultures aside from the Chinese culture. Many consider the Chinese culture as the dominant culture they practice. Their hybrid nature is evident in the fact they call themselves Tsinoy; are trilingual in conversation; read and write in English; no longer read and write in Putonghua; and mix different cultures and beliefs in some aspects of their lives, including the religious aspect. They have produced a third culture, uniquely their own. The Tsinoys may have similarities with other Chinese in diaspora. However, they are culturally distinct as a whole. Their knowledge of different cultures enables them to switch from one to another as situations arise. They also adapt to and adopt these cultures, adding them to their culture and making them part of their own.

The discussion on hybridity continues with the Tsinoys as unhomed. They are suspended in what Bhabha calls a third space. This third space or unhomely state is where ambiguity and uncertainty dominate. Such circumstances develop as their physical features or accent become avenues for discrimination and prejudices; or when those with Chinese citizenships go abroad with China or Taiwan passports. Their "imaginary"

Chinese citizenship has left them confused, marginalized, displaced, and with no country to call their own.

The Tsinoy's cultural hybridity is also developed in Barth's situational approach and Robbins's mixed yet unmixed nature. This research discovers that the Tsinoy informants compartmentalize their hybrid nature as they negotiate, adapt, and adopt different cultures in different situations. They are "mixed yet unmixed" or compartmentalized because they often can still distinguish which language or practice belongs to which culture. And yet, there are instances they cannot be certain which belongs to which. Another example, the Chinese or Chinese Mestizo spouses in inter-ethnic marriages tend to be Filipinized rather than Sinicized. They experience Reversed Identities. Some allow themselves to be assimilated into the dominant Filipino community which they are now part of. Most of those interviewed fail to Sinicize their partners. Very few of the Filipino spouses were Sinicized as evident in their failure to speak or understand the Minnanhua language. Although the Filipino spouses admit that they learn some Chinese cultural practices as they deal with their in-laws.

Fourth, the present Chinese Filipinos still practice endogamy and this seems to be the main cause for the continuing existence of their ethnic group. Endogamy and adhering to Chinese culture can be viewed as preference and celebration of one's cultural heritage. At times, they are associated with ethnocentrism. But ethnocentrism is discrimination and prejudice that must be dealt with intentionally to prevent it from serving as a barrier to unity, equality, and harmony in a multicultural society like in the Philippines. There is a diminishing prejudice against the Chinese Mestizos and even toward the Filipinos as evident in the diminishing use of offensive labels and names against these.

The relationship of endogamy and Sinicization or Filipinization is obvious in the inter-ethnic marriages and the Chinese Mestizos. The CMs are both cultural and biological hybrids. The process of Sinicization, Filipinization, or Resinification can be more understood and evaluated by studying three or more generations. It is evident from the interviews that Filipinization often happens in inter-ethnic marriages, thus, the first-generation CMs will be more inclined to Filipinization than Sinicization. Unless the parents and the children altogether will intentionally learn Minnanhua or apply Chinese culture, chances are Filipinization happens more than Sinicization. However, if the first-generation CMs choose to marry Chinese or more Sinicized CMs, there is a higher probability that

Resinification will happen. If endogamy is continually practiced, then, the following generation will likely be more Sinicized than Filipinized.

Fifth, the Chinese Filipinos are constructivists not primordialists. The fact that they see themselves as cultural hybrids connotes a constant mixing and construction. Sinicization, Filipinization, and Resinification are intentional constructs that the Chinese Filipino will have to decide in their continuing construction of their culture and identity as they are being exposed to different cultures. Moreover, culture and identity change as times change, and the socio-political, ecological, and historical dimensions in which the Chinese Filipino are situated must be considered. However, the inclination of most Tsinoy to remain essentially a Chinese is ethnification in process. But then, with global and technological advancement, they are not immune to outside influences and their cultural practices are in constant negotiation, adaptation, adoption, or elimination.

Sixth, the ethnic identification of the Chinese Filipinos affect other aspects of their lives such as in relation to education, language, marriage, family, and even in religion.

Seventh, their hybrid nature also affects their mindset as they apply this in relation to their religious life. The Chinese Filipinos tend to add rather than replace gods and produce a mixed belief system. The Chinese Filipino evangelical churches need to help these Chinese Filipinos to become authentic believers rooted in biblical truths.

This research has not fully covered the ethnicity, cultural hybridity, or religious facets of the Chinese Filipinos. The author recommends more studies and further research in recognition of continual change of culture over time. In terms of ethnicity, further studies are needed to explore the persisting Chineseness of present Chinese Filipinos and the process of constructing their identities. This research can serve as a baseline study of identity, church, and mission which can then be compared with other ethnic groups.

Cultural hybridity opens many avenues and prospects for research and discoveries. This study discusses the hybrid nature of the Chinese Filipinos in the area of identity as they are hybrids in cultural practices and in bloodline. It also raises the issue of ambivalence in mixed or not yet mixed nature and unhomely situations. It presents their negotiating tendencies, as they employ different cultures on different occasions. The most obvious marker for cultural hybridity discovered in this study is the mixing of three languages in conversation. More subtle is the deeply rooted pragmatism that has served Chinese Filipinos so well over the years, but inclines them toward participating in several religions, each for different purposes. More work could be done on how to harness this pragmatism in the service of Christianity. What does this mean to discipleship? What is the response of the Chinese churches in relation to this?

In addition, more research can be done on the cultural practices or how Confucianism is mixed with other Filipino or American values and practices. In the area of religion, this study brings out the syncretistic nature of the Chinese Filipinos. There is a need to study appropriate local theologies to address these issues and create methods of evangelism and discipleship appropriate for each kind of Chinese Filipinos.

Another recommended topic is raising institutional (churches or para-churches) problems and issues and finding solutions in this global age with the reality of cultural hybridity. The following are some of the issues and concerns:

How do they intend to respond to the issues of EngChiLog, En-RAWGen, lack of fluency in Minnanhua and Putonghua, and preference for the English language among the Tsinoys today? What about the elderlies who still employ Minnanhua as their heart language or the influx of NIs who speak Putonghua? What will happen to the Chinese Christians who intermarry with Filipinos? Should we just lose them to the Filipino churches? How will the church address this issue of an increasing number of inter-ethnic marriages? How do the CFEC respond to issues like non-Chinese membership and leadership in their churches? What will the CFEC look like in the next ten years with the tension of Sinicization and Filipinization?

Along with evangelism and discipleship, there is a pressing concern among the Chinese Filipino evangelical churches today regarding the exiting of many young CFEC to non-Chinese mega churches. This leads to a study made by Stewart Young for the BSOP Research Office in 2013. His research concludes that:

- The Chinese Church is very traditional, culture-laden (i.e., the good, bad, and ugly) and largely irrelevant (not contextualized) to contemporary life.

- There is an urgent need for liberation from the externals within the Chinese Church. There is a great need "*to be*" than "*to do.*"

- The primary reasons for many leaving the Chinese Church has more to do with cultural factors than the spiritual; the cultural affects the spiritual.[1]

This study along with more studies are needed to help the Chinese evangelical churches face the challenges and appropriate strategies and changes in doing mission among the Chinese Filipinos. Despite the fact that there are many leaving the churches, there are even more who have yet to be evangelized and discipled. The *chap chay lomi* nature of the Chinese Filipinos in relation to faith and spirituality is enough to convince us that we need to go to them and help them understand the gospel truths.

The CFEC are pivotal in reaching their fellow Chinese in the Philippines and abroad. They are also able to minister to the Filipinos here and abroad. They are also possible missionaries in cross-cultural ministry here and abroad. More research is needed in the area of partnership and coordination among the Chinese Filipino evangelical churches. Partnership and joint projects are already ongoing but studies need to be made to understand the processes and evaluate their effectiveness. Unity and coordination among these churches are also crucial in working for the same vision and mission for God's kingdom and glory. Further studies can be made on possible mission work among Chinese in China or Filipinos in the Philippines. CFEC can dream big by studying opportunities on how to make an impact in their community, society, country, and worldwide. With the frequent calamities in the Philippines, the CFEC can also do research and create feasible studies on proper procedure and training for pre-, during, and post-calamity scenarios. This is to avoid so much waste in time, energy, and money as compared to each church doing their own thing.

This research has established that there are many kinds of Chinese Filipinos; that there is still a need to evangelize and disciple them to the knowledge and truth of the Scriptures; and that they can be used greatly as God's channels of blessings to their own kind and to the rest of the world. This research can serve as a comparative study for other ethnic groups in the Philippines or even ethnic groups or diaspora groups in other parts of the world.

1. Young, "Why Chinese Church Members Are Leaving."

APPENDIX A

List of Key Informants for the Present Chinese Filipino Profile[1]

Table 5. Old Immigrants

Informant	Birth	Birth Place	Date of Interview	Residence	Status	Religion
Un Tién	1927	Fujian	June 15, 2012	Quezon City	Widow	Protestant
Luther	1929	Fujian	August 1, 2012	San Juan	Married	Protestant
Jimmy	1936	Fujian	July 4, 2012	San Juan	Married	Buddhist
Ahbi	1936	Philippines	August 1, 2012	San Juan	Married	None

Focus Group A-OI in Malabon City, five people, June 14, 2012.
Focus Group B-OI in Quezon City, five people, July 11, 2012.

TOTAL: 14

Table 6. New Immigrants

Informant	Birth	Birth Place	Date of Interview	Residence	Status	Religion
Mr. Chia	1949	Fujian	July 27, 2012	Binondo	Married	Protestant
Peter	1959	Inner Mongolia	July 24, 2012	Binondo	Married	None
Ping	1962	Fujian	July 25, 2012	Binondo	Married	None
Kerri	1962	Hong Kong	June 13, 2012	Quezon City	Married	Protestant

1. Pseudonyms are given to all key informants whether individually interviewed or in focus groups.

Informant	Birth	Birth Place	Date of Interview	Residence	Status	Religion
Li	1964	Fujian	July 24, 2012	Binondo	Married	None
Carla	1987	Fujian	June 20, 2012	Binondo	Single	Protestant
Mina	1990	Taiwan	July 27, 2012	San Juan	Single	Mixed Religions

Focus Group C-NI Youth in Binondo, four people, July 13, 2012.

TOTAL: 11

Table 7. Tsinoys, Local Born Second Generation Chinese Filipinos

Informant	Birth	Date of Interview	Residence	Status	Primary Language/s*	Religion
Pepito	1941	June 26, 2012	Binondo	Married	Minnanhua	Buddhist
Rose	1944	June 18, 2012	Binondo	Married	Cantonese and Minnanhua	Protestant
Martha	1946	June 29, 2012	Binondo	Married	Minnanhua	Protestant
Nellie	1946	June 25, 2012	Binondo	Married	Minnanhua	None
Ludy	1962	June 17, 2012	Quezon City	Married	Minnanhua and Filipino	Protestant
Mr. John	Did not mention	June 23, 2012	Did not mention	Married	Minnanhua	Protestant
Milo	1950	June 23, 2012	Binondo	Married	Minnanhua	Protestant
Dan	1969	June 21, 2012	Tondo	Married	Minnanhua and Filipino	Mixed Religions
Paolo	1977	July 19, 2012	Sta. Mesa	Married	Minnanhua and Filipino	Mixed Religions

TOTAL: 9

*Primary language is the first language or heart language that one is most fluent and comfortable with.

Table 8. Tsinoys, Local Born Third Generation Chinese Filipinos

Informant	Birth	Date of Interview	Residence	Status	Primary Language/s	Religion
Hendrick	1973	June 16, 2012	Quezon City	Married	English	Protestant
Benjie	1981	July 21, 2012	Caloocan City	Single	Cantonese and Filipino	Roman Catholic
Sunny	1978	June 23, 2012	Binondo	Single	Filipino	Protestant
Bert	1992	July 21, 2012	Binondo	Single	Minnanhua	Protestant

Focus Group D-T3 in Quezon City, thirteen people, June 17, 2012

TOTAL: 17

Table 9. Tsinoys, Local Born Fourth and Fifth Generation Chinese Filipinos

Informant	Birth	Date Of Interview	Residence	Status	Primary Language/s	Religion
Halley	1971	July 23, 2012	Binondo	Single	Minnanhua and Filipino	Protestant
Nolan	1972	June 25, 2012	Quezon City	Single	Minnanhua and Filipino	Protestant
Anne	1998	July 21, 2012	Binondo	Single	Minnanhua and Filipino	Protestant
Ellis	1998	June 11, 2012	Mandaluyong	Single	Minnanhua and Filipino	Protestant

TOTAL: 4

Table 10. Overseas Chinese Filipino Workers

Informant	Birth	Date of Interview	Country / No. of Years	Status	Fluent Language/s	Religion
Wendel*	1961	July 4, 2012	Saudi Arabia, 2	Married	English, Filipino, and Minnanhua	Roman Catholic
Arlene	1981	June 26, 2012	Singapore, 2	Single	English, Filipino, Mandarin, and Minnanhua	Roman Catholic

Informant	Birth	Date of Interview	Country / No. of Years	Status	Fluent Language/s	Religion
Robert	1974	June 28, 2012	Taiwan, 13	Single	English, Filipino, Mandarin, and Minnanhua	Protestant
Margaret	1981	June 29, 2012	Australia, 6	Single	English, Filipino, and Minnanhua	Protestant
James	1986	June 3, 2012	Taiwan, 2	Single	English, Filipino, and Minnanhua	Protestant

TOTAL: 4

*Wendel also contributed in the Chinese Spouse category.

Table 11. Chinese Mestizos, First Generation

Informant	Birth	Date of Interview	Residence	Status	Primary Language/s	Religion
Gregorio	1933	July 23, 2012	Quezon City	Married	Filipino	Roman Catholic
Fely	1955	July 15, 2012	Antipolo, Rizal	Married	Filipino	Roman Catholic
Billy	Did not mention	July 4, 2012	Bulacan	Married	Filipino	Roman Catholic
Darla	1958	July 4, 2012	Tondo	Married	Minnanhua and Filipino	Roman Catholic
Jennet	1963	June 13, 2012	Quezon City	Single	Filipino, English, and Minnanhua	Protestant
Arian	1979	June 9, 2012	Quezon City	Married	English and Filipino	Protestant
Chris	1988	July 22, 2012	Quezon City	Single	Filipino	Protestant

TOTAL: 7

Table 12 Chinese Mestizos, Second Generation

Informant	Birth	Date of Interview	Residence	Status	Primary Language/s	Religion
Benson	1941	June 19, 2012	Binondo	Married	Minnanhua	Mixed Religions
Nadine	1975	June 21, 2012	Tondo	Single	Minnanhua and Filipino	Mixed Religions
Lani	1981	July 19, 2012	Sta. Mesa	Married	Filipino and English	Mixed Religions
Steven	1988	July 15, 2012	Quezon City	Single	Filipino	Protestant
Casey	Did not mention	June 10, 2012	Quezon City	Single	Filipino, English, and Minnanhua	Protestant

TOTAL: 5

Table 13. Chinese Mestizos, Third Generation

Informant	Birth	Date of Interview	Residence	Status	Primary Language/s	Religion
Carding	1982	July 21, 2012	Quezon City	Single	Filipino	Roman Catholic
Rick	1996	July 22, 2012	Binondo	Single	Minnanhua	Protestant
Joshua	2001	July 16, 2012	Mandaluyong	Single	Minnanhua	Protestant
Harry	1999	July 24, 2012	Binondo	Single	English and Filipino	Protestant
Hal	1999	July 24, 2012	Binondo	Single	English and Filipino	Protestant

TOTAL: 5

Table 14. Chinese Spouses in Inter-Ethnic Marriages

Informant	Birth	Date of Interview	Spouse	Birth	Opposition	Religion
Nara	1955	July 19, 2012	Chester	Did not mention	Chinese side	Protestant
Andrew	1957	July 13, 2012	Sally	1967	Sally herself struggling	Roman Catholic
Adam	1959	July 4, 2012	Jenny	1973	Filipino side	Roman Catholic
Wendel	1961	July 4, 2012	Rachel	1972	None	Roman Catholic
Lovely	Did not mention	July 4, 2012	Miguel	Did not mention	None	Roman Catholic

TOTAL: 5

Table 15. Filipino Spouses in Inter-Ethnic Marriages

Informant	Birth	Date of Interview	Spouse	Birth	Opposition	Religion
Ace	1957	July 21, 2012	Ellen	1958	Chinese side	Roman Catholic
Faustino	1957	July 25, 2012	Ashley	1960	Chinese side	Protestant
Edna	1957	July 16, 2012	Art	1950	Filipino side	Protestant
Glenda	1959	July 24, 2012	Teddy	1941	Both	Protestant
Bernice	1970	July 23, 2012	Eddie	1972	Both	Roman Catholic

TOTAL: 5

The number of individually interviewed informants are 59.
These are in-depth interviews.

There are four focus groups facilitated by the author with
a total of 27 people.

Total number of key informants for the profile is 86 people.

APPENDIX B

Basic Questionnaire for All Informants

Name:

Birth:

Birthplace:

Home Address:

Contact number:

Email:

Sex:

Status: ☐ Student

         ☐ Married

         ☐ Working (name workplace and position)

FAMILY BACKGROUND

1. Father's name/birthday/birthplace.

2. Is he a Filipino/Chinese/Chinese Mestizo?

3. If he is a Chinese, is he a native born/what generation/Chinese immigrant/Filipino or Chinese citizen?

4. If he is a Chinese immigrant, please indicate what province in China did he come from? Does he visit China and connect with people back there?

5. Mother's name/birthday/birthplace.

6. Is she a Filipino/Chinese/Chinese Mestizo?

7. If she is a Chinese, is he a native born/what generation/Chinese immigrant/Filipino or Chinese citizen?

8. If she is a Chinese immigrant, please indicate what province in China did she come from? Does she visit China and connect with people back there?

9. What is your birth order?

10. No. of siblings (specify how many male and female).

11. Are you influenced/pressured/forced in choice of peers, college course, career, and spouse?

EDUCATION (Please indicate name of school, year entered
and year graduated)

Elementary:

High School:

College/Course:

Graduate/Post-Graduate/Areas of Discipline:

1. In what way is your ethnicity/identity an advantage or disadvantage to you as a student? How would you compare studying in a Chinese school versus in a Filipino school? Did you experience discrimination or prejudice of any sort in school because of your ethnicity? Give examples.

2. Describe your peers in college. Do your parents approve of your Filipino peers if you have one or more?

3. Do your parents influence/persuade/force you in what course/career you should pursue? If you have a choice, what course/career would you choose?

RELIGION

1. Which of the following best describe your religious affiliation or practice? You can check more than one.

☐ Roman Catholic [God, Jesus, Holy Spirit, Virgin Mary, other saints]

☐ Protestant [God, Jesus, Holy Spirit]

☐ Buddhist [Sakyamuni Buddha (釋迦牟尼菩薩), Bodhisattvas (菩提薩睡)]

☐ Daoist [Jade Emperor/Yu Huang (玉皇), Kuan Yin(觀音), Sam Po (三保), Xianshi (先師), Sanqing (三清), Sanzunfo (三尊佛)]

☐ Muslim [Allah, Mohammed the Prophet]

☐ Chinese Beliefs, Traditions and Practices [Thi Kong (天公) god in heaven, Tu Ti Kong (土地公) god of earth/soil, Teh KhiChu (地基主) god of foundation]

☐ Others

2. From whom or how did you arrive to your religious affiliation or choices? Are there opposition to your choice of religion or you had no choice at all?

☐ School

☐ Friend

☐ Family

☐ Relative

☐ Others

3. How often do you go to church or attend mass (for Roman Catholics) or go to temples (Buddhists)?

☐ Weekly

☐ 3 times a month

☐ Twice a month

☐ Monthly

☐ Seldom

☐ On special occasions only (Christmas or Easter)

☐ Never

4. Do you have an altar (based on your religious affiliation) in your home? Who decide what idol to place and how to venerate it?

☐ Yes

☐ No

5. Do you practice ancestral veneration? Can you tell me more about it in your understanding and practice? Is this enforced by your parents?

☐ Yes

☐ No

6. Do you believe and practice any of the Chinese religious beliefs and practices?

☐ Pat kua or Ba gua (八卦)

☐ Fortune telling

☐ Yin-Yang Principle

☐ Feng Shui

☐ Ha ha Popi (burning incense to gods)

☐ Others (please specify as many as you can)_____

LANGUAGE & CULTURE

1. Have you heard of Kaisa Para Sa Kaunlaran or Teresita Ang See?

2. What do you think is the mission of Kaisa?

☐ A foundation to help the less fortunate Chinese Filipinos

☐ A charitable organization for the Filipinos

☐ A cooperative for the Chinese Filipinos

☐ A business association for Chinese Filipinos

☐ A cultural center for the Chinese Filipinos

☐ A channel to promote mutual understanding between Chinese and Filipinos

3. Have you been helped personally by Kaisa through their projects or by Teresita Ang See?

4. Have you heard of Bahay Tsinoy? Have you visited Bahay Tsinoy? What can you say about it? Do you echo their way of presenting the Chinese in the Philippines?

5. Do you subscribe to the fortnightly issue of Tulay? Have you read any of the books published by Kaisa?

6. Do you think the Chinese Filipinos need to be integrated (i.e., to be acknowledged as part of the mainstream Philippine societies though not necessarily losing one's ethnic identity and culture)? Do you think they have truly integrated in the present? How it should look like for you?

7. Do you think the Chinese Filipinos need to be assimilated instead and there should be no adherence to Chinese culture but only Filipino?

8. Why do you think the Chinese want to stay Chinese? Why some want to become Filipinos?

9. What do you think are the issues of the Chinese Filipinos today in the Philippine society?
   - ☐ Ethnic identity
   - ☐ Unequal opportunities in business or profession
   - ☐ Racial prejudice from Filipinos
   - ☐ Racial prejudice towards Filipinos
   - ☐ Bribery
   - ☐ Tax Issues
   - ☐ Business/Economy instability
   - ☐ Poverty
   - ☐ Education
   - ☐ Language
   - ☐ Chinese Traditional Practices
   - ☐ Acquiring Filipino citizenship
   - ☐ Immigration problems
   - ☐ Kidnapping/Peace and order
   - ☐ Others (please specify as many as you can)_____

10. How many languages can you speak or understand?

11. What language or languages do you speak at home? Is this enforced by parents? Do you get confused with the different languages while growing up or this comes naturally for you? Which you prefer and most natural to you (Minnanhua, Filipino, mixed)?

12. Do you read Chinese newspaper or Chinese books? Watch Chinese movies (in Mandarin or with English subtitles)? Listen to Chinese songs?

13. Do you mostly eat Chinese food? Do you prefer Chinese food? Why?

14. What do you do for leisure?

15. Do you see yourself as?
    - ☐ Mono-cultural (Purely ethnic Chinese culturally)
    - ☐ Bicultural (Mixed Chinese and Filipino cultures)

    If bicultural, please check which is dominant.
    - ☐ Chinese
    - ☐ Filipino
    - ☐ Western

16. If people were to ask you about your identity, are you a Chinese or a Filipino? How do you see yourself? Would you agree to be called a Tsinoy? Chinese? Chinese Filipino? Do you have your loyalty to the Philippines or to China?

17. Do you see yourself homogenous or hybrid in the sense you acknowledge the influences of Filipino and Western cultures? Do you prefer to be homogenous or hybrid in culture? Would you say your identity has evolved throughout the years? Why or why not?

18. Manila Chinatown is the oldest existing Chinatown. What are your thoughts on segregation/separation of races? (Chinese schools, Chinese fire station, Chinese association) What do you think are the advantages and disadvantages? Do you agree with such kind of set up?

19. Would you see it ethnocentric if one seeks to retain and maintain their cultural heritage? How do you think should the Philippine government solve the issues of different ethnic groups such as Chinese, Igorots, or Koreans? Would you agree a multicultural setting or assimilated one?

20. Do you see yourself a stranger in this country or part of it?

21. Do you see yourself mainly pure and mono-cultural? If you see yourself a hybrid or mixed, do you think these cultures have been infused and cannot be separated from one to another? Or do you

see yourself with multiple "selfs" and able to compartmentalized cultures as need situationally?

MARRIAGE AND FAMILY (For married informants)

Spouse's name:

Birth:

Birthplace:

Please identify his/her race/ethnicity:

    ☐ Filipino

    ☐ Chinese Mestizo

    ☐ Chinese

If Chinese, choose one of the following:

    ☐ Native born

    ☐ Chinese immigrant (indicate what province in China)_____

    ☐ Chinese or Filipino citizen

    ☐ Others (please specify)_____

Educational Background:

Child/Children: (Please specify name/birthday/educational background)

COURTSHIP & MARRIAGE

1. How or where did you meet your spouse?

2. What qualities that made you attracted to him/her?

3. Was there opposition to your relationship? (e.g., family, faith) If yes, how did you respond to the opposition?

4. How long did your courtship go before deciding to get married?

5. Date and place of your wedding.

6. How do you complement and help each other as husband and wife?

7. What are some of the big challenges your marriage has faced and how did you overcome?

8. What are some of the things you wish you knew before and could have saved you and your spouse from much trouble or could have helped your marriage early on?

APPENDIX C

Note to All Participants

MY NAME IS JULIET Lee Uytanlet. I am doing a PhD in Intercultural Studies at Asbury Theological Seminary. For my dissertation, I am writing about the ethnic identity of the present Chinese in the Philippines. The working title of my dissertation is "The Hybrid Tsinoys: Challenges of Hybridity and Homogeneity as Sociocultural Constructs among the Chinese in the Philippines in the Twenty-First Century." The research seeks to discover how the Chinese Filipinos today identify themselves ethnically (whether as a Chinese, Filipino, or both) and how this classification affects other aspects of their lives.

I am hoping that through this research, I will be able to contribute to the following:

1. To provide an anthropological study on the ethnic identity of the twenty-first century Chinese in the Philippines through an ethnographic research method.

2. To contribute in the literature of cultural hybridity and ethnic identity.

3. To construct a profile of the present Chinese in the Philippines as oppose to the generalized understanding on Chinese Diaspora.

4. To aid Chinese churches in facing issues on multilingual services, inter-ethnic marriages, and Filipino memberships.

Thank you for your willingness to participate in this study. I am indebted to your commitment to help provide important data for this research. I hope this will spur further research in the future and be an encouragement to many. To do this study, I have formulated a two-part-questionnaire. The questions for each part are so constructed to acquire information essential for writing the paper. The first part will be answered in paper form. The second part will be an oral interview. Some information may not be included in the paper but may be important in the analysis and drawing conclusions. Further, your anonymity is a choice. Pseudo names will be provided if you choose to remain anonymous for your protection. However, for purposes of accuracy in collecting data, voice recording and video recording will be necessary as well as still shots photos. I believe many will benefit from your invaluable sharing. For purposes of formality and possible publication, I request your signature to prove your consent to allow me the right to publish data acquired from this interview. Again, thank you.

Sincerely,
Juliet Lee Uytanlet
Summer 2012

Informant Printed Name/Signature/Date

APPENDIX D

Timeline of Important Dates and Events of Chinese in Spanish Period Philippines

THE FOLLOWING IS A timeline of dates, events, and laws to aid in understanding why and how the Chinese were engaged mostly in trade, segregated, Hispanized or Christianized, expelled, and massacred during the Spanish Period based on the accounts of Abinales and Amoroso's book *State and Society in the Philippines* unless stated otherwise.[1]

❖ 1561—(TRADE) The Spaniards found a settlement of 150 Chinese and 20 Japanese in Manila. They also discovered that Chinese trading vessels made frequent visits to trade with native products.[2] Manila was chosen as the capital city by the Spaniards since the presence of 150 Chinese raised hopes for trade and mission work in China. The new colonizers increased the trade in the Philippines which in turn increased the influx of Chinese migrants. The Chinese were not only merchants but artisans and laborers that helped build establishments for the Spaniards. The increasing number of Chinese eventually exceeded the number of Spaniards which caused suspicion and alarm and led to distrust and restrictions. The Spaniards early on saw the Chinese as Jews or Moors. They imposed segregation, Hispanization, and expulsion on them as they did on the two other groups back home.

❖ 1572—(TRADE) When Guido de Lavezares was then governor, three ships from China docked in Manila while five went to the

1. Abinales and Amoroso, *State and Society*, 64–66.
2. See, *Tsinoy*, 45.

southern islands. This showed the growth of commerce and trade between the two countries.[3]

❖ 1574—(RESISTANCE) Lim A-Hong, the Chinese pirate, attacked the friars, churches, and Spanish residents in Manila. Some Chinese residents fought alongside him against the Spaniards, which widened the rift of distrust. The Sangleys became a despised minority. Since then, the Chinese were not allowed to travel freely into other parts of the Philippines without a permit. The Spaniards feared they would incite revolt or led revolts with the Filipinos. They segregated them from the Filipinos. However, this restriction only led the Chinese to become wholesalers, distributors, and shopkeepers, befriending the *alcalde mayores* and lay administrators of friar estates as they traveled into other parts of the country. Kaisa posed the possibility that Lim A-Hong was actually finding refuge in the Philippines to escape imprisonment and cruelties in China. Though he was outlawed as a pirate by the Chinese emperor, it was important to understand that during the Ming Dynasty, the peasants were taxed heavily to finance the extravagant lives of the rulers. This led to peasants uprising and rebelling much like Lim A-Hong's case. See argues that considering the fact that he came with 62 junk ships that included women and children aside from domestic animals and all sorts of treasures, could he have jeopardized them by attacking the Philippines? She infers that the lack of an interpreter and prejudice against the Chinese might have prompted the Spaniards to fight Lim A-Hong.[4]

❖ 1581—(SEGREGATON) The Spaniards forced the Chinese to live in the Parián. This way the Chinese could easily be controlled and administered. The Parián was situated outside the walled city of Intramuros with the cannons on top of the walls pointing in its direction. The Parián was the place where one could buy goods from East and West. The Parián in Manila changed location nine times but there were no records of their exact locations. The houses built were made of light materials that easily burned down after each massacre.[5] Phelan wrote that the Chinese were said to have a monopoly over the retail business. In response to this, the Spaniards imposed

3. Benitez, *History of the Philippines*, 73.
4. See, *Tsinoy*, 55–58.
5. Ibid., 62.

taxes on them, requiring them to pay a yearly license fee, tribute, and house tax amounting to a total of eighty-one *reales* (compared to the *indio* who paid only ten), in addition to unpaid labor and occasional arbitrary taxes. They had the highest level of taxation in the colony aside from the arbitrary taxes.[6] The Manila Chinese might have enjoyed the most successful trades, and yet, on the other hand, they experienced the worst atrocities.

❖ 1587—(TRADE) Under Governor Santiago de Vera, more than thirty large Chinese vessels had arrived Manila with merchandise, horses, and cows. These goods were taken to the Parián to be sold. Only silver or *reales* were accepted to purchase these goods, unlike in the early days when goods could be traded with other goods.[7] *Reales* or *real* was the Spanish word for royal. The *reales* or Spanish coins, specifically the *de a ocho reales* or "pieces of eight," became the international currency at the end of the sixteenth century until it was replaced by the British pound sterling silver in the nineteenth century. It was called the "Spanish dollar" in the United States.[8]

❖ 1589—(EXPULSION/HISPANIZATION) Governor de Vera reported that there were about four thousand Chinese found in the city, both as merchants and workmen. These Chinese men either stayed temporarily or permanently, changing citizenships and building houses.[9] That same year, a decree was made that expelled all Chinese, except farmers, carpenters, and mechanics from the colony. Many of those who remained converted to Roman Catholicism for fear of expulsion and to show loyalty to the Spanish regime. Nevertheless, the Spaniards eventually realized the Chinese's conversion was purely for economic reasons. Their visions of seeing China opened up for trade and mission through these Chinese in the Philippines turned out to be just a dream.

❖ 1593—(RESISTANCE/EXPULSION) Four hundred Chinese were drafted by force to row vessels in a military expedition against Maluku. The Chinese responded with mutiny and killed the governor of the colony. Because of this fateful event, half of the Chinese

---

6. Phelan, *Hispanization of the Philippines*, 11.

7. Benitez, *History of the Philippines*, 73.

8. Allen, *Encyclopedia of Money*, 107.

9. Benitez, *History of the Philippines*, 73.

population were deported back to China and the rest placed under guard. In the accounts of See, the rowers were untrained in systemized rowing, still they were punished severely and kept rowing without rest. P'an Ho Wu learned that they were going to war. Consequently, he challenged his fellow rowers to die fighting these Spaniards rather than die meaninglessly in a war that was not theirs. The Governor General Gomez Perez Dasmariñas was killed along with his men. This event led to deeper hate and distrust toward the Chinese especially by the son of the governor general, Luis Perez Dasmariñas. As the son took over his father's position, he led the massacre of 20,000 Chinese in 1603.[10]

❖ 1594—(SEGREGATION/HISPANIZATION) Binondo was established as a Chinese town.[11] It was the result of a royal order for the expulsion of all Chinese from the Philippines possibly due to the mutiny of 1593. Interestingly, Governor Luis Dasmariñas intervened because he recognized the important role played by the Chinese people as merchants and artisans. He retained a small number of Chinese instead of removing the whole race. The Spaniards were not able to give up their dependence on the Chinese for certain services like butchery and baking, as well as trade and other jobs.[12] Binondo was originally established for the availability of Chinese

10. See, *Tsinoy*, 58.

11. Hence, Binondo was the first officially established Chinese town or Chinatown. Today, it is the oldest that is still in existence. According to Teresita Ang See, Binondo was bought from Don Antonio Velada by Dasmariñas for 200 pesos. "Known as Binunduc (hilly place), the land was given to the Catholic Chinese in perpetuity, tax-free, and self-governing privileges to mitigate the damages caused by the expulsion. The adjoining village of Baybay was also acquired and was merged with it, creating the sub-district of San Nicolas, where many of the streets were named after Spanish cities and towns - Madrid, Sevilla, Barcelona, Numancia. Eventually, Binondo became a center of catechization and a commercial hub. Its inhabitants were mostly Christian Chinese, their Tagalog wives, and their mestizo offspring who were brought up as Malays, not as Chinese." See, "Binondo's Byways," 142. By 1858, Caoili recorded that Binondo had a population of 27,557. 21,002 were natives and mestizos. He added that 25,000 to 30,000 Chinese lived in the suburbs of Manila, mostly in Binondo. He described Binondo as "where the rich merchants—foreign, Chinese mestizos, and natives—resided, in the newest, most elegant houses along the Pasig River. Escolta and Rosario were the principal streets in the district, where most of the Chinese shops could be found . . . The first big hotel (Hotel Oriente) was opened in Binondo in January 1889 with 83 rooms and stabling for 25 horses. It ranked with the best hotels in the East." Caoili, *The Origins of Metropolitan Manila*, 42–43.

12. Chia, "The Butcher, the Baker, and the Carpenter," 517.

services and not for religious or cultural reasons. But the Dominican fathers turned the place into what Wickberg called an "acculturation laboratory" by marrying the Chinese with "*indias*" or local women. This resulted in the first generation of Chinese Mestizos. The non-Catholic Chinese were "missionized, baptized, married, and added to the community of married Catholics." By 1600, this group reached five or six hundred. The Dominicans were hoping that these mestizos would be well educated and assisted them in their mission to China.[13] The Parián was supposed to be evacuated at this time. Nevertheless, the Chinese population once again increased in number, and in a decade they reached 25,000.

❖ 1603—(RESISTANCE/MASSACRE) Manila became prosperous with the unrestricted trade from the number of ships to the value of goods and even to what countries conducted business. Further, there were many Europeans and Asians settling in Manila that made the city so diverse and considered the greatest in the world at that time. Azcárraga y Palmero recorded that about 25,000 Chinese could be found and numerous Japanese as well. That same year, the Spanish fortified Manila as the phantom Chinese invasion played in their minds. Meanwhile, the Chinese, fearing a massacre, rose up in revolt. The Spaniards almost wiped out the whole community of twenty thousand. Benitez noted that the Chinese could have overthrown the Spanish sovereignty if not for the 1,000 soldiers from Pampanga that saved the Spaniards. Moreover, when the Chinese fled to San Pablo, Laguna, they were defeated with the aid of 400 Japanese, 2,000 Pampangan Filipino soldiers, 200 Muslims, and 300 blacks.[14] Interestingly, the Spaniards feared retaliation from the Chinese, and they sent envoys to China. Sadly, the emperor saw those Chinese in the Philippines as "unfilial sons who left their ancestral home and did not deserve sympathy."[15]

❖ 1639—(RESISTANCE/MASSACRE) The Chinese were also encouraged to be farmers. They worked in the royal and friar estates and provided sustenance to Manila.[16] Unfortunately, three hundred

13. Wickberg, "Chinese Mestizo in Philippine History," 69; *Chinese in Philippine Life*, 18–19.

14. Benitez, *History of the Philippines*, 181.

15. See, *Tsinoy*, 60.

16. The Jesuits who became successful in agrarian enterprises employed the

Chinese died while clearing the land for cultivation because of demanding and tough conditions. This led to agrarian resistance of Chinese tenants in the royal haciendas. See added that the inhumane treatment of the alcalde-mayor Don Luis Arias de Mora drove Chinese farmers to revolt and attacked the town of Calamba. The revolt spread from Laguna to nearby towns like Rizal, Cavite, and Manila. The Spaniards in return massacred the Chinese worse than the 1603 incident. Based on Spanish sources, there were more than 25,000 killed, but the Chinese Ming annals recorded more than 33,000.[17]

❖ 1663—(SEGREGATION/MASSACRE) Koxinga (Zheng Cheng Gong, 鄭成功) was a Ming loyalist and considered a rebel during the Qing Dynasty. He was considered a pirate by the Europeans. He defeated the Dutch colonists in Taiwan. The Spaniards were afraid of his possible invasion of the Philippines. Troops concentrated in Manila. Governor General Sabiniano Manrique de Lara feared the Chinese would assist if Koxinga attacked, ordered them to stay in Binondo and Parián and disarmed the non-Catholic Chinese. The Chinese, on the other hand, were afraid of another massacre. The Parián residents had a demonstration to voice their fear, but it was mistaken for an uprising. The Spanish soldiers killed 9,000 residents. "Many tried to escape, some drowned in the ditches, while others hanged themselves. About 2,000 rose in arms to protect themselves but were all killed with the help of Pampangueño forces."[18] Ironically, Koxinga did not invade Manila.

❖ 1686—(PUNISHMENT) Lucille Chia narrates the horrible turnout on the eve of May 28 when a band of eleven Chinese robbers attacked and killed the constable responsible for residence permits while the governor of Parián managed to escape. The eleven Chinese were immediately caught, hanged, and quartered. Their chopped corpses were put on display along river Pasig. Further, rumors spread that Chinese employees planned to put "ground glass and burned bits of pottery into the bread they made." These rumors strengthened the Spanish resolution to expel all non-Catholic Chinese within two months. However, the real deportation took place from 1690 until

Chinese laborers in their estate. Benitez, *History of the Philippines*, 109.

17. See, *Tsinoy*, 60.

18. Ibid., 60–61.

1700.[19] See noted that Tingco was a fugitive. He and his men were trying to raise enough money to go back home to China. Sadly, their looting and robbing led to their own doom. Moreover, the rumors about Chinese conspiracy led to more restrictions and persecutions on Chinese residents.[20]

❖ 1700s—(HISPANIZATION) Many Chinese intermarried with Filipinos to be able to stay in the country and gained more advantages in trade. This resulted in what the Spaniards referred as *mestizos* (half bred) or Chinese Mestizos as distinguished from the Spanish Mestizos. Later in the nineteenth century, it was the Chinese Mestizos who became the leading entrepreneurs of the country.[21]

❖ Mid 1700s—(EXPULSION) The Spanish government sought to establish self-sufficiency in the country with the Bourbon Reforms. They believed it was necessary to expel all Chinese to achieve this goal. They believed that the Chinese controlled the wholesale and retail trade and that made them rich, leaving the Spaniards and the Filipinos with nothing to gain. They believed that when the Chinese were gone, they could take over and could even put in new industries to add revenues for the new self-sufficient colony.[22]

❖ 1755—(HISPANIZATION/EXPULSION) Many Chinese converted to Roman Catholicism in order to escape being expelled from the country.[23] The Spaniards decided to reduce the number of Chinese to four or five thousand all over the Philippines. Again, this resulted in the decline of the Chinese population in the country.[24]

❖ 1762—(RESISTANCE/MASSACRE) Six thousand Chinese were killed after the Chinese sided with the short-lived British invasion. The Chinese were hoping to have better treatment under the supposed new colonizers.[25]

❖ 1766—(EXPULSION) Pampanga-based Spanish governor-in-exile ordered a preemptive massacre on the Chinese in Manila. Five

19. Chia, "The Butcher, the Baker, and the Carpenter," 509–10.

20. See, *Tsinoy*, 61.

21. Caoili, *Origins of Metropolitan Manila*, 37.

22. Sugaya, "Expulsion of Non-Christian Chinese," 111.

23. Ibid., 114.

24. Wickberg, "Early Chinese Economic Influence," 277.

25. See, *Tsinoy*, 61.

thousand Catholic Chinese in Manila rose up in revolt which led to the last expulsion of the Chinese in the country that greatly reduced their number.[26]

❖ 1778—(RESTRICTION) Governor General José de Basco y Vargas allowed the Chinese to return but limited their number to four thousand.[27]

❖ 1800—(MESTIZOS) This period saw the rise of Chinese Mestizos in replacing the Chinese in some occupations and challenging Chinese monopoly.[28]

❖ 1820—(MESTIZOS) The Chinese Mestizos dominated with great profit the new commercial agriculture where rural produce were bought wholesale and sent to market in Manila or overseas. They eventually became money lenders in rice-growing areas.[29]

❖ 1850—(BAN LIFTED) Spanish government removed the restrictions on Chinese immigrants to promote economic development of the Philippines. Not only were the Chinese not restricted in numbers, they were also not restricted to travel or stay anywhere in the archipelago.[30]

❖ 1869—(TRADE) Opening of Suez Canal shortened the travel time from Europe. British and Chinese dominated the import and export trade, such that the country became known informally as "Anglo-Chinese."[31]

---

26. Abinales and Amoroso, *State and Society*, 72.
27. Ibid., 76–77.
28. Wickberg, "Early Chinese Economic Influence," 278.
29. Ibid.
30. Ibid.
31. Abinales and Amoroso, *State and Society*, 80.

APPENDIX E

Labels and Names Given to the Chinese in the Philippines

Table 16. Labels and Names Given To the Chinese in the Philippines

Spanish	American	Filipino	Chinese	Social Scientists	Missionaries or Missiologists	Academicians
Sangleys	Chinamen	Barok	Tsinoy	Huáshāng 華商 or traders or merchants	Heathen	Chinese
Chinos	Coolies	Beho	Chinoy	Huágōng 華工 or Coolies	Pagans	Philippine Chinese
	Aliens	Buchiki	Chinese	Huáqiáo 華僑 or overseas Chinese	Buddhists	Filipino-Chinese
	Non-Christian Tribe	Bulol	*Tiong-Kok Lâng*	Jìjū 寄居 or sojourners	Daoists	Chinese-Filipino
		Kabise	*Lanlâng*	Huárén 華人 or Chinese people in diaspora	Syncretistic	Chinese Filipino
	Intsik		*Banlam Lâng*	Huá-yi 華裔 or of Chinese descent	Split level Christians	

Tsino	*Huakiao*	Jews of the East	Folk Roman Catholics
Tsinito, Tsinita	*Hua din*	Immigrants	Folk Evangelical Christians
Tsekwa	*Hua si*	Transnationals	*Chap Chay Lomi*
Chinky-eyed, Chinks	*Tsiá lanlâng*	Essential Outsiders	
Singkit, Singkot	*Chhut-sì-á*	Market-Dominant Minorities	
	Hoan-á	Flexible Identities	
	Hoan-á gong	Cosmopolitan Capitalists	
	Hoan-á kúy	Global Cosmopolitans	
	Hoan-á thé		
	Siõng Hoan		

APPENDIX F

Da Chen and Chinese Emigrations

DA CHEN (TA CHEN) evaluated Chinese emigration in his dissertation *Chinese Migrations* in 1923 from historical, social, and economic perspectives. Historically, there were three important Chinese emigration periods: the seventh, the fifteenth, and the nineteenth century. The seventh-century migration began with the Chinese colonists settling in Taiwan and the Pescadores Islands. Many of those who emigrated were people who lived in coastal ports. The Hakkas or Kèjiā 客家 were the first to trade with the original inhabitants of Taiwan that led to settlement.[1] Eventually, the Chinese partnered with friends back home and decided to trade with neighboring countries. The seventh-century migration opened the main trade routes that led to the British Malacca, to the Dutch East Indies, and to the Philippines.[2]

The second wave of migration started in the fifteenth century when the imperial eunuch Zhèng Hé (Cheng Ho) 鄭和 returned from his trips to western oceans.[3] Stories of El Dorado spread like wildfire in Fujian and Guangdong. There were also exaggerated miracles and distorted tales that led to the exodus of large numbers of Chinese. It was during

1. Ethan J. Christofferson's informants claimed that the Hakkas' ancestors originated from the central part of China. Harsh life drove them to different migration periods that eventually led them to Taiwan. Christofferson, *Negotiating Identities,* 112–13.

2. Da Chen, "Chinese Migrations," 4.

3. In 1405, Ming emperor Yung Lo appointed Admiral Zhèng Hé to be the governor over *Liu Sung* (Luzon) to impose China's supremacy over the Philippines. Karnow, *In Our Image,* 9.

this period that the junk trade flourished.[4] Further, the Ming emperors extended their rule over neighboring countries, extracting tributes from them. All these led to Chinese settling in the Malay Archipelago and the Philippines.[5]

The last wave of migration was in the nineteenth century[6] and particularly in 1860 when the Coolie Trade was legalized.[7] Spain, Portugal, Holland, Great Britain, and other European powers looked to China for supply of manual labor as the African slave trade began to decline in popularity. Most of the Chinese emigrated on their own free will under treaty provisions or labor contracts. They usually sought to stay for a limited time to earn money. Unfortunately, many were tricked in their contracts and sold as slaves.[8]

Da Chen enumerated what he called the "driving forces" of Chinese emigration. These push factors were social and economic. First, the increase in population led to inadequacy of food. Based on his tabulation, there was an increase of 15 percent of the population in China from 1812 to 1842. In Fujian alone, there was a huge increase of 75 percent in population.

Second, droughts, famines and wars pushed people out of the country. A significant decrease of 20 percent in population from 1842 to 1882 testified to the atrocious consequences of famines and wars. It was

4 Anthony Reid argues that the word "junk" derived from the Javanese and Malay word *jong* and not the Chinese Fuzhou dialect *song*; cf. Mandarin chuán 船. *Jong* is an older known Javanese word appearing as early as AD ninth-century literature. However, it may have derived from the Minnanhua word for boat which was *tsûn*. The Fujian people had been engaging in trade since the Tang Dynasty (618–907). Zhou, *Contemporary Chinese America*, 24–25. The junks are described as follows: "East Asian trading vessel came into European languages from the reports of travelers as early as the fourteenth century, though far more frequently in the sixteenth ... these junks were large cargo vessels of 500 to 600 tonnes, with the hold divided into variable partitions and the hulls able to have extra planks fastened to them as they grew unseaworthy." Reid, "Flows and Seepages," 18; *Southeast Asia in the Age of Commerce*, 36–39.

5. Da Chen, "Chinese Migrations," 4.

6. In 1850, Spanish government in the Philippines lifted the ban on Chinese immigrants to promote economic development. Wickberg, "Early Chinese Economic Influence," 278. In 1860, the opening of Suez Canal shortened the travel time from Europe to the Philippines. British and Chinese dominated the import and export trade the country became known informally as "Anglo-Chinese." Abinales and Amoroso, *State and Society*, 80.

7. See appendix G.

8. Da Chen, "Chinese Migrations," 4–5. See also Benitez, *History of the Philippines*, 157; Alejandrino, *Chinese Exclusion Act*, 8.

estimated that a total of 44,475,000 lives were lost due to famine and wars from 1846 to 1878. Considering the fact that 75 percent of the people in China at this time were farmers with an average number of five people in each family, famines and wars rendered them helpless and hopeless.

Table 17. Da Chen on Wars and Famine

Year	Calamity	Estimated Loss of Population
1846	Famine	225,000
1849	Famine	13,750,000
1854 to 1864	Taiping Rebellion	20,000,000
1861 to 1878	Mohammedan Rebellion	1,000,000
1877 to 1878	Famine	9,500,000

[9]Third, the nature of their environment added to their mobility. People living near ports and seas had more access to venture abroad. I will add that those living in port areas had the opportunity to do trade locally and internationally. Migrating for business purposes was also promising.

Fourth, Da Chen saw that their mental and physical abilities enabled them to endure and persevere in emigrating, acclimating to new places.

Lastly, the wage issue was an attraction to work abroad. Based on 1920 statistics, the daily wage in China was ten to fifty cents per day. With ten cents a day wage, a year's wage was about thirty dollars. Those working abroad like in Hawaii received as much as a dollar a day, or three hundred dollars a year.[10]

With all these driving forces, it was no wonder that the Chinese embarked on such a journey in search of greener pastures. The desire to alleviate hunger, escape the horrors of wars, and the tempting possibility of finding fortune and wealth pushed thousands of Chinese to migrate in the nineteenth and twentieth centuries.

9. Da Chen, "Chinese Migrations," 6.
10. Ibid., 5–12. See also appendix G.

APPENDIX G

The Coolie Trade: A Historical Backdrop

HARDSHIP SEEMS TO BE the last name of every Chinese in China during the nineteenth century. Russell Conwell investigated in 1871 why the Chinese left their beloved country for the United States even in the midst of warnings from their Majesty that they would be considered disloyal to China. He could not simply accept the popular belief that these people desired gold more than anything. He proposed another explanation. The Chinese left their country to escape oppression from their own people.[1]

Conwell used Chinese and Coolies[2] interchangeably in his book since the masses were the poor hired workers. He discussed the severe corruption of the government officials reducing the people to poverty and slavery. He described the poor roads from Nanking to Jinjiang that caused poor distribution of goods. He mentioned the increase in taxes while wages actually lessened; how the children were destroyed as a necessity. He believed that hardships and tyranny produced superstitious Coolies who tried to find answers in life. He concluded that the Coolies wanted to return to China when they grew older. They went to the United States simply to earn money and not be tormented by superstitions, calamities, and oppressions back home.[3]

Labor wage in China during the 1870s was very low. A Chinese working in a farm earned eight to ten dollars a year. Carpenters and

1. Conwell, *Why and How*, 10.

2. The word "Coolie" originally refers to an aboriginal Gujarat tribe of India, and stretches to mean migrant laborer or hireling. It later refers to Chinese contract laborers. Pan, *Sons of the Yellow Emperor*, 45. See also Watt, *Chinese Bondage in Peru*, 16. Coolie means cheap Chinese labor. Alejandrino, *Chinese Exclusion Act*, 8.

3. Conwell, *Why and How*, 31–32, 39, 41–43.

masons earned twenty two cents a day but with heavier tax. Clerks earned twelve to fifteen dollars a year. Out of his salary, he had to provide for his boarding for two dollars; tax for eighty cents; worship for a dollar; food for sixty cents; and clothing for a dollar. How much then would be left for his family? If he had a big family, the remaining amount from his salary could not be sufficient to feed, board, and clothe them all for the whole year. They would eventually fall into debt. Compare that to a Chinese of that same period working as a servant in San Francisco who earned twenty five dollars a year.[4] No wonder the Chinese in general were likely to leave the country in search of a better life. They were desperate to find more money. Tragically, many were fooled into signing contracts as indentured laborers in strange countries with little or no pay at all.

The Don Pedro was a Portuguese vessel with a capacity weight of eight hundred tons. The ship arrived in the early spring of 1847 in the port of Macao. The captain was impatient with the delay of the tea cargo. He got into a fight with the senior partner of the firm that cost him his charter. As he searched for new cargo, he met a Spanish businessman from Peru. The Spanish was surprised with the Chinese cheap labor and wished he had a thousand Chinese. The two planned to load the ship with Coolies for Peru under the pretense of shipping them to Java. They acquired three hundred men. It was not clear whether these Chinese were given contracts or at least had understood what they were about to enter into.[5] Conwell reported,

> Near the first day of June the "Don Pedro" sailed out of the port of Macaow with three hundred as happy men as ever trod the planks of a ship. Believing the falsehoods that had been told them, and expecting soon to return to their homes wealthier men, they looked back upon the disappearing shores, sighing only for the time when they should see them again. It is doubtful if any one of them has yet seen their native land, and as doubtful as any of them will do so.[6]

After one hundred days of exposure to storm, sun, hunger, and thirst, only one hundred and seventy five survived and landed in Callao, Peru. The Coolies endured inhumane conditions. They were placed in the interior plantations to prevent them from escaping. Their inability to

4. Ibid., 62–63, 69.
5. Ibid., 82–83.
6. Ibid., 83.

communicate in Spanish became the Spaniard's alibi for no complaints. The success of employing Chinese Coolies quickly spread to Spanish and Portuguese colonies. Demands for Coolies increased but obtaining that many voluntary workers seemed impossible. Back in China, rumors about the horrible fate of the Chinese on board the Don Pedro began to spread as wives waited in vain for their husbands, mothers for their sons, and children for their fathers. As the brokers had difficulty convincing the Chinese to work abroad, the system of kidnapping, chaining, starving, and murdering of Chinese as Coolies began and lasted for twenty years.[7]

> Fathers and mothers sold their sons, fugitives bargained away themselves, banditti brought in their male and female prisoners and sold them in lots to the traders, for which sums never exceeding ten dollars per person were thankfully received. The market being ill supplied with purchasable human beings, the traders organized bands of night-thieves whose business it was to steal into the cabins of the laborers and carry on board the ship the father and sons, and sometimes the whole family.[8]

Conwell described how the Coolies were poorly treated. They were given little food on board and on land. They were whipped and tasked to work night and day. They were considered prisoners. The saddest part of his account was the fact that the Chinese sold fellow Chinese as their government connived or turned a blind eye. There were clan wars that resulted in the capture and sale of Chinese. Many of these Coolies stabbed themselves or hung on trees out of severe hardship. There were mutinies and murders.[9]

In 1856, three hundred drowned themselves in the ocean near the Guano Islands. In 1857, the Coolies murdered their captors while on board the ship. In 1867, the Coolies butchered the officers and crews out of rage and ate human flesh to alleviate their hunger while on board the ship. Each Coolie was sold for ten to twenty seven dollars depending on physical strength. They were sold in bulk to the highest bidder. In 1864 and 1865, nine thousand seven hundred Coolies were sold to Cuban traders in the port of Macao and around three thousand were sold in the port of Canton. All Coolies were forced to sign a contract by which each

7. Ibid., 83–85.

8. Ibid., 85.

9. Ibid., 86–89.

was sold for three hundred fifty to six hundred dollars for eight years of contract after which the Coolie was at the disposal of the purchaser. It was doubtful if there were five hundred who were able to return to China out of the one hundred fifty thousand Chinese taken to Spanish and South American colonies before 1865.[10]

By 1854, the British government had taken measures to regulate the emigration of Coolies. British and German vessels were not allowed to carry Coolies. According to Da Chen, Coolie Trade was first legalized in the province of Guangdong in 1859. A year later, the whole of China allowed emigration of Chinese beyond its borders. In 1866, France and Great Britain refused to approve the reiteration of the emigration law because of its added provision for the death penalty for illegal recruitment and kidnapping of Coolies. Both countries acknowledged their dependence on illegal recruitment of laborers. China, nevertheless, promulgated the decree.[11]

These laws did not stop the trafficking of Chinese as contract laborers or slaves. The *London and China Telegraph* dated January 4, 1869, chronicled the condemnation of the Coolie Trade by the Governor Antonio Sergio de Souza of Macao and Timor. News received from the Portuguese Consul of Callao, Peru, that a certain farmer marked forty-eight Coolies with red hot iron as practiced for African slaves. Further, Coolies were found roaming the streets of the city begging for charity after they were mutilated and abandoned by their masters for they were deemed useless. In another report dated January 25, 1869, the American vessel *Cayalti* surfaced in Hakodadi. It carried Coolies who staged a mutiny and killed the crews but spared the captain.[12]

The Coolie Trade was dispensable. Immigration laws were tightened or loosened depending on the foreign countries' needs and situations. When the economy of the United States went down, the immigration laws were tightened and the country executed the Chinese Exclusion Law of 1882. After the First World War, France and Great Britain loosened their immigration laws to accommodate the much-needed Coolies to meet their shortage of workers.[13] Likewise, in the present, immigration

10. Ibid.

11. Da Chen, "Chinese Migrations," 17–20. See also Conwell, *Why and How*, 86, 89–91, 93.

12. *London and China Telegraph*, "Coolie Trade;" *London and China Telegraph*, "Last Coolie Tragedy."

13. Da Chen, "Chinese Migrations," 19; Alejandrino, *Chinese Exclusion Act*, 7–10.

laws tightened or loosened depending on the needs and situations of the host countries. Therefore, the migrants or immigrants will also be at the mercy of the changing times and the changing policies of nations.

APPENDIX H

NHI and Kaisa Project

THE KAISA AND THE National Historical Institute (NHI) had conducted a very interesting joint research project in which they photographed Chinese tombstones all over the archipelago from Aparri to Jolo. This project was accomplished through the journey of a photographer from the NHI and a Chinese researcher from 1992 to 1994. With a total of 39,479 tombstones, 7,377 were written in English or Spanish but the rest were in Chinese. The data gathered confirmed 90 percent of the Chinese in the country traced their origin from Fujian while 10 percent from Guangdong.[1] There were 238 tombstones that indicated other Chinese provinces. Those tombstones that indicated Fujian also indicated specific municipalities and 66.46 percent claimed to be from Jinjiang.[2]

Table 18 Places of Origin

Province		Number of Tombstones	Percentage
福建	Fujian	27,373	89.260
廣東	Guangdong	3,025	9.860
北京	Beijing	3	.010
上海	Shanghai	2	.006
山東	Shandong	9	.030
山西	Shanxi	1	.003

1. 30,637 tombstones indicate the origin of the deceased. 27,373 or 89.26 percent indicate that they are from Fujian province while 3,025 or 9.86 percent indicate that they are from Guangdong.

2. See, *Chinese in the Philippines*, 3:196–201.

台灣	Taiwan	7	.023
金門	Jinmen	180	5.880
安徽	Anhui	7	.023
江西	Jiangxi	1	.003
江蘇	Jiangsu	4	.013
西安	Xian	1	.003
浙江	Zhejiang	9	.030
奉天	Fongtian	3	.010
南海	Nanhai	5	.016
河北	Hebei	3	.010
廣西	Guangxi	1	.003
湖北	Hubei	1	.003
湖南	Hunan	1	.003

Originally published in See, *Chinese in the Philippines*, 3:197.

Table 19. Fujian Municipalities of Origin

	Province	Number of Tombstones	Percentage
晉江	Jinjiang	18,193	66.46
南安	Nan-an	4,826	17.63
廈門	Xiamen	854	3.12
惠安	Hui-a	810	2.96
龍溪	Longxi	425	1.55
思明	Si-ming	339	1.24
泉州	Quanzhou	319	1.17
同安	Tong-an	307	1.12
石獅	Shishi	234	0.85
永春	Yongchun	160	0.58
安溪	An-xi	149	0.54

Originally published in See, *Chinese in the Philippines*, 3:198.

Table 20. Guangdong Municipalities of Origin

	Province	Number of Tombstones
台山	Taishan	17
開平	Kaiping	6
中山	Zhongshan	2
汕頭	Shantou	2
潮州	Chaozhou	1

Originally published in See, *Chinese in the Philippines*, 3:198.

APPENDIX I

Acquiring Filipino Citizenships during the American Period

Kwok-Chu Wong cites three possible avenues for the Chinese in the Philippines to acquire Filipino citizenship during the American Period in his *The Chinese in Philippine Economy, 1898–1941*. First, they are citizens if they were considered "Spanish subjects" on April 11, 1899.[1] During the mid-nineteenth-century Spanish Period, the Chinese no longer needed to be converted to Roman Catholicism to become subjects of Spain. The liberal policies during this time period gave the Chinese fewer restrictions and the freedom to engage in trade or reside in the country. This enabled them to remain as they were, Chinese. They were still subjects of the Chinese Empire. Only a minority acquired Filipino citizenship or became Spanish subjects. The majority of them carried on their Chinese citizenship into the American Period.[2]

The second legal avenue was that the Chinese Mestizos born in the country of a Chinese father and a Filipina mother could claim Filipino citizenship by following the mother's citizenship. The precedent was set

---

1. "Sec. 4. That all inhabitants of the Philippine Islands continuing to reside therein who were Spanish subjects on the eleventh day of April, eighteen hundred and ninety-nine, and then resided in the Philippine Islands, and their children born subsequent thereto, shall be deemed and held to be citizens of the Philippine Islands and as such entitled to the protection of the United States, except such as shall have elected to preserve their allegiance to the Crown of Spain in accordance with the provisions of the treaty of peace between the United States and Spain signed at Paris December tenth, eighteen hundred and ninety-eight." Chan Robles Virtual Law Library, "Philippine Bill of July 1902."

2. Wong, *Chinese in Philippine Economy*, 6.

in the case of *Tranquilino Roa vs. the Insular Collector of Customs* of October 1912. The Philippine Supreme Court decided then that the child followed the nationality of the mother, thus becoming a Filipino citizen.[3]

Tranquilino Roa was born in Mindanao on July 6, 1889. His father was a Chinese immigrant while his mother was a Filipina. After his father's death in 1900, he went to China to study but with the intention to return. In 1910, he was not admitted to enter the Philippines because of the Chinese Exclusion Act that had been extended to the new colony of the United States. He appealed for reconsideration as a citizen of this country by virtue of election in between *jus soli* and *jus sanguinis*.[4] In other words, Roa sought to forego his Chinese citizenship since he had almost reached his age of maturity by the time he arrived in the country. He also argued that since his father died before he left for China, his mother in effect reacquired her Filipina citizenship. Hence, he automatically became a subject of Spain and not China. The Philippine Bill of July 1902 was therefore applicable to his case.

The third legal avenue to acquire Filipino citizenship was through naturalization. Early in the American Period, the Chinese, did not see the necessity to apply for Filipino citizenship. Eventually, the Act of Congress of August 1916 gave the Philippine legislature the autonomy to set the naturalization laws, and they barred most alien Chinese from applying for Filipino citizenship. With this, not more than 500 had applied for naturalization by 1936. Further, with the blossoming nationalism in China and Sino-Japanese Wars, the idea of getting Filipino citizenship seemed not to be a priority at that time.[5]

3. Ibid., 6–7.

4. "This is an appeal from an order of the Court of First Instance of Cebu recommitting the appellant, Tranquilino Roa, to the custody of the Collector of Customs and declaring the Collector's right to effect appellant's deportation to China as being a subject of the Chinese Empire and without right to enter and reside in the Philippine Islands. There is no dispute as to the facts." Chan Robles Virtual Law Library, "Tranquilino Roa."

5. Wong, *Chinese in Philippine Economy*, 8.

APPENDIX J

Mixed Breed in Colonial Period

DURING COLONIALISM, HYBRIDITY WAS viewed negatively. Conversely, it was during this period that products of mixed union increases. The intermingling of different ethnic groups due to trade, conquests, and migration since ancient times have been avenues for inter-ethnic relationships. Those living on the borders cannot escape the possibility of contact and union that gives birth to hybrid people. This echoes with Young's premise in his book that the colonizers actually desires the goods and the women of the colonized. In the chapter "White Men, White Desire," Young explores Edward Long's writings that many were the white women who turned into spinsters in the West Indies. This was because the white men desired the black women. This was not for the lack of white women but the mere desire for the black colored flesh.[1]

In the Spanish Period Philippines, inter-ethnic marriage was not discouraged but even encouraged for the purposes of converting the Chinese. However, "mixed breed" was still looked upon with condescension. Young's discussion on hybrids and mixed unions reveals the prejudices of the Europeans on the colonized and deemed them as from a different human species, possibly not fully humans. This created both a fear and fantasy for the colonized women. Likewise, the colonized also feared and fantasize about their colonizers. This inevitably produced the "horror of racial mixing" and the hybrid products. Theorists in the nineteenth century attempted to discourage inter-ethnic marriages by putting labels or names on the offspring of mixed unions; stating fertility theories such

---

1. Young, *Colonial Desire*, 150–51.

as amalgamation or miscegenation.[2] In retrospect, the idea behind the theory of diminishing fertility was in a sense to assure the European's purity of race since the mixed breed will eventually die out with their infertile nature. Unfortunately, mixed breeds continued to multiply.

The purity of blood was very important for the Spaniards for social ranking. This is evident in their meticulous classification system during their conquest in the Philippines. From the recognition of three races in the islands in the beginning of conquest, Spaniards, *indios*, and Chinese. The colonizers developed five social classes by the nineteenth century. This may have in part influenced by the European ideas and writings of this time period. The Spaniards born in Spain were called *peninsulares*. They were on top of the social classes. Next in line are the *insulares* or Spaniards born in the country. They are the first to be called Filipinos. They are also called *creoles*. The Spanish Mestizos or *mestizos de español* were also included in this category as Constantino described them like "apes" mimicking their creole brothers and regarding themselves of higher stature than their brown brothers. They are of Spanish and *indias* (indigenous Filipino) descent. Distinguished from the Spanish Mestizos, the Chinese Mestizos or *mestizos de Sangley* are of Chinese and *indias* descent. They belonged to the third class. Then the *indios* or *indios naturales*, they are pure natives emphasizing that they have no traces of Chinese or Spanish ancestry. The fifth and lowest class who are deemed as pagans are the Chinese.[3]

Edgar Wickberg argues that the Chinese Mestizos were a distinct group already during the Spanish Period.[4] They were classified separately from the *indios* and from the Chinese. They were also different from the Spanish Mestizos. They were the offspring of Chinese and *indios*, specifi-

2. Ibid., 4–19, 112–15.

3. Constantino and Constantino, *Past Revisited*, 120; Halili, *Philippine History*, 86–87. The *indios* are reserved for Christianized natives. The Muslims are called *Moros* while those who neither adhere to Christianity or Muslims are called *infieles* or pagans by the Spaniards. Tan, *History of the Philippines*, 44.

4. Joaquin Sy writes in response to Wickberg's article, "It is noteworthy that it was mainly during the latter part of the nineteenth century or towards the end of the Spanish colonial rule that the Chinese mestizos played a significant role in society as a distinct social class. After the Philippines gained independence from Spain in 1898 and up to the present, never again did the Chinese mestizos play a role and exert influence in society as a distinct social class or political force." In his article, Sy believes that the Chinese Mestizos are the most qualified people in promoting harmony and unity between the Chinese and Filipinos. Sy, "Changing Role," 124.

cally the *indias*, that is, Spanish for female natives. The Spanish government early on exempted the Spaniards and Spanish Mestizos from tribute. The *indios* paid the lowest, the Chinese Mestizos paid doubles, and the Chinese paid the highest tribute.[5] On the other hand, the Chinese were exempted from *polo* or forced labor but not the Chinese Mestizos and the *indios*. Wickberg believes that the Chinese were exempted because the Spaniards saw their potential in generating more money through commerce than agricultural labor.[6]

The Chinese, the *indios*, and the Chinese Mestizos were segregated to easily control them, a "divide and conquer" tactic. Furthermore, the Spaniards believed that a healthy society was a segregated society. People of different cultural backgrounds should not be allowed to live together in order to maintain harmony in the society. Social compartmentalization was implemented mid-way through their colonization of the country.[7]

The Spanish classification of legal statuses was based on the parental ethnicity. The child was classified as *mestizo de Sangley* if the father was a Chinese and *mestizo de Español* if the father was a Spaniard. The descendants of *mestizos* remained in *mestizo* classification. However, a *mestiza* could remain in the *mestizo* classification along with her children when married to a Chinese or *mestizo*. Her classification was moved to *indio* if married to an *indio*. This system encouraged the growth and development of the *mestizo* class. The problem came when a person desired to move from *mestizo* class to either Chinese or *indio*. Wickberg contends that this rarely happened since the *mestizo* class carried more privilege and favor than either of the other two classes.[8]

5. The Spaniards found the Chinese monopolizing retail trade. They extracted taxes by requiring them to pay yearly license fees, tributes and house taxes amounting to a total of eighty-one *reales* (compared to the Filipinos who only paid ten), aside from unpaid labor, and occasional arbitrary taxes. The Chinese had the highest level of taxation in the colony aside from the arbitrary taxes. Phelan, *Hispanization of the Philippines*, 11.

6. Wickberg, "Chinese Mestizo in Philippine History," 63.

7. Ibid., 62–64.

8. Ibid., 65–66. During the American Period, the legal classification of ethnicities was simplified to Filipinos and non-Filipinos or non-Christian Tribes. The *mestizo* classification was removed. The legal status of the child was based largely on the father's ethnic status. If the father was a Chinese and the mother a Filipina, the child would still be classified as non-Filipino by virtue of the father's ethnic status. Abinales and Amoroso, *State and Society*, 124. See also Chu, *Chinese and Chinese Mestizos*, 251. This system of classification is presently employed by the Philippine Bureau of Immigration.

Lynne Pan entitles her chapter on the Chinese Mestizos of the Philippines as "Hybrids" in the book *Sons of the Yellow Emperor*. She argues that being a Chinese Mestizos does not necessarily mean identifying oneself as Chinese. Jose Rizal, the Philippine national hero, was a fifth-generation Chinese Mestizo. As he was about to be executed for sedition and treason, he wanted to be identified as *indio* and not a Chinese Mestizo or a Chinese. Cory Aquino used her Chinese descent as a means to gain the support of the Chinese community during her administration as president of the country.[9] The "Hybrid" Chinese Mestizo had the advantage of using either Chinese ancestry or Filipino descent as means for negotiating in the society. Nonetheless, their hybrid nature could also be to their disadvantage. There were prejudices against them. They were also labeled as impure.

9. Pan, *Sons of the Yellow Emperor*, 153–54, 165.

APPENDIX K

Tracing Chinese Ethnocentrism

IN AN ATTEMPT TO trace the Chinese disdain for hybridity, I present the works of Edward Schafer. Edward Schafer (1913–1991) was an American sinologist and expert on the Tang Dynasty. In his book *The Golden Peaches of Samarkand,* he discusses China's interactions with foreigners during the Tang Dynasty. Ye Yiliang mentions that Chinese contact with foreign traders can be trace way back the fourth century BC through what they called the Maritime Silk Road.[1] Nevertheless, the residence and intermingling of foreigners and Chinese in China was explicitly described by Schafer in his work. Schafer describes Yangzhou 揚州 as the jewel city of China during AD eighth century. Yangzhou or Yangchou or Yangchow was a bustling city with a strategic location for trade. Schafer points out that it was inevitable that many foreign merchants lived and established shops there. In AD 760, Tian Shen-Gong's (T'ien Shen-kung) 田神功 rebel soldiers entered the city and killed thousands of Persians and Arabs.[2]

Schafer also talks about foreigners' tendency to congregate in commercial cities and major cities in China in the Tang Dynasty. They were even allowed to build their own temples and worship their own gods. Among the many foreigners such as the Turks, Uighurs, Tocharians, and Sogdians, they tended to stay in Chang'an. The Chams, Khmers, Javanese, and Singhalese crowded in Canton. Nevertheless, the Arabs, Persians, and Hindus were numerous in both cities. But the Iranians were the most

1. Ye, "Introductory Essay," 3.
2. Schafer, *Golden Peaches,* 17–18.

numerous since the Tang government even gave them their own office of the Sarthavak to watch over their own matters.[3]

Chinese treatment of foreigners changed from time to time. Though there was the desire for the exotic, there were still limits on Chinese interactions with others, thereby compelling the foreigners to learn and adapt Chinese manners and even dressing to freely mingle with the local people. However, Schafer notes that the Uighurs in particular were forbade to dress in Chinese manner but to wear their native clothing as not to be mistaken by Chinese women as Chinese men. The Uighurs were singled out since they were mostly moneylenders and were resented by many Chinese. Schafer adds that forbidding inter-ethnic marriage at this point could be simply the zeal of an ethnic puritan named Lu Chun. Lu Chun was a pious magistrate of Canton in AD 836 who sought to protect the purity of the Chinese culture by imposing segregation. He outlawed inter-ethnic marriage to protect the Chinese women. He also forbade aliens from owning lands and houses.[4]

Schafer resonates Young's premise of colonial desire or to aptly put in the context of the Chinese in the Tang Dynasty, "exotic desire." The ambivalent nature of both desire for and disgust of foreigners and anything they had to offer plagued the Chinese. The desire for ethnic purity struggled with the desire for exotic Central Asian harpers and dancers. Schafer concludes,

> Distrust or hatred of the foreigners was, in short, not at all incompatible with the love of exotic things. This love was realistic in the fine new days of the seventh and eight centuries, and embalmed in the literature of the ninth and tenth centuries. Then it recalled the fine old days, when the foreigners universally recognized the superiority of Chinese arms and Chinese arts, and when the ordinary Chinese citizen might expect to enjoy the rare goods of distant places.[5]

Chao Ju-Kua's 1225 sinological scholarship entitled *Description of the Barbarous Peoples* referred to all people except Chinese as "fan" 蕃 or barbarians. The word "fan" was applied impartially by Chinese to all non-Chinese from hunting cannibals to European monarchs.[6] When the

3. Ibid., 19–20.

4. Ibid., 20, 22.

5. Ibid., 23.

6. Chao, *Chu-Fan-Chï*, 159–62. See also Scott, *Prehispanic Source Materials*, n18,

Chinese settled in the country, they perceived the Filipinos as barbarians. Their fear of mixed marriages was rooted in their fear of the other and the possible monstrous child produced from such a union. The hybrid child could not be trusted as two kinds of blood ran in their veins.[7] Their hybrid nature portrayed the unsettling loyalty of this child to China and to the Philippines. There was the fear of betrayal and losing connection with homeland and kin. It was no wonder that they abhorred the hybrids.

According to the *Oxford Dictionary* online, the name China was designated by the Europeans during the sixteenth century. It originated from the Persian *chīnī* to attribute to anything made from China such as chinaware or porcelain. The name the Chinese called their country was Zhongguo 中國 or Middle Kingdom. It connotes being the center or the most important country in the world. It had a rich culture and long history. It had a vast and prosperous land matched with numerous people. Their pride for their heritage and nation had led many to ethnocentrism. Ethnocentrism had led to many broken hearts, broken hopes, and broken lives.

71, 73; ch. 2.

7. In cursing someone, the Chinese Filipino might say *tsáp tséng* 雜種 (lit. hybrid) to express their abhorrence of that person whom they equate to a mixed breed.

Bibliography

Abinales, Patricio N., and Donna J. Amoroso. *State and Society in the Philippines*. New York: Rowman & Littlefield, 2005.

Acosta, Persida. "Resolving Citizenship Issue, jus soli or jus sanguinis." *Manila Times*, March 18, 2009. http://archives.manilatimes.net/national/2009/march/18/yehey/metro/20090318 met5.html.

Agoncillo, Teodoro A. *History of the Filipino People*. 8th ed. Quezon City: Garo Tech, 1990.

Alejandrino, Clark L. *A History of the 1902 Chinese Exclusion Act: American Colonial Transmission and Deterioration of the Filipino-Chinese Relations*. Manila: Kaisa, 2003.

Allen, Larry. *The Encyclopedia of Money*. 2nd ed. Santa Barbara, CA: ABC-CLIO, 2009.

Alfonso, Amelia B., et al. *Culture and Fertility: The Case of the Philippines*. Singapore: Institute of Southeast Asian Studies, 1980.

Anderson, Benedict R. O'G. *Imagined Communities: Reflections on the Origin and Spread of Nationalism*. London: Verso, 1991.

Appadurai, Arjun. *Modernity At Large: Cultural Dimensions of Globalization*. Minneapolis: University of Minnesota Press, 1996.

Arroyo, Joker. "Rizal Yuyitung: A Tribute to an Ideal Filipino," *Inquirer*, April 26, 2007. http://globalnation.inquirer.net/news/news/view/20070426-62548/Rizal_C.K._Yuyitung:__Tribute_to_ideal_Filipino.

Barth, Fredrik. *Ethnic Groups and Boundaries: The Social Organization of Culture Difference*. Bergen, Norway: Universitesforlaget, 1969.

Basch, Linda G., et al. *Nations Unbound: Transnational Projects, Postcolonial Predicaments, and Deterritorialized Nation-States*. [S.l.]: Gordon & Breach, 1994.

Bayar, Murat. "Reconsidering Primordialism: An Alternative Approach to the Study of Ethnicity." *Ethnic & Racial Studies* 32 (2009) 1639–57.

Beyer, Henry Otley. "The Philippines before Magellan." *Asia Magazine* (November 1921) 861, 865, and 892.

Bhabha, Homi. *The Location of Cultures*. London: Routledge, 2004.

Benitez, Conrado O. *History of the Philippines*. Manila: Ginn, 1954.

Brettell, Caroline. *Anthropology and Migration: Essays on Transnationalism, Ethnicity, and Identity*. Walnut Creek, CA: Altamira, 2003.

Brown, Abram. "Philippines' 50 Richest." *Forbes*, August 27, 2014. http://www.forbes. com/philippines-billionaires/.

Brown, William N. *Amoy Magic*. Xiamen, China: Xiamen University Press, 2000.

Bulatao, Jaime C. *Split-Level Christianity*. Manila: Ateneo de Manila, 1966.

Bureau of Immigration. "The ACR I-Card." http://www.immigration.gov.ph/index. php/services/acr-i-card.

———. "Administrative Naturalization Law of 2000." http://www.immigration.gov.ph/ index.php/information/immigration-law/117-the-administrative-naturalization- law-of-2000?showall=1&limitstart=.

———. "Immigrant Visa." http://www.immigration.gov.ph/visa-requirements/ immigrant-visa/quota-visa.

Burke, Peter. *Cultural Hybridity*. Cambridge, UK: Polity, 2009.

Caoili, Manuel A. *The Origins of Metropolitan Manila: A Political and Social Analysis*. Quezon City: New Day, 1988.

Catindig, Raymund. "Gen. Jose Paua, the Chinese in Philippine Revolution." *Philippine Star*, February 10, 2013. http://www.philstar.com/headlines/2013/02/10/906952/ gen.-jose-paua-chinese-philippine-revolution.

CBCP [Christian Bible Church of the Philippines]. "Ministries." http://cbcp.org/ ministries.

Chan Robles Virtual Law Library. "The Philippine Bill of July 1902." http://www. chanrobles.com/philippinebillof1902.htm#.UnmR3lOZWF0.

———. "Tranquilino Roa, *Petitioner-Appellant*, vs. Insular Collector of Customs, *Respondent-Appellee*." http://www.chanrobles.com/scdecisions/ jurisprudence1912/oct1912/gr_l-7011_1912.php.

Chan-Yap, Gloria. "Hokkien Chinese Loanwords in Tagalog." *Studies in Philippine Linguistics* 1 (1977) 17–49.

Chandra, Kanchan. *Constructivist Theories of Ethnic Politics*. New York: Oxford University Press, 2012.

Chao, Ju-Kua. *Chau Ju-Kua: His Work on the Chinese and Arab Trade in the Twelfth and Thirteenth Centuries, Entitled Chu-Fan-Chï*. Translated and annotated by Friedrich Hirth and William Woodville Rockhill. St. Petersburg: Imperial Academy of Sciences, 1911.

Cheung, David. "The Chinese-Filipino Profile." *Philippine-Chinese Mission 2000* 3 (1994) 1–2, 6, 9, 11, 13.

———. *Christianity in Modern China: The Making of the First Native Protestant Church*. Leiden: Brill, 2004.

———. "EnRAWGen Ministry and the Phil-Chinese Church Growth." *Philippine- Chinese Mission 2000* 4 (1995) 1.

Chia, Lucille. "The Butcher, the Baker, and the Carpenter: Chinese Sojourners in the Spanish Philippines and Their Impact on Southern Fujian (Sixteenth-Eighteenth Centuries)." *Journal of the Economic and Social History of the Orient* 4 (2006) 509–34.

Christofferson, Ethan J. *Negotiating Identity: Exploring Tensions between Being Hakka and Being Christian in Northwestern Taiwan*. Eugene, OR: Pickwick, 2012.

Chu, Richard T. *Chinese and Chinese Mestizos of Manila: Family, Identity, and Culture, 1860s–1930s*. Leiden: Brill, 2010.

Chua, Amy. *World on Fire: How Exporting Free Market Democracy Breeds Ethnic Hatred and Global Instability*. New York: First Anchor, 2003.

Clifford, James, and George E. Marcus. *Writing Culture: The Poetics and Politics of Ethnography: A School of American Research Advanced Seminar.* Berkeley: University of California Press, 1986.

Constantino, Renato. *The Making of a Filipino.* Manila: Malaya, 1969.

Constantino, Renato, and Letizia R. Constantino. *The Philippines: A Past Revisited.* Quezon City: Tala, 1975.

Conwell, Russell H. *Why and How: Why the Chinese Emigrate, and the Means They Adopt for the Purpose of Reaching America; with Sketches of Travel, Amusing Incidents, Social Customs.* Boston: Lee & Shepard, 1871.

Corpuz, Onofre D. *The Roots of the Filipino Nation.* 2 vols. Quezon City: University of the Philippines Press, 2006.

Da Chen (Ta Chen). *Chinese Migrations, with Special Reference to Labor Conditions.* Washington, DC: Government Printing Office, 1923.

Daquila, Teofilo C. *The Economies of Southeast Asia: Indonesia, Malaysia, Philippines, Singapore and Thailand.* Hauppauge, NY: Nova Science, 2005.

David, E. J. R. *Filipino-American Postcolonial Psychology: Oppression, Colonial Mentality, and Decolonization.* Bloomington, IN: Authorhouse, 2011.

Felix, Alfonso, Jr. "How We Stand." In *The Chinese in the Philippines*, edited by Alfonso Felix Jr., 1:1–14. 2 vols. Manila: Solidaridad, 1966–69.

Foreign Aid Transparency Hub. "Total Foreign Aid Pledge." January 21, 2014. http://www.gov.ph/faith/.

Friedman, Jonathan. "The Politics of De-Authentication: Escaping from Identity, a Response to 'Beyond Authenticity' by Mark Rogers." *Identities* 3 (1996) 127–36.

Gannett, Henry, et al. *Census of the Philippine Islands, Taken under the Direction of the Philippine Commission in the Year 1903, in Four Volumes.* Washington, DC: US Government, 1905.

Geertz, Clifford. *The Interpretation of Cultures.* New York: Basic, 1973.

Gessner, Volkmar, and Angelika Schade. "Conflicts of Culture in Cross-Border Legal Relations: The Conception of a Research Topic in the Sociology of Law." In *Global Culture: Nationalism, Globalization, and Modernity*, edited by Mike Featherstone, 253–77. London: Sage, 1990.

Go, Bon Juan. "Kennon Road's Chinese Laborers." In *Tsinoy: The Story of the Chinese in Philippine Life*, edited by Teresita Ang See, 122–23. Manila: Kaisa, 2005.

———. *Myths about the Ethnic Chinese: Economic Miracle.* Manila: Kaisa, 1996.

———. "Old and New Immigrants from China: Comparative Dimension." In *Globalizing Chinese Migration: Trends in Europe and Asia*, edited by Pál Nyíri and I. R. Savel'ev, 309–19. Aldershot, UK: Ashgate, 2002.

Grace Christian College. "Campus Bulletin: Special Announcement." Accessed January 27, 2014. http://www.gcc.edu.ph/.

Guéguen, Catherine. "Boundaries, Spaces and Populations in the Study of Binondo, the Manila Chinatown." Our Own Voice. December 2010. http://www.oovrag.com/essays/essay2010c-2.shtml.

———. "Moving from Binondo to the 'Chinese Villages' of the Suburbs: A Geographical Study of the Chinese in Metro Manila." *Journal of Chinese Overseas* 6 (2010) 119–37.

Halili, Maria Christine. *Philippine History.* Manila: Rex, 2004.

Hamilton, Gary G., ed. *Cosmopolitan Capitalists: Hong Kong and the Chinese Diaspora at the End of the Twentieth Century.* Seattle: University of Washington Press, 1999.

Hansen, Valerie. *The Silk Road: A New History*. Oxford: Oxford University Press, 2012.

Harris, Marvin. *Theories of Culture in Postmodern Times*. Walnut Creek, CA: AltaMira, 1999.

Hiebert, Paul G., *Anthropological Insights for Missionaries*. Grand Rapids: Baker, 1985.

Hiebert, Paul G., et al. *Understanding Folk Religion: A Christian Response to Popular Beliefs and Practices*. Grand Rapids: Baker, 1999.

Hill, Jonathan. *Zondervan Handbook to the History of Christianity*. Grand Rapids: Zondervan, 2006.

Hoeffel, Elizabeth, et al. "The Asian Population 2010: 2010 Census Briefs." Issued March 2012. http://www.census.gov/prod/cen2010/briefs/c2010br-11.pdf.

Hutchinson, John, and Anthony D. Smith, eds. *Ethnicity*. Oxford: Oxford University Press, 1996.

Indiana University Bloomington. "The Lilly Library Digital Collection: Boxer Codex." http://www.indiana.edu/~liblilly/digital/collections/items/browse/tag/Spain.

Jones, Arun W. *Christian Missions in the American Empire*. Studies of Intercultural History of Christianity 132. Frankfurt: Peter Lang, 2003.

Kaisa Para Sa Kaunlaran, Inc. "Declaration of Principles." http://kaisa.org.ph/.

——— "Kaisa Para Sa Kaunlaran, Inc.: Projects." http://www.kaisa.org.ph/.

———."Tsinoy National Conventions and Local Conferences." http://www.kaisa.org.ph/conventions.html.

Karnow, Stanley. *In Our Image*. New York: Random House, 1989.

Lewellen, Ted C. *The Anthropology of Globalization*. Westport, CT: Bergin & Garvey, 2002.

Lim, Ka-Tong. *The Life and Ministry of John Sung*. Singapore: Genesis. 2012.

London and China Telegraph. "The Coolie Trade." *London and China Telegraph* 11, no. 302 (January 4, 1869) 4.

———. "The Last Coolie Tragedy." *London and China Telegraph* 11, no. 304 (January 25, 1869) 36.

Macgowan, John. *English and Chinese Dictionary of the Amoy Dialect*. Amoy, China: A. A. Marcal, 1883.

Mann, Charles. *1493: Uncovering the New World Columbus Created*. New York: Knopf, 2011.

McConnell, C Douglas. "Confronting Racism and Prejudice in Our Kind of People." *Missiology* 25, no. 4 (October 1, 1997) 387–404.

McCurdy, David W., et al. *The Cultural Experience: Ethnography in Complex Society*. 2nd ed. Long Grove, IL: Waveland, 2005.

Mydans, Seth. "Kidnapping of Ethnic Chinese Rises in Philippines." *New York Times*, March 17, 1996. http://www.nytimes.com/1996/03/17/world/kidnapping-of-ethnic-chinese-rises-in-philippines.html?pagewanted=1.

National Statistics Office. "Population and Housing." Last modified April 4, 2012. http://census.gov.ph/sites/default/files/attachments/hsd/pressrelease/National%20Capital%20Region.pdf.

Nederveen Pieterse, Jan. *Globalization and Culture: Global Mélange*. Oxford: Rowman & Littlefield, 2004.

Ngo, Hope. "Kidnapping on the Rise, Say Philippines Chinese." *CNN*, May 5, 2001. http://edition.cnn.com/2001/WORLD/asiapcf/southeast/05/04/philippines.kidnap/.

Norval, Aletta J. "The Politics of Ethnicity and Identity." In *The Blackwell Companion to Political Sociology*, edited by Kate Nash and Allan Scott, 271–80. Malden, MA: Blackwell, 2001.

Novak, Michael. *Unmeltable Ethnics: Politics and Culture in American Life.* 2nd ed. New Brunswick: Transaction, 1996.

Official Gazette. "Proclamation no. 295, s. 2011." November 28, 2011. http://www.gov.ph/2011/11/24/proclamation-no-295-s-2011/.

———. "Typhoon Yolanda." November 6, 2013. http://www.gov.ph/crisis-response/updates-typhoon-yolanda/.

Ong, Aihwa. *Flexible Citizenship: The Cultural Logics of Transnationality.* Durham: Duke University Press, 1999.

Ong, Aihwa, and Donald M. Nonini. *Ungrounded Empires: The Cultural Politics of Modern Chinese Transnationalism.* New York: Routledge, 1997.

Osias, Camilo, and Avelina Lorenzana. *Evangelical Christianity in the Philippines.* Dayton, OH: United Brethren, 1931.

Overseas Community Affairs Council Republic of China (Taiwan). "Overseas Chinese Population Count." http://www.ocac.gov.tw/OCAC/Eng/Pages/VDetail.aspx?nodeid=414&pid=1168.

———. "Overseas Chinese Population Distribution: Overseas Chinese Population by Country 2012." http://www.ocac.gov.tw/english/public/public.asp?selno=8889&no=8889&level=B.

Oxford Dictionaries. "China." http://www.oxforddictionaries.com/us/definition/american_english/china?q=china.

Pan, Lynn. *Sons of the Yellow Emperor: A History of the Chinese Diaspora.* Boston: Little, Brown, 1990.

Phelan, John Leddy. *The Hispanization of the Philippines.* Madison: University of Wisconsin Press, 1959.

Philippine Retirement Authority. "Special Resident Retiree's Visa." http://www.pra.gov.ph/main/srrv_program?page=1.

Reid, Anthony. "Flows and Seepages in the Long-Term Chinese Interaction with Southeast Asia." In *Sojourners and Settlers*, edited by Anthony Reid, 15–50. Honolulu: University of Hawaii Press, 1996.

———. *Southeast Asia in the Age of Commerce 1450–1680: Volume Two Expansion and Crisis.* New Haven: Yale University Press, 1993.

Rizal, Jose. *Noli me Tángere.* Translated by Ma. Soledad Lacson-Locsin. Edited by Raul L. Locsin. Honolulu: University of Hawaiian Press, 1997.

Robbins, Joel. *Becoming Sinners: Christianity and Moral Torment in a Papua New Guinea Society.* Berkeley: University of California Press, 2004.

Roberts, John A. G. *A Concise History of China.* Cambridge: Harvard University Press, 1999.

Rodell, Paul A. *Culture and Customs of the Philippines.* Westport, CT: Greenwood, 2002.

Rynkiewich, Michael A. "A New Heaven and a New Earth? The Future of Missiological Anthropology." In *Paradigm Shifts in Christian Witness: Insights from Anthropology, Communication, and Spiritual Power; Essays in Honor of Charles H. Kraft*, edited by Charles H. Kraft et al., 33–41. Maryknoll: Orbis, 2008.

———. *Soul, Self, and Society: A Postmodern Anthropology for Mission in a Postcolonial World.* Eugene, OR: Cascade, 2011.

————"The World in My Parish: Rethinking the Standard Missiological Model." *Missiology* 30 (2002) 301–21.

Schafer, Edward H. *The Golden Peaches of Samarkand: A Study of T'ang Exotics.* Berkeley: University of California Press, 1963.

Schottenhammer, Angela. "Transfer of Xiangyao 香藥 from Iran and Arabia to China." In *Aspects of the Maritime Silk Road: From the Persian Gulf to the East China Sea*, edited by Ralph Kauz, 117–49. Wiesbaden: Harrassowitz, 2010.

Schreiter, Robert J. *The New Catholicity: Theology between the Global and the Local.* Maryknoll: Orbis, 1997.

Scott, William Henry. *A Critical Study of the Prehispanic Source Materials for the Study of Philippine History.* Manila: University of Santo Tomas Press, 1968.

See, Carmelea Ang. "Roman Ongpin." In *Tsinoy: The Story of the Chinese in the Philippines*, edited by Teresita Ang See, 145. Manila: Kaisa, 2005.

See, Teresita Ang. "Bridge-Builders in Our Midst: The Story of Professor Chinben See, Anthropologist." In *The Chinese Immigrants: Selected Writings of Professor Chinben See*, by Chinben See and Teresita Ang See, 500–510. Manila: Kaisa, 1992.

————. "The Case of the Chinese in the Philippines." In *The State, Development and Identity in Multi-Ethnic Societies: Ethnicity, Equity and the Nation*, edited by Nicolas Tarling and Edmund Terence Gomez, 154–71. London: Routledge, 2008.

————. *The Chinese in the Philippines: Problems and Perspectives.* 3 vols. Manila: Kaisa, 1990–2004.

————. "The Ethnic Chinese as Filipinos." In *Ethnic Chinese as Southeast Asians*, edited by Leo Suryadinata, 158–202. Singapore: Institute of Southeast Asian Studies, 1997.

————. "Influx of New Chinese Immigrants to the Philippines: Problems and Challenges." In *Beyond Chinatown: New Chinese Migration and the Global Expansion of China*, edited by Mette Thunø, 137–62. Malaysia: NIAS, 2007.

————. "Jose Ignacio Paua: Chinese General in the Philippine Revolution." In *Tsinoy: The Story of the Chinese in the Philippines*, edited by Teresita Ang See, 90–93. Manila: Kaisa, 2005.

————. "Long Wait for Justice." *Philippine Center for Investigative Journalism*, October–December 2004. http://www.pcij.org/imag/Yearend2004/crime.html.

————, ed. *Tsinoy: The Story of the Chinese in Philippine Life.* Manila: Kaisa, 2005.

Severino, Howie. "Pagbalik sa Karagatan." I-Witness. July 30, 2012. http://www.gmanetwork.com/news/video/128917/iwitness/howie-severino-traces-what-happened-to-the-npa-s-cargo-ship-in-pagbabalik-sa-karagatan.

Shao, Joseph. "A Channel of Blessings in God's Hands: Chinese Protestant Churches in the Philippines." In *Chapters in Philippine Church History*, edited by Anne Kwantes, 413–28. Colorado Springs: International Academic, 2002.

Shao, Rosa C. "Chinese-Filipino Adolescents' Developing Autonomy in the Context of Parent-Adolescent Conflict and Family Cohesion." PhD diss., Ateneo de Manila University, 2006.

Sugaya, Nariko. "The Expulsion of Non-Christian Chinese in the Mid-18th Century Chinese: It's Relevance to the Rise of Chinese Mestizos." In *Ethnic Chinese: Proceedings of the International Conference on Changing Identities and Relations in Southeast Asia*, edited by Teresita Ang See and Go Bun Juan, 111–19. Manila: Kaisa, 1994.

Suryadinata, Leo. "Government Policies towards the Ethnic Chinese in the ASEAN States: Comparative Analysis." In *The Ethnic Chinese: Proceedings of the International Conference on Changing Identities and Relations in Southeast Asia*, edited by Teresita Ang See and Go Bun Juan, 67–80. Manila: Kaisa, 1994.

Sy, Joaquin. "The Changing Role of Chinese Mestizos in Philippine History." In *The Ethnic Chinese: Proceedings of the International Conference on Changing Identities and Relations in Southeast Asia*, edited by Teresita Ang See and Go Bun Juan, 121–25. Manila: Kaisa, 1994.

Szanton Blanc, Cristina. "The Thoroughly Modern 'Asian': Capital, Culture, and Nation in Thailand and the Philippines." In *Ungrounded Empires: The Cultural Politics of Modern Transnationalism*, edited by Aihwa Ong and Donald Nonini, 261–86. New York: Routledge, 1997.

Tan, Chiu-Eng. "The Cosmos, Humans, and Gods: A Comparison of Non-Christians and Christians on Chinese Beliefs in Metro-Manila." PhD diss., Trinity International University, 1996.

———— "A Descriptive Study of Mission Programs of Selected Philippine-Chinese Churches in Metro Manila: Policies, Motives, and Views of Mission." In *Asian Church and God's Mission*, edited by Wonsuk Ma and Julie Ma, 211–32. Manila: OMF, 2003.

Tan, Samuel K. *A History of the Philippines*. Quezon City: University of the Philippines Press, 2008.

Tanganco, Joyce. "Bringing God's Love to the Elderly." United Evangelical Church of Malabon. http://uecmalabon.org/?page_id=132.

Te, Melchor. "CKSC Cares for Typhoon Yolanda Victims." Chiang Kai Shek College. November 25, 2013. http://cksc.edu.ph/news/student-life/734-cksc-cares-for-typhoon-yolanda-victims.

Tira, Sadiri Joy. "Preface." In *Scattered and Gathered: A Global Compendium of Diaspora Missiology*, edited by Sadiri Joy Tira and Tetsunao Yamamori, xv–xix. Oxford: Regnum, 2016.

Tong, Chee Kiong. *Identity and Ethnic Relations in Southeast Asia: Racializing Chineseness*. London: Springer, 2010.

Tuggy, Arthur. *The Philippine Church: Growth in Changing Society*. Grand Rapids: Eerdmans, 1971.

Uayan, Jean U. "Chap Chay Lo Mi: Disentangling the Chinese-Filipino Worldview." In *Doing Theology in the Philippines*, edited by John D. Suk, 65–77. Mandaluyong: OMF, 2005.

————. "A Study on the Emergence and Early Development of Selected Protestant Chinese Churches in the Philippines." PhD diss., Asia Graduate School of Theology, 2007.

United States, Philippine Commission (1900–1916). *Report of the United States Philippine Commission to the Secretary of War*. Washington, DC: US Government, 1904.

Uytanlet, Juliet Lee. "Pride and Prejudice, Colonialism and Post-Colonialism in the Philippine Chinese Context: How IBS Can Be a Liberating Methodology to Find the Truth to Be Set Free." *Asbury Journal* 68 (2013) 56–68.

Walls, Andrew. *The Missionary Movement in Christian History: Studies in the Transmission of Faith*. Maryknoll: Orbis, 1996.

Wan, Enoch. "Mission among the Chinese Diaspora: A Case Study of Migration and Mission." *Missiology* 31 (2003) 35–44.

Wang, Gungwu. "Chineseness: The Dilemmas of Place and Practice." In *Cosmopolitan Capitalists: Hong Kong and the Chinese Diaspora at the End of the Twentieth Century*, edited by Gary G. Hamilton, 118–34. Seattle: University of Washington Press, 1999.

———. "Sojourning: The Chinese Experience in Southeast Asia." In *Sojourners and Settlers*, edited by Anthony Reid, 1–14. Honolulu: University of Hawaii Press, 1996.

Watt, Stewart. *Chinese Bondage in Peru: A History of the Chinese Coolie in Peru, 1849–1874*. Westport: Greenwood, 1970.

Wickberg, Edgar. "Anti-Sinicism and Chinese Identity Options in the Philippines." In *Essential Outsiders: Chinese and Jews in the Modern Transformation of Southeast Asia and Central Europe*, edited by Daniel Chirot and Anthony Reid, 153–83. Seattle: University of Washington Press, 1997.

———. *The Chinese in Philippine Life 1850–1898*. New Haven: Yale University Press, 1965.

———. "The Chinese Mestizo in Philippine History." *Journal of Southeast Asian History* 5 (1964) 62–100.

———. "Early Chinese Economic Influence in the Philippines, 1850–1898." *East Asian Series Reprint* 3 (1962) 275–85.

Wong, Kwok-Chu. *The Chinese in the Philippine Economy 1898–1941*. Quezon City: Ateneo de Manila Press, 1999.

Xinhua News Agency. "China to send 119 language teachers to Southeast Asia." April 13, 2009. http://www.china.org.cn/china/news/2009-04/13/content_17598549.htm.

Yang, Fenggang. "Chinese Conversion to Evangelical Christianity: The Importance of Social and Cultural Contexts." *Sociology of Religion* 59 (1998) 237–57.

Ybarrola, Steven. "Opening Session." MC980: Ethnographic Field Methods. Class lecture at Asbury Theological Seminary, Kentucky, September 9, 2010.

Ye, Yiliang. "Introductory Essay: Outline of the Political Relations between Iran and China." In *Aspects of the Maritime Silk Road: From the Persian Gulf to the East China Sea*, edited by Ralph Kauz, 3–6. Wiesbaden, Germany: Harrassowitz, 2010.

Young, Robert. *Colonial Desire: Hybridity in Theory, Culture, and Race*. London: Routledge, 1995.

Young, Stewart. "Why Chinese Church Members Are Leaving for Philippine Megachurches?" Presentation, Biblical Seminary of the Philippines faculty meeting, February 19, 2014.

Yu, Jose Vidamor B. *Inculturation of Filipino-Chinese Cultural Mentality*. Interreligious and Intercultural Investigation 3. Rome: EPUG, 2000.

Zhou, Min. *Contemporary Chinese America*. Philadelphia: Temple University Press, 2009.

Subject Index

Author Index